SUITORS AND SUPPLIANTS

The Little Nations at Versailles

SUITORS AND SUPPLIANTS

The Little Nations at Versailles

by

STEPHEN BONSAL

Introduction by

Arthur Krock

New York PRENTICE-HALL, INC. *1946*

To my four indulgent sons

STEPHEN AND PHILIP, RICHARD AND DUDLEY

In gratitude and with the proud confidence that they and their contemporaries will cope more successfully with the problems of a war-wracked world than did the generation that now passes from the troubled scene

J SHALL BE content if those shall pronounce my history useful who desire to give a view of events as they really did happen and as they are very likely in accordance with human nature to repeat themselves at some future time—if not exactly the same yet very similar.

—THUCYDIDES

Introduction

$\mathcal{T}$HE CAUSES of war vary in détail, although in most instances they have their source in the expansionist policies of a nation of people on the make, or in the determination of a fading power to hold what it acquired when it was young and strong and relatively virtuous.

Nations in the first category which have made war have usually been egged on to it by a chorus of ancestral voices both jingo and traditional—of whom Wagner and Hegel are good examples—and this cultural voodoo has usually evoked an uncultured but more effective demagogic leader—of whom Hitler will serve as well as any in history as the illustration.

Nations in the second category need no such mental preparation for war—their principal requirement is a seneschal with a good loud horn to rouse them unwillingly from their slumbers with the news that the rustlers are among their fat sheep and cattle.

But the occasions of war nearly always have been the outgrowth of the conflicting policies of such nations as these in the territory of small or weak peoples, strategically located for this purpose by the curse of geography or natural riches. Because the peoples at the point of conflict are small or weak this enables the new aggressor or the hold-fast overlord to play appealingly on the strings of the instruments of virtue, assuring one or all of these several results:

> The masses in the strong nations are presented with a handmade set of idealistic objectives, which many require for spiritual consolation and the rest for a dignified excuse.
>
> The military and civil leaders of the nations which engage in the war can publicly summon God to their standards with every mark of belief that He could not possibly make another choice, and this comforts the upright whom they summon to the colors.

The victims who furnish the occasions of war and most of the battle areas are thus held in the supply system of the victors, who always stand in need of abnormal supply quotas after they have won their wars.

If the small or weak peoples who furnish most of the occasions and areas for large conflict could ever have their grievances reasonably redressed, if the promises of the great were ever fully kept to them, and if those forced onto the losing side were not stripped of the opportunities for a fair existence, it would be much more difficult for the great nations to justify this hypocritical use of them in the rhetoric which always precedes and accompanies it. And the difficulty would be greater in this period of the world's history for these reasons:

> A Second World War, twenty-five years after the First (and with the Twentieth Century in which they were fought not yet half over) has produced a real determination in every nation to try to space these conflicts more widely.
>
> Those who feel this determination, currently expressed in the United Nations Organization, are more attracted than ever before by the thesis that in a successful league to keep the peace all nations must be heard and heeded, and some of the sovereignty of the great must go into a world pool with that of the small.
>
> War has demonstrated twice, emphatically, and in the sight of millions of living men and women, that it is the eternal vanguard of the Four Horsemen, however pious and idealistic the assertions of any who participated may be.

Because of these things, Colonel Bonsal's book is more timely, and could have more lasting benefit, than at any period of the past in which it might have appeared. The story, documented by the records of the author in his official capacity at Paris in 1919, is that of the efforts of the small nations to remove themselves thereafter as the occasions of war. And it is the story of their failure to get from the victors the assistance essential to that objective.

The direct consequence, as these pages make plain, was another and larger and more terrible war. Nor is the atmosphere of the ante-rooms of the next peace conference, in which the "suitors and sup-pliants" are again forgathering for the same purpose, very favorable to a wiser and fairer arbitrament of their claims than that, related by Colonel Bonsal, in which was spawned the Axis and the hideous war that followed.

But man somehow and at times progresses and learns from the lessons of the past when they are written down plain and the span of human experience is as brief as that from 1919 to 1946. The plain writing is here and the lesson is obvious. Also, the author speaks by facts within his own sight and knowledge.

This is no "analysis," no assumption "on reliable witness." It is the group photograph of the small nations at Paris and Versailles, illuminated but not posed by the ablest and best-informed foreign correspondent in the history of the American press, and a diplomat and statesman when called upon to be.

Once when he felt obliged to relate what he thought to be too tall a tale of history, Gibbon countered with this footnote: "Abu Rafe says he will be witness for this fact, but who will be witness for Abu Rafe?" That question does not arise in the contents of the following pages. The facts themselves, expertly assembled by Colonel Bonsal, and with foreboding, are sufficient witness.

ARTHUR KROCK

Preface

IN THE FOLLOWING section of my chronicle of things seen and heard at the Peace Conference, I have in pursuit of clarity, an ideal so often praised by our French friends, withdrawn from the body of my diary many entries dealing with issues with which in my subordinate capacity I was closely concerned or which for a variety of reasons were of special interest to me. Also, in order to present in as straightforward and lucid a manner as possible the complex pleas of the many suitors and suppliants at the bar of the Great Assizes, I have made changes in the day-by-day chronological order of my diary, though each individual entry, of course, retains its original date. I can see objections to such rearrangement, but it does avoid much acrobatic springing from one topic to another, from the familiar home front to distant lands, from an involved ethnic factor to a remote boundary dispute.

In the main these excerpts deal with ancient questions once again become present-day problems which the Conference, and particularly the Great Four, pressed as they were for more urgent decisions, regarded as of such minor importance that they might be postponed, or, with advantage, could be relegated to the League of Nations then a-borning. Even before the League died, however, several of these neglected issues had developed into a menace to the public law so recently and so hopefully proclaimed throughout the world, and this neglect paved the way to the catastrophic situation in which all the nations of the world have for a second time been involved.

The proceedings in this impromptu world court, for such was the Peace Conference, have often been described as forensic battles between the Good and the Bad nations. This seems an illustration of a tendency toward over-simplification to which particularly in times of stress we are so often prone. This statement may be accepted as a half truth, but during the Conference I came across the illuminating words (and indeed was fascinated by them) which Thomas Carlyle, that Titan among the thinkers, applied to a somewhat similar but less tragic situation in his day. He wrote: "Formula and Reality wrestle it out"—words that are truly descriptive of what happened then and are appropriate to what is happening today. The wrestling has brought widespread misery to the world and it is only too clear that the cut-and-dried formalist has not been silenced. He is heard today in the market places and in the forum and, as always before, he will put in an appearance at the Peace Conference.

While admitting failure in many regions where complete success had been too confidently expected, it should be stressed that no single feature of his programme was nearer to the heart of our crusading President than the fate of the submerged nationalities and the widely scattered ethnic factors (only too often but forlorn fragments) who presented themselves at the Great Assizes with their petitions, supplications and pleas. One of the basic mistakes in Mr. Wilson's campaign was, however, that he almost invariably ignored the experts who could have told him that his belief in "easily recognizable frontiers of nationality" was not based on accurate knowledge, that frequently they did not exist, and that the traditional ties between reputedly sister nations were often tenuous and frequently snapped without warning. Yet it cannot be denied that the President, although the outstanding formalist, made a gallant fight in Paris for what he thought to be right and most certainly often was. He was slow in perceiving that many of his fellow delegates, blinded by racial or national ambition, seeking only what seemed economic advantages or a winning election slogan, were turning deaf ears to the voices of humanity and were not fearful of that unenviable pre-eminence in history which the President had in the opening skirmish predicted for them—if only they could boost trade and maintain their parliamentary majorities.

The first trumpet note with which President Wilson electrified the world in that dark moment of world history should be recorded here. His words were:

> The voices of humanity insist that no nation or peoples
> shall be robbed or punished because the irresponsible rulers

of a single country have themselves done deep and abominable wrong. *(Dec. 4, 1917)*

Then getting down to details he insisted: "There shall be no more bartering of peoples and provinces as mere chattels and pawns in a game. Every territorial settlement is to be made in the interests of the populations concerned." And last but by no means least, he demanded "the destruction of any arbitrary power anywhere that can disturb the peace of the world." (The full text of the Wilson programme is detailed in the Appendix.)

By April 1919 the President came to a truer appreciation of his situation and he saw, as General Smuts put it in words a few days later, "that humanity was failing him." It was then on May 31st that he summed up the pleas he had so often made in the sessions of the League and Covenant Commission, where he had so frequently insisted that the treatment of the submerged and the oppressed nationalities would prove the acid test of the Conference. But by this time his confidence in the outcome of the good fight was weakening. He asked questions and his words were pleading, unlike the tone of perhaps unconscious arrogance with which he had opened his campaign. In this mood his words were:

> Nothing I venture to say is more likely to disturb the peace of the world than the treatment which might in certain circumstances be meted out to minorities and, therefore, if the Great Powers are to guarantee the peace of the world in any sense, is it unjust that they should be satisfied that the proper and necessary guarantees have been given? If we agree to the additions of territory asked for in this instance (particularly by Prime Minister Bratianu of Rumania), we have the vested right to insist upon certain guarantees of peace.

They were not forthcoming. There was an epidemic of side-stepping among the war-worn nations and unfortunately in the backward movement the people of America were not the hindmost. It is to be hoped that we have learned our costly lesson.

STEPHEN BONSAL

Washington, D.C.

Contents

SUITORS AND SUPPLIANTS

The Little Nations at Versailles

CHAPTER I

From a Front-Line Cellar
To the Hotel Crillon

Troyon, October 8, 1918

I am writing this by the feeble light of a smelly bicycle lamp in a damp cellar under a ruined house somewhere near the front. By pulling a brick from my barricaded window, and with the aid of a little imagination, anyone can see the *voie sacrée*, the great Chaussée, the life line of Verdun which the Crown Prince and all his armies have failed to cut. My sergeant tells me the place is called Rottentout and he asserts that it is "rotten all through." I have been here for four days and I am inclined to agree with him.

"All the folks were evacuated before we Americans arrived," he explains, "and you can't find the place on the map. Even the town major does not know its name, so we just call it 'Rotten-all-through.'"

But we are not lost; our collection of ruined houses is a short mile from Troyon, the headquarters of the 26th or Yankee Division, the first National Guard division to see service on the fighting front and now forming a part, a very important part (we number over 30,000) of the French Army under General Degoutte.

Difficult as it must be I shall try to explain the vicissitudes of fortune which I have suffered, I must admit gladly, during the last week. As I face the squalor of the humid cellar in which I live, more suitable for the cultivation of mushrooms than for human habitation, and view the sagging cot upon which I recline in my few hours of ease, it is hard to believe that I am the same soldier-diplomat who only a few days ago voiced the sentiments of America at the Congress of Submerged Nationalities * and lunched with M. Pichon in the stately precincts of the Quai d'Orsay, sipping rich wines and talking of our experiences in distant Peking in far-off Boxer days. But here goes:

Two days after M. Selves had adjourned the Congress without fixing a definite date for the renewal of our labors, I found myself continually wandering along the boulevards with uncertain step and certainly in a mental quandary. Right in front of the Café de la Paix, the scene of many important meetings that have so often shaped my life lines, I ran into Clarence Edwards, an old friend from the "days of the Empire" in the Philippines. Then he was aide to General Lawton, stood by his side indeed on that unlucky day when Lawton fell mortally wounded in a petty skirmish on the banks of the Pasig River. Now Edwards was a major general and had commanded a fighting division at the active front for a longer period than any of his brother officers. Strangely enough he had come across my name in a memorandum which we had drawn up at the War College a year ago explaining how we could best undermine the loyalty of troops with whom we might be confronted, men whose allegiance to the Central Empire could not be regarded as above suspicion.

"We have the plan in operation now," explained Edwards. "Before me is an Austro-Hungarian division filled with Rumanians from Transylvania and a Prussian Landwehr division of second-line troops. We have editors from Cleveland and Detroit and one from Milwaukee, and whenever the opportunity presents we bombard them with Mr. Wilson's notes translated into their various lingoes. We were getting results, but last week the officer in charge of the unit died of pneumonia and confusion resulted. What are you doing here?"

I told him, and he did not think much of it—and, well, before I knew what was up I found that I had agreed to take up the new job. That evening before he returned to the front Edwards arranged all the details; orders and travel orders were forthcoming, and it was agreed that Simpkins, his aide whom I knew, would drive me to Troyon and induct me into my new post.

* This was the second Congress of Submerged Nationalities (the first met in Rome in the spring), and Major Bonsal was the American delegate at Paris in September, 1918. It suddenly adjourned to make way for the Armistice proceedings and the Peace Conference, and Bonsal rejoined his outfit at the Verdun Front.

Forty-eight hours later I was dining very simply but very well at my general's headquarters and for that night at least I slept in his guest chamber which had so often lodged a marshal of France. It was only twenty-four hours later that I subsided into my cellar and got in touch with the propaganda machinery for which the general assigned me greater credit than I deserved.

October 18, 1918

Today the sergeant brought me a message that came over the telephone from headquarters. It was not in the romantic Choctaw that was supposed to baffle the wily Germans, always suspected of listening in, but in plain English. It directed me to present myself to General Edwards as soon as possible. It was about ten-thirty and I had on my desk several rather important letters to be translated, and then —well, I was nearly starving. Our mess arrangements were beneath contempt. If I tarried over my work I could arrange to arrive at the general's at lunchtime. While nothing extravagant or luxurious, I knew from several happy experiences that the general sets an excellent table. I also knew that General Degoutte, our army commander, had recently sent several cases of an excellent *petit vin* to the headquarters mess. Most of all, I remembered that slogan of my friend Conte in Paris: "*On cause mieux, on cause beaucoup mieux, en déjeunant.*"

So I kept on with my translations, only putting my sergeant on the lookout for a passing lorry. In places the mud on the road to Troyon was at least a foot deep, and I did not want to appear before my general as a mudlarker. Like many old soldiers, Edwards has the knack of always looking well groomed. So, acting as a shrewd "rustler" rather than as a smart soldier (I think you have to be that to survive in army circles), I arrived just as the general was going to the mess hall. He took me by the arm and ushered me in:

"This is your last army ration," he said; "you are ordered to Paris to await Colonel House who is coming over to initiate the peace negotiations. Your orders have come by telephone."

"Why," I interrupted him in astonishment, "I did not think anyone but you—and Nolan—had the remotest idea of where I was."

"Do not speak disrespectfully of the army," said Edwards, trying to look severe but soon relaxing into a broad smile. "But I suppose it is natural. East and West you have been an independent camp follower for years. You had so much seniority in that capacity that when old General Bliss [U. S. military representative at the Peace Conference] heard you had been commissioned a mere major he thought you had been demoted. But demoted or promoted, remember you are in the army now, and what you have just said might mean a court-martial.

"You are to return to Paris and report to Colonel House for special duty on his arrival. Official orders may or may not be here in a few hours, but in any event I authorize you to leave in the morning, especially as I am then sending Simpkins to Bar-le-Duc in my car on an important errand. Going with him you will have the right of way on the cluttered-up road, and that will save you many hours. I am going the rounds of the field hospitals now to cheer up the boys who were wounded or gassed at Marchville. Come along with me. I want to discuss with you the future of your cohort of polyglots, then to supper and you to pack."

"That will not take much time," I admitted, and the general smiled. "Yes, we are all traveling a bit light. You will have to spruce up quite a bit when you reach Paris. After what you have experienced here, peace-talking will be dress parade."

*   *   *   *

Well, I pulled out of that damp, moss-grown cellar none too soon; for days now I had been coughing with increasing violence and intensity. I once heard the sergeant say in an undertone which, however, reached me, "There's one good thing about the major's cough; it drowns out the artillery fire"—a statement that was not quite the truth but certainly approximated it. Simpkins * came for me before daylight, and I was glad he had with him the general's chauffeur, because he too was suffering from paroxysms of coughing which, whatever may have been the sergeant's opinion, were even more violent than mine.

All of my detail who were off duty, including the Cleveland and Detroit editors, saw me off and gave me the best of wishes for the best of luck.

* A week later "Nat" Simpkins died of septic pneumonia.

Paris, October 20, 1918

In the gray light of a misty morning I had my last glimpse in war-time of the Verdun salient and of the shell-pitted route which had proved to be the life line of France. There were many fires glowing in the beleaguered city, but outside in the shadows the graveyard of half-a-million unburied Germans and as many gallant sons of France was veiled in a heavy mist. Overhead many invisible planes were droning about upon their deadly missions, and the roar of the never-ceasing bombardment made all conversation impossible. At first the road was fairly passable, and shunning shell holes and soft shoulders we progressed at the rate of five miles the hour, although we natu-rally gave the right of way to ambulances with their sad freight and to the on-coming convoys of munition trucks. But even before Souilly was reached we ran into traffic congestions which the frantic efforts of the exasperated French gendarmes could not straighten out.

Hour after hour we plugged along, enveloped and involved in the confusion and all the disarray in the rear of the armies. Indeed, when but five miles out from Rottentout we were forced to halt, all traffic being blocked by disabled lorries. We skirted through a field that was pitted with fresh shell holes, pushed up a hill, and there upon the crest there came to us a symbol of hope. An old woman was plow-ing. Harnessed to her unconquerable will and to her plow was an emaciated cow and a little barefooted girl.

"*Hein*," she said, "I must get in my winter wheat, or else what shall we eat in the spring?" As we looked on, the whole strange outfit capsized into an unsuspected shell hole. We backed up and rescued her. With brief thanks she started another furrow. "I must get in my winter wheat," she repeated. At last we got back on the main road, and then simultaneously from Simpkins and myself came the words, "We should have no fear; France cannot die."

Darkness had fallen when we reached the railhead, and but for the major general's pennant flying over our car we would in all proba-bility have spent the night on the road.

October 27, 1918

My new Colonel [House] tiptoed into Paris so softly yesterday morning that I only reported to him today at the house that had been arranged for his reception in the Rue de L'Université. He immediately installed me in his official family on the same familiar footing that I had enjoyed in Berlin three years before:

"The President has given me no instructions; he said I would know what he wanted me to do and then told me to shove off. For the next few days we shall be very busy debating the terms of the Armistice, and you and Frazier and all of us will have to work long hours.* Today I am just talking with all and sundry [by this I suppose he referred to the two prime ministers and the three war ministers who were cooling their heels in the anteroom as Frazier passed me through their ranks], but tomorrow we shall get down to brass tacks. Come in at nine, prepared to make a day and perhaps a night of it."

Then a moment later, "I will follow the President's example and give you no definite instructions but just a hazy idea of what I shall expect from you. I think I can handle Lloyd George and the "Tiger" [Clemenceau] without much help, but into your hands I commit all the mighty men of the rest of the world. I shall expect you to call at least once a day and my door will always be open to you. From time to time, if inconvenient to call, send me a memo—or better still, leave it with the sailors who will guard my gate."

After a moment's reflection he continued, "You have seen all these strange people with whom Paris now is swarming on their native heaths. Most of them you knew and appraised before they were built up by war propaganda and nationalistic inflation. The war that has destroyed cities has puffed up some little men until they find their hats and their boots too small, much too small for them. I shall count on you to present them to me in their original proportions. That will be an invaluable service."

I went out of the room gasping. It was certainly quite a job I had fallen into by "picking up" Colonel House on the streets of Berlin in March, 1915!

[One winter's afternoon in Berlin, Stephen Bonsal spied a fellow American who seemed lost and confused, unable to extract directions from the hurried German pedestrians who jostled by him without notice. Bonsal came to the rescue, led the stranger to his destination,

---

* Arthur Hugh Frazier of the Foreign Service, who had been secretary of the American Embassy in Vienna and Paris, was one of the three aides to Colonel House. Major Bonsal and Gordon Auchincloss, son-in-law and private secretary to House, comprised the nucleus of the Colonel's "family."

and in fluent German interpreted for him. Not until the next day at the American Embassy where they met again were they formally introduced. The two became firm friends, and when House was sent abroad to initiate the Armistice negotiations, he cabled General Pershing and asked for Bonsal's services as interpreter. Eventually Bonsal was picked to sit in on the most "graveyard" secret sessions of the Peace Conference and interpret for President Wilson and Colonel House. This diary is the record of such meetings and was used by the President as a reminder of what had taken place from one important session to another.]

October 29, 1918

House received his credentials at the White House on October the fourteenth (1918). Several days before that, aware of the mission upon which he was about to set out and impressed with the fact from the day that the Bulgars capitulated to the Army of the East (September 29th) that more local knowledge was needed than he possessed, he sent a cable to Pershing asking that someone familiar with Balkan conditions be attached to his staff. This cable resulted in my recall from the 26th Division and my being attached for duty with the Armistice Commission and the Peace Delegation.

The colonel picked me up exactly where our relations had ended in Berlin:

"I'm afraid I shall want you to be at my beck and call throughout the Armistice proceedings. If this should leave any free time on your hands, which I doubt, I want you to keep in touch with the strange peoples from Southeastern Europe who are assembling in such numbers in Paris in expectation, I fear, of the millennium—which may not be so near at hand as we all hope. This is to be your job. Of course when the Germans come, you are to be, as you were in Berlin, my interpreter and intermediary, and then indeed your hands will be full."

[From this and another statement which he made to me a few days later, it is quite clear that House had expected to enter into direct negotiations with the Germans at an early day; and his disappointment that these expectations were not realized was very great. Bearing on this phase of the problem with which he and the other delegates were confronted were these, his often-repeated words:

"It took many of us to win the war, and each one of the powers will have to be consulted in winning the peace. In adjusting these different points of view, our principal difficulty will lie."]

October 29, 1918

A very momentous meeting *chez* House this morning. Everybody was there, but Foch, the Generalissimo, had the floor and did not seem inclined to share time with any of the civilian chiefs. Lloyd George remarked in a petulant aside, "I think we are wasting precious hours. The Germans are beaten but not down on their knees as yet. They are not thinking of surrender."

If Foch heard this he paid no attention to it. He described at considerable length the operations that he was planning, that were indeed under way. "In view of the information I have from many quarters and all in agreement as to the morale and the physical condition of the German armies, these operations will undoubtedly prove successful. Your military advisers, I am happy to say, are in complete agreement as to the armistice terms we are prepared to offer, should the Germans ask for them. They do not differ in any way from the terms we would impose upon the Germans after the success of the operations we are about to undertake. [The march to Berlin.] So it is clear that if the Germans accept the terms we are willing to grant them today, when they ask formally for the armistice, *il est inutile de continuer la Bataille*—nothing would be gained by continuing the fighting."

House made now an inquiry—not on his own behalf, he stated, but voicing the views of others who were not present and yet wanted to be heard and informed:

"M. le Field-Marshal, would our victory not be more complete if terms were only granted after the Germans had been expelled from the territory they invaded and driven back across the Rhine?"

"I think not," answered Foch. "The terms which I have drawn up, with the advice and approval of all the Allied commanders, are identical with the terms that I think we should impose if our armies had reached Berlin. The march to the Prussian capital in the present state of affairs would not be difficult, but we would lose men. Why lose them if we secure all we desire without undertaking the march?"

November 4, 1918

Mermeix, the venerable journalist, came in today and gave us some interesting details as to certain aspects of the pending armistice negotiations hitherto unknown to us. In their discussion on October 25, he says, Pétain insisted, as did Foch, upon the complete disarmament of all German troops in France with the exception of what he called carrying arms (I suppose small arms are meant). He further demanded a broad strip of German territory as a protection against a renewal of invasion and as a pledge for carrying out the other stipulations of the capitulation. He insists that the Germans should only be allowed ten days in which to leave French territory. In this way they would be prevented from taking with them their stores and war supplies. He insists that the French armed forces should occupy the left bank of the Rhine and a zone fifty kilometers deep on the right bank. This, he said, was his minimum demand, but he was quite confident that the Germans would not accept it.

Haig,* according to Mermeix, expressed his belief that the whole discussion was a waste of time and that the Germans were not ready to accept such enormous demands. He added that if an armistice is really desired at the present moment more modest terms should be offered. While the Allied armies are victorious, they are worn down and have gotten far ahead of their supplies and have also outrun their communications. And, while the German forces are in a measure disorganized, their spirit of resistance is not entirely broken. As for himself, he contended that the evacuation of Alsace-Lorraine, and of course of all French territory, would seal the victory.

General Pershing, Mermeix reports, was far from enthusiastic for an armistice at this time, but he conceded that he would approve any terms that Foch approved of. Lord Milner, British delegate, expressed great fear of the growing strength of the Bolsheviki and he contended that as the first bulwark against the Red flood Germany should be given sufficient armament to cope with this menace.

November 10, 1918

Here is Colonel Boyd's version as to what really happened, and he ought to know because he is Pershing's brilliant military secretary

---

* General Haig was commander in chief of the British forces on the Western Front.

and interprets for him in all his contacts with French officials. Of course Black Jack [Pershing] wanted to push on to Berlin, as did every soldier in the army, but at the Senlis Conference on October 25 he agreed with Haig and Pétain and Bliss that if the Germans asked for an armistice the terms we had agreed upon must be submitted to them. They were, none of them, enthusiastic for the terms that Foch had drawn up, but as they were convinced that the Germans would not accept them, they agreed that it was just as well to let the Generalissimo get the idea out of his system and go on with the war. Pershing was confident, and said so quite frankly, that in view of the defense the Germans were putting up on his, the Sedan, front, it was absurd and worse to think that Ludendorff would accept any terms that we would feel inclined to offer. Haig and Pétain were in full agreement that the negotiations had not been opened in good faith, that Ludendorff was simply sparring for time.

"I think it fair to say," concluded Boyd, "that all the generals bowed to Foch's wishes because they were confident his terms would be rejected—that a rotund 'no' would be the answer from the German lines."

However, the generals were mistaken, and soon the impression, the very unwelcome impression, grew that the Germans would accept. It was then that Pershing went back to what was undoubtedly his original thought and tried to block the Armistice, although he knew at the time that the prime ministers, who had been as skeptical as he in the beginning, were now behind the Foch terms if the Germans asked for them.

It was in a letter which reached House on October 30 that Pershing explained his new position and why he had reverted to his original thought on the vital matter. On the twenty-fifth he had agreed with Foch out of courtesy to the Commander in Chief and also because he had been convinced that the Germans would not consider the Allied terms. He again asserted that the Germans were not acting in good faith, that they were hoping by securing a breathing spell of a few days to extricate themselves from their present unfortunate positions.

House cabled the letter and the memorandum on to Washington and also some of the explanatory remarks that Boyd had been authorized to make to me. Not a word was said about continuing the march to Berlin, but of course that was implicit in the Pershing attitude. House also discussed the memo with Clemenceau and with Lloyd

George, but the discussion did not detain them long because the evidence was mounting every hour that whether in good faith or in bad the Germans were preparing to accept the Foch terms.

As a matter of fact, all the civilian leaders were pleased with this conclusion to the long debate. Foch had convinced them all that while the march to Berlin was practicable it would take at least two months' time and would be costly in casualties, and that once on the [River] Spree the Allies would not be able to demand, or at least would not be justified in demanding, terms more exacting than those that had been drawn up at Senlis—terms approved by men who, however, regarded them as more of a gesture than as the historic instrument that would bring the war to an end.

The changes of thought among the generals and the civilian chiefs are difficult to follow and out of them legends will grow; but I believe that these are the facts, although I am not at all certain they will find their place in the official histories.

November 11, 1918

Colonel House treated us to a bit of acting this morning, which left Frazier and myself abashed and ashamed of our own poor performances. At what seemed to us the crack of dawn, although it was really after eight, General Mordacq appeared. He is the principal military aid of the Tiger; he wore the formal uniform of great occasions and was covered with decorations, and his mien was portentous. "I have come to tell you, at the express orders of the president of the Council of Ministers, that the armistice terms have been accepted and signed. M. Clemenceau wished that you, who have contributed so notably to the happy result of the negotiations, should be first advised and by word direct from him."

As a matter of fact, through our own official channels some hours before we had been advised of all that had happened at the Rethondes meeting, but the Colonel acted as though the news came to him like a bolt from a blue sky. He thanked Mordacq warmly, patted both his hands affectionately, only stopping short of the *accolade*. When the General left the Colonel explained, "He would have been mortified if after 'deranging' himself at this early hour he had seen that the news he brought was a twice-told tale."

November 12, 1918

Suddenly in the hour of victory the President has changed his mind as to where the Peace Conference should be held. He had hitherto openly, indeed even boisterously, favored Lausanne, Geneva, any place in Switzerland. But now he vetoes all these places and plunges for Paris. "In Switzerland," he cables, "the Conference would be saturated by every poisonous element and very accessible to hostile influences." House is amazed and not a little disappointed. He was against Paris as the meeting place; but as to the other cities, he was without a favorite.

With characteristic energy the Colonel sets about carrying out the President's plan, however unwise he may think it. For the last twenty-four hours he has so harassed Northcliffe--the great editor and British propaganda chief who is over here hoping (against hope, I fear) that Lloyd George will make him one of the delegates—that he has abandoned his own personal plan of having the conference meet in Belgium ("Make 'em crawl on their knees to where they disgraced themselves and our civilization," was his slogan) and has submitted to House for his approval an editorial to appear in the London *Times* which says roundly: "It would be egregious folly to have the Conference convene anywhere but in Paris." The Colonel has a way with the press lords!

Now that the Germans are beaten and the great host that was so formidable ten weeks ago is disintegrating, with many units of the "ever-victorious army" sneaking over the frontiers into Holland, the light-hearted Parisians are saying, "It was easy; no army can stand up to ours." There are some who quite openly seek to minimize the recent achievements of the Allies and above all of the Tiger. They have quite forgotten the dark days when they said, "What is the matter with the Allied armies?—After all, the Tiger is not a worker of miracles."

Now that the danger is gone it is forgotten. No one recalls the twenty-eighth of May when the French lost the Chemin des Dames and Paris was again in grave danger. Even the memory of July 15 is effaced, when the Germans advanced on Rheims, crossed the Marne, and Paris was menaced for the third and last time, and no one knew it was to be the last time.

In military history there is no such striking reversal of fortune, and so I suppose it is natural that soldiers and civilians alike fail to comprehend it. How did it happen? The Germans lost men and the reserves were few; and they had lost guns, and replacements were not in sight. But what they had lost, and what in my judgment explains their disaster, is the fact they had lost their morale. Fed upon lies for four years, this "cannon fodder" at long last saw how they had been deceived and caved in by regiments, brigades, and divisions. Only to hold their way of escape and the road home they fought desperately on the Sedan front. The dream of conquest had given way to *heimweh*.

* * * *

Today, after a long eclipse through the days of imperial expansion and overseas adventures, I am hearing again the words that foreshadowed a new era which I so often listened to a generation ago in London as they fell from the lips of Kropotkin, the battle-scarred Russian prince, the descendant of Rurik whom the parvenu Romanoffs had driven into exile. I heard them cheered to the echo in the saloons of London's East End and in the meeting place in Hammersmith where the poet William Morris presided over gatherings of exiles from all over Europe and Asia. "All history must be rewritten," Kropotkin would say; "rewritten from the point of view of the people."

Well, here they are, gathered together not only from Dan and Beersheba but from the more spacious if more troubled world of our day. But alas, divergent views are very vocal, and it is quite apparent that the making of history is a difficult task whether undertaken by the philosophers in their closets or by the orators in the market places.

CHAPTER II

Russians: Reds, Whites, and Pinks

"Whither then are you speeding, Russia of mine?" asked Gogol in 1841. I quote him and shall endeavor to give some of the very contradictory answers that are given me here today.

Paris, January 6, 1919

The Russian groups are sweeping down upon me in ever-increasing numbers. I give them a loose rein, and after they have delivered themselves of what they have to say, more or less exhausted they retire. I remain silent. I am at the receiving end, but when I have to say something I confine my words to the President's Russian message of 1917. Then it had an excellent reception, but today it would seem to have lost its savor.

In his clarion call Mr. Wilson said: "The day has come to conquer or submit; if the forces of autocracy can divide us, we shall be overcome; if we stand together, victory is certain and also the liberties which only victory can secure. Then we could afford to be generous, but now we cannot afford to be weak or omit a single guarantee of justice and security. We are fighting for no selfish object but for the liberation of peoples everywhere from the aggression of autocratic forces."

It has been well said that the voice of Wilson was the voice of freedom, but it should be admitted that he spoke a language which more than 99 per cent of the Russian people at that time did not understand. His objective was splendidly stated, but in the same manifesto, as though at last seeing the obstacles in his path (among them the

14

mountains of ignorance which would have to be surmounted), he added: "Practical questions can only be settled by practical means; phrases will not right wrongs; remedies must be found as well as statements of principles that have a pleasing sound." Well, I keep that manifesto on my desk in Russian, in French, and in a number of other languages. It is our avenue of approach to the Russian problem, also our point of departure when and if we give it up.

Of course the present, the new rulers of Russia are ruling by the only methods they have any knowledge of, those of the tyrant and the autocrat, and this is perhaps, as many think, the only ideology that the liberated but still benighted serfs can understand. In his talk with the Colonel several days ago, Iswolsky, long ambassador for the Tsar in Paris and twice minister of Foreign Affairs, amazed the Colonel, and he is not easily surprised, by stating:

"From 1906 on we were working toward democracy, the grave need of which the disasters in the war with Japan disclosed. With this purpose, my august master summoned the First Duma; its members were incompetent, the outcome was disgraceful, and he 'discharged' it. He then convened the Second Duma; if possible, it was still more incompetent and disgraceful in its behavior, and he dispersed it. The Tsar was still with infinite patience seeking another and perhaps a better way to share his burdens with the people when the hoodlums got the upper hand and—well, you know what happened."

I am afraid there are many who share Iswolsky's depressing thoughts and carry them out to what they consider their logical conclusion. Better to have had no revolution at all than the anarchy with which the Russian people are now confronted—and also their neighbors.

Here I shall make as plain as I can how our negotiations with the Soviets got under way and also the circumstances under which they bogged down. Hopefully, President Wilson fired the opening salute on March 11, 1918, with this cable to the Soviet Congress recently assembled. It reads:

May I not take advantage of the meeting of the Congress of the Soviets to express the sincere sympathy which the people of the United States feel for the Russian people at this moment when the German power has been thrust in to interrupt and turn back the whole struggle for freedom, and substitute the wishes of Germany for the purpose of the people of Russia?

The whole heart of the people of the United States is with the people of Russia in the attempt to free themselves forever from autocratic government and become the masters of their own life.

Four days later (March 15, 1918) the following reply was received from Moscow:

The Russian Socialistic Federative Republic of Soviets takes advantage of President Wilson's communication to express to all peoples perishing and suffering from the horrors of imperialistic war its warm sympathy and firm belief that the happy time is not far distant when the laboring masses of all countries will throw off the yoke of Capitalism and will establish a socialistic state of society which alone is capable of securing just and lasting peace, as well as the culture and well-being of all laboring people.

In his confidential file, there is a note in the Colonel's handwriting. "That is a tough one to answer! I think formal correspondence had best be discontinued." And as a matter of fact it was. Some weeks later Mr. Francis, our envoy in Moscow, wrote: "I am informed that Zinoviev, the Soviet Foreign Minister, boasted that 'with these words we slapped President Wilson in the face.'"

February—undated, 1919

When Kerensky called today, I took this opportunity of relating to him an episode of my war days in Russia. It proved far from comforting and added to his burden of doubt and anxiety which, despite his brave words, is evidently very heavy. [Kerensky, former prime minister of the short-lived Provisional government (July-November, 1917), was one of the many fugitive "Pinks" in Paris representing Russian liberalism.]

In November, 1915, I traveled through Russia on my way back to my post in the Philippines. The English, for war purposes, had bought up all the trans-Pacific liners, and so I was compelled to proceed to the Far East by an unusual route, through war-stricken Europe. Certainly this was the only way that would bring me to Manila before my leave expired. I crossed the Atlantic on a Danish steamer, the *Frederick VIII*, and after landing in Copenhagen I went by rail to Stockholm and from there by the so-called Lapland Express around the Gulf, via Tornea and Haparanda to St. Petersburg, since this was at the time the only rail route across Europe that had not been interrupted.

Peter's improvised city, his "window" on Europe, presented a tragic spectacle. It was bitter cold and the streets were crowded with hundreds and thousands of half-frozen peasants who, fleeing from their homes in the border provinces, were seeking what shelter they could find from the advancing German armies. I stayed as always at the little Hotel de France, awaiting the departure of the Trans-Siberian Express which, owing to lack of fuel, now only ran once a week. This hotel had been the rendezvous of all the correspondents during the first revolution (1905–1906), and there I had foregathered with them. They were widely scattered now. Of all the familiar faces, only that of the trusty Beringer of Reuter's was in evidence.

For the first day I wandered about, depressed by the sad spectacle which the once gay capital presented. In the great square by the Winter Palace, thousands of thinly clad peasants were being put through the manual of arms; but in lieu of rifles, which were not available, they were being drilled with sticks. I lunched at the Hotel d'Europe, where the war profiteers, still in fine fettle, were eating and drinking copiously. At a prominent table sat General Rennenkampf, responsible for the loss of two battles and the captivity of thousands of Russians now in the prison camps of East Prussia. He was on trial for incompetence and with having had treasonable relations with the German General Staff; but as an evidence of the weakness of the government, the trial or the inquiry hung fire and the general drank champagne. The Great White Tsar? Was he living or dead? With certainty no one knew. If alive, he was leading a hermit's existence in Tsarskoe Selo while the walls of his once mighty empire tumbled about him.

That evening I dined in the almost deserted *salle* of the Hotel de France. At an adjacent table, also alone, sat Prince Lvoff, whom I had come to know quite intimately during the revolutionary movement of 1905. He was at that time the leading spirit in the Zemstvo organization which, in spite of the open opposition of the imperial bureaucrats, made some headway in securing popular participation in local and provincial government. I had described his work in my cabled letters to the *New York Times* (sent via Germany of course) and had hailed his work as perhaps the only healthy and hopeful sign visible on the somber horizon.

The Prince recognized me, although he did not place me after all these intervening years until I made myself known to him. Then with the coffee, at his request, I moved over to his table. He seemed greatly interested in my proposed journey across Siberia and then, growing thoughtful, he asked me to his apartment where, as he said, it would be safer to discuss the present situation than in a public place where "walls have ears."

Once in his apartment Lvoff admitted frankly that the imperial regime was headed for disaster; that the prevailing misery was more than flesh and blood could stand. He went on to say: "The more intelligent of the bureaucrats have read the handwriting on the wall and are conceding to my organization some power and a little authority. Many of our leaders have been placed with the war industries, and in many provincial governments our Zemstvo organizations have been given an opportunity to work. It is difficult to get this or any other news out of the country, but it is most desirable that our friends in Western Europe, and above all in America, should be advised of our hopes and our expectations. They must be advised of this trend in our affairs so that they may not be surprised by developments that cannot be much longer delayed. I have a letter to Charles Crane in America, always our good friend and always so helpful to the liberal movement in Russia, but it would be unwise to entrust it to the mail. I wonder if you would be so kind as to take the letter to Peking and mail it there, or better still, once there open it and cable the contents to Mr. Crane?"

I assured the Prince I would be pleased to do him this favor and then we parted for the night, and for good, as we thought, because he was leaving for Mohileff in the morning and my train left for the Urals a few hours later.

Back in my room I did a little packing and was preparing for bed, when suddenly (late in the day, I must admit) it occurred to me that I had let myself in for an act that was quite reprehensible under the circumstances. I now remembered that I was traveling under the safeguard of a diplomatic passport, and that it would be most improper for me to aid in the transmission of a letter which the government whose favor I enjoyed would have intercepted had they known of its existence. I hastened back to Lvoff, and my call, it was long after midnight, evidently startled him. I explained my dilemma and he was greatly distressed. Sadly he said: "I had regarded you as a messenger from heaven. The service I asked of you would be valuable to our cause, but I understand your scruples and respect them."

As I handed back the letter and saw his disappointment, suddenly a way of escape occurred to me. "I suppose it is a quibble, a mere quibble," I admitted, "but still quibbles so often ease the pangs of conscience. If you should care to read the letter to me and then destroy it, I could on my arrival in China cable Crane that I had chanced to meet you and give him your message."

"Splendid," assented Lvoff, and he opened the letter and read it aloud twice. It was short and easy to commit to memory. It ran:

We are making great progress. We have now at least three hundred thousand men in the Zemstvo organization and there are many more in minor government jobs who are acquiring valuable experience and above all confidence in their ability to meet the emergency that will shortly arise. At the proper moment we shall take hold and the transition will be orderly. Your fear of anarchy is natural but unfounded. We shall not push matters but shall be ready to take the rudder when the discredited helmsmen jump or are thrown overboard.

When I reached this point in my story, Kerensky interrupted me with what was almost a wail. "Ah, what a mistake! What a tragic mistake—that delay. Our Liberals lost hope. They concluded that our leaders were talkers, not doers. And the criminals? They indeed were doers. They saw their chance and pitched in. No man's life was safe, and the Zemstvos and the other liberal organizations were swept away in a maelstrom of anarchy." Then rallying, Kerensky added: "It is heartening to see that once again the outlook is bright but, had not Lvoff waited so long, while the powers of darkness grew bold, thousands of lives would have been saved and Russia would not sit there as she does today, the Niobe of the nations, mourning for her children. But after darkness and death, the dawn is coming. It is unmistakable . . ."—and a prey to emotions which I, in part, at least, had aroused, the poor fellow ran out of my room.

I cabled Lvoff's message to Mr. Crane from Peking but did not see him again until he appeared at the Peace Conference four years later. Then he simply said, "Lvoff was an excellent man, but a poor timer. And as a prophet . . ."

January 4, 1919

Prince Lvoff, president of the deposed and fugitive Kerensky government and the founder of the Zemstvos, came in this morning. He brought no encouraging news, only complaints, and that was not news. He stated that the promised arms and ammunition [for use against the Reds] were only reaching the Omsk government with great delay or not at all. I had to tell him this was not surprising as so much of it fell into the hands of the Bolsheviki even when we placed it at points represented as being safely in the possession of his forces. The old man has aged twenty years since I saw him last in Petrograd, and yet but a scant four years have elapsed. These years of *Sturm und Drang* count as double time, I suppose, for all who are closely involved.

Not so Boris Savinkov, however; he looks ten years younger than he did during our clandestine meetings in the Tartar Market of Moscow, now some twelve or thirteen years ago. Then he was a terrorist to be shot on sight. Now he claims to be still Minister of War, although the Bolsheviki have expelled him. Now he twirls a cane and wears a gardenia in his buttonhole. He could pass for a boulevardier of the latest vintage, but he says he is returning to Russia very shortly, where, he asserts, the Bolsheviki are at the end of their tether.

[Savinkov, a born revolutionary, is credited with having organized the assassination of Grand Duke Sergius in 1905. As Minister of War in the short-lived Kerensky regime, he fought the Bolsheviks in Russia, Poland, and then in Paris. Apparently believing all this was forgiven, he did return to Russia in 1924, was promptly arrested, and, while being questioned by the secret police at their headquarters, either leaped or was pushed to his death from a window.]

January 14, 1919

I have taken a night off and I spent it with Savinkov. At night he is fearless and will go anywhere, but, like the bats and the owls, with the coming of the sun he disappears. He explains that many men are seeking to kill him. In restaurants and cafés he invariably sits with his back to the wall and facing the entrance. And the Browning he always carries is near at hand. He told me this evening the story of Aseff, the spy, and if you want to know a revolutionist, this one was certainly quite a contrast to my good friends of the earlier days, Stepniak and Prince Kropotkin.

"He was not a bloodthirsty man," maintained Savinkov. "Out of pure malice he would not kill a fly. He assassinated Plehve, Minister of the Interior, to get a much needed bonus from the Revolution, and he safeguarded the Tsar to secure a reward from the police. He had to live, and as he lived on a large scale he had to have money—quite a lot of money. No, I don't think you met him in our hide-away in the Tartar Market in 1906, where you met so many of the 'comrades.' You were lucky, as most of the men assembled there he later brought to the gallows.

"I think, however, you must have met Stalin; he is from the Caucasus and at birth was handicapped by a name as long as the Volga. So they called him Stalin—and hard as steel he is, but true? Certainly not true as steel, I would not say so. Many of the new comrades fear him, and not without reason. Now he has left us and he is working against the only people who can save Russia; but I admit, he is a man of infinite resource, *tiens*, let me tell you about that. You have heard of the looting of the Tiflis Bank. It happened while you were in Moscow. That was a great coup and it came at an opportune moment for us. There wasn't a sound kopek or even a counterfeit note in our treasury. Stalin heard that a million rubles were coming from Moscow for the monthly pay-off and he determined to intercept it. He contrived the whole business, but physically he decided he did not want to take an active part in it; he was the executive of the affair.

"One of the guards of the treasure wagon was in his pay, and at a signal from Stalin, who stood on the sidewalk, he ran a knife in the heart of the driver. Just at that moment, most unfortunately, a file of *gardevois* (transport police) came around the corner and took in the situation. And so did Stalin. You would think a thing like that would rattle a man, but not one of Stalin's caliber. He grabbed one of his own men and, as the treasure wagon was driven away by his other confederate, he shouted, 'Comrades, I have him!' And indeed he had. Speechless with amazement, the fellow was delivered to the police. When he recovered his rattled wits, the victim, his fellow conspirator, charged Stalin with being the ringleader; but the police paid no attention to his protestations, and when he began to bore them, they stood him up against a wall and filled him full of lead. Yes, Comrade Stalin is a quick thinker, a man of infinite resource.*

"Well, I have almost forgotten to tell you—they got away with the wagon and the booty was distributed where it was needed. With the small notes, that was not difficult; but there were also big notes, five-thousand-ruble notes, and that was not easy; so they passed them

---

* It is only fair to say that Savinkov hated Stalin as the Devil hates Holy Water.

along to Comrade Litvinoff, who had traveled abroad, who could speak languages, who knew his way about and could eat soup without making too much noise. But they caught him the first time he tried to change a note in Paris. You see the Bank of Russia had advised the French authorities of the numbers; and it was now that Litvinoff made his debut in diplomacy. He explained that the democratic groups in Russia had sent him to pay at least part interest on the loans that in happier days the French people had made to the Russians, and that the note he had been caught trying to change was but to meet his paltry living expenses while on this noble mission. They sent him to prison for six months, but he was pardoned out in a few weeks by a radical minister of the interior, who was convinced, or pretended to be, that he was the only Russian who had ever attempted to pay interest on the Russian loan! Keep an eye on him, and on Stalin. They will go far if they do not have their throats cut."

Then Savinkov resumed his revelations as to Aseff, so long his idol.

"If I were not held here by a still more important duty, I would go after Aseff because I was hoodwinked by him and because many of my comrades were delivered by him to the hangman, partly, at least, as a result of my sponsorship. The man was an artist in his line, which was double-dealing. I can think of no one in history to compare with him. It is now clear that he betrayed all of us to the police. You probably met at our hideaway Gershuni, an artist in terror if there ever was one. He had the power of influencing people to an extraordinary degree. Some thought he was an adept in black magic— perhaps it was only hypnotism. He was sold out by Aseff in our first attempt to murder Plehve. He, our chief, yielding to our insistence, retired to Vilna, there to await the news of our success. But the coup failed, and many were gathered in and died to whom Aseff had given the kiss of death.

"At this time, our master plotter fell under the suspicion of some of the comrades, most unjustly, I thought. Indeed, I threatened to withdraw from the organization unless he was given a clean bill of health. Under this suspicion Aseff decided that Plehve must die. This was necessary if he were to retain the confidence of both his employers. I also think the Ochrana [the Tsar's secret police] had been short-sighted and stingy; they had not given him a bonus at all commensurate with his betrayal of all those involved in the first attempt.

"You should not think that I am the only one of the comrades who was fascinated by Aseff, the master spy. No, there were many of them, although perhaps I am the only one alive today. Gershuni, that apostle of the Terror, the young man with the ikon face, worshipped the very ground he walked on. While still a student, Gershuni had been sent to Siberia for revolutionary activities, but he soon made his escape. He was smuggled out of the prison yard in a barrel of sauerkraut and he made his way to America via Vladivostok. In grateful memory of the vehicle of escape he assumed and ever after bore the name of Kapusta, or 'Mr. Cabbage.' Once back in our circle he volunteered for most dangerous duty in connection with the second and successful attempt to kill Plehve, the hated Minister of the Interior. In taking his leave of us he asked for one favor and it was, of course, granted.

" 'If I fail, and in that case I shall not return,' he said, 'I ask that you restore Aseff to your full confidence and make him your leader. He is the master mind of the revolutionary movement and we shall not succeed until he is given full powers.'

"As a general practice Aseff would turn suspicion from himself to others, and it was at his suggestion that Gershuni and I killed Comrade Tataroff in Warsaw. Yes, we killed him, although it was Gershuni who wielded the dagger. No, I have no remorse. True, he was not guilty of the crimes with which Aseff, to shield himself, charged him, but he was an informer and should have been put out of the way.

"After the first and the second attempts to kill Plehve had failed, doubtless through the information which Aseff furnished the police, many more of our group became suspicious. Aseff recognized that his complete rehabilitation required that he must at last pull off a big coup. He went about among us saying, 'Plehve must die. His responsibility for the Kichenew pogrom makes him our outstanding enemy. His execution will please the Jews throughout the world and from them will come the sinews of war we are in such great need of.'

"Aseff was not a Jew," explained Savinkov, "but as an abandoned child he was adopted into a Jewish family and he had a grateful remembrance of their kindness."

Some weeks later Savinkov came in to see me again. He seemed depressed and so, unwisely, I asked him if he had news of the great spy. "Yes," he answered, "bad news. He has escaped me. He is dead. His last coup was to escape my dagger." Then, at some length, which I shall condense, he gave me the last chapter of this strange history.

"We have now learned what happened to him. When he saw that even my faith in him was wavering, by night he fled from Paris, taking with him all our funds. With a stout lady of his choice he sailed for months through the isles of Greece. Then he established himself in Berlin as a stockbroker under the name of Alexander Neumeyer. He was quite successful and was doing very well until the war came. His money was in Russian bonds; at first their sale was forbidden and then they became valueless. With the stout lady he opened a corset business and was again doing well when the German police gathered him in. They said they were holding him because he was an anarchist, but after some months they offered to let him out but merely for the purpose of transferring him to a Russian concentration camp. Aseff knew what fate would overtake him there, so he prevailed on the Germans to keep him in prison. When all Germans began to starve, they turned him loose and starvation and gallstones ended his career in the spring of 1918. The scoundrel has escaped my dagger. The great cheat; he has even cheated the gallows!"

February 4, 1919

Today, for perhaps the hundredth time in this catastrophic year, I witnessed an incident which reminded me of how quickly the pomp of power passes, how near to the highest place in the capitol yawns the abyss by the Tarpeian Rock. I saw Count Cassini, so long ambassador extraordinary of Holy Russia, running through the sleet and rain on the Place de la Madeleine to catch a bus to take him to the modest suburban retreat, or refuge, with which the French government has provided him.

I grant you that thousands of other people were doing the very same thing at this crowded hour, but the difference is that they have done it every day of their lives; they are inured to it. But Cassini! When I saw him first (1896), he was lording it over all China. He was practically Viceroy of the Far East. When he moved through the streets of Peking, sotnias of Cossacks dashed ahead and cleared the way for the little man with the monocle who for four years, with the dreaded power of Russia behind him, dominated four hundred million Chinese and made them do his bidding.

"I want a railway to run across China from the Amoor to the sea."

"Excellency, we shall be delighted."

"But," he explained, "unfortunately, there are many, so many Hunhuzes in that territory, outlaws who respect neither Russian nor Chinese culture, I shall have to have guards, perhaps a little army, in that zone to protect our rails."

"Undoubtedly, Excellency, it shall be as you say."

As these pictures passed before me, the little man, now almost blind and evidently quite lame, was climbing onto the tail board of the bus and the conductress was giving him a piece of her mind and a push with her stout arm. She did not want him to clutter up the platform, and it was there he wanted to smoke a cigarette; the two purposes clashed, and I hung back. Perhaps I was a fair-weather friend, but I did not want the great man of former days to know that I witnessed his hour of humiliation. And help him I could not. The French government was doling out to him, as to the other great ones now in exile from Unholy Russia, a meager monthly stipend which at least keeps the wolf from the door. Of course all these advances are being entered on the Grand Livre of the Russian debt in the hope, a forlorn one I think, that Russia will pay up when, as the expression is, "things once again become normal."

February 10, 1919

I have neglected serious Russian affairs hitherto, as far as my diary is concerned at least, and yet the fact is they have been with us from the start of the Conference and I was immersed in their affairs even before the talk fest began. President Wilson never said a truer word than when he announced his belief that the treatment of Russia presented the acid test to the peacemakers. Up to the present the result of the acid test has been negative and the outlook for the future is far from reassuring.

At the first meeting (January 16), when the Russian problem was broached, Lloyd George threw a bombshell by announcing that while he was helping Kolchak [leader of the White Russian Armies in Siberia who was captured and shot in 1920] with money and munitions, he was convinced that the Admiral was a monarchist. According to some accounts he called him a Tsarist. Many plans were then proposed, and according to the announcement of my cheerful Colonel, the four powers present divided into six groups. But at least three definite and distinct plans were immediately advanced to deal with the spreading "plague spot."

The first plan was military intervention, sponsored by Winston Churchill, the dispatch of an army of one hundred thousand men to Moscow, not of course "with hostile intent or imperialistic purpose," merely to open a political kindergarten in which the "Ruskies" might be taught the difficult task of governing themselves. Second, the *cordon sanitaire*, to make it impossible for the crazy moujiks to infect Europe with their weird but most infectious malady. The third plan, sponsored by the British, was to summon the leaders of all the Russian fractions and factions to Paris in the hope of bringing them into agreement among themselves and, if possible, to concerted action with the Allies.

Many thought well of this third plan; at least it committed no one to a line of policy and it would postpone decision and action, but M. Clemenceau smashed it with: "I cannot permit the Soviet agents to enter France, much less come to Paris, where we have already so many Bolsheviki of varied nationalities."

Disappointed but not discouraged, the President after this setback decided to go it alone, at least temporarily. He sent out invitations to all the Russian groups to assemble at Prinkipo, the pleasant summer resort on the Bosphorus, for the purpose of having a "good talk." He hoped it would lead to disarmament and the holding of a "free and fair" election. The plan did not prosper. Unfortunately, almost before it was sent out (the invitation, I mean) Miliukoff, the leader of the Cadet party, the most progressive and responsible in Russia, who like most of his adherents is living in exile, issued a statement deploring the call and declining it for himself and his adherents.

This action was immediately followed by refusals from the so-called governments of Omsk, Ekaterindor, Archangel, and the Crimea. The Soviets now joined in the chorus and made the rejection of the project unanimous, or nearly so. [They accepted, indeed, but with reservations and limitations on the scope of the Conference that robbed the meeting of any chance of a successful issue.]

It is true that the Baltic republics, Esthonia, Latvia, and Lithuania, were willing to put in an appearance, but they wanted transportation and assurances of protection from enemies on sea and land. As the President saw no advantage in a rump congress, he let the matter slide

and turned to other equally thorny problems. I regaled the Colonel
with a Homeric sentence of Bismarck to me in Friedrichsruh thirty
years ago, *"Diese verdamte Russen geben uns viel zu shaffen."* ("These
—— Russians give us a lot of trouble.")

"And it is true today and will be true tomorrow, I fear," said the
Colonel.

April 20, 1919

I have been canny, perhaps even "ca' canny," to use Lloyd George's
favorite expression, in my relations with the Russians. The fact is
that with the exception of Prince Lvow, in whom I have full confidence that dates back to and was tested by our close relations during
the first revolution (1906), I frankly distrust them all. When they
came to the Crillon, and they came from the beginning in droves
(now they are fighting among themselves and come singly), I would
introduce them to House and when he requested it to the other commissioners with the simple statement, "This is M. Kerensky, of whom
you have heard," or "This is M. Boris Savinkov, his former minister
of war."

It was a wise precaution and I congratulate myself upon my unusual
reserve. I do not know what has happened, but I can see that the
President is far from pleased with the Russians and if, as reported,
Uncle Sam's money bags were ever open to them they are closed
now.

Yesterday the President, Lloyd George, and House were in a hud-
dle as I brought the Colonel an important telegram. Lloyd George
was telling the President about how Russia might yet be saved and
the President was smiling sourly. Lloyd George said he could get
plenty of volunteers for a Russian expedition, British and others and,
with fifty thousand men, Moscow, "that den of vipers," could be
cleaned out in a jiffy—"But," he added, "America must provide the
funds." The President refused point-blank and then added: "Every
time we have given your Russians a subsidy they have backed away
from their objective. I have no further patience with them."

From this and other incidents I gather that Kolchak has not only
lost ground in Russia but also in the favor of the Big Four. He has,
it is true, agreed verbally, at least, to order a constituent assembly
when and if he reaches Moscow, but the formal promise has never

reached here in official form and there are in his council undoubtedly many men long and closely associated with the imperial regime.

May 5, 1919

Yesterday Kerensky, prime minister of the short-lived liberal Provisional government (July-November, 1917), came in, this time bubbling over with optimism. The Colonel let him bubble for about ten minutes and then turned him over to me.

"This news is so important," said the Colonel, "that I shall ask you to draw up a formal memo to be distributed to our delegation and to others."

Well, this is what Kerensky said: "The Bolsheviki are at the end of their rope. Their complete overthrow is more a matter of weeks than of months. Admiral Kolchak is sweeping the country, but I fear that success is mounting to his head like strong wine. I fear that the excited admiral will inaugurate a regime as repressive and as sanguinary as did the Bolshe. The danger is clear, and none too soon I must point out that the true interests of Russia, and of the civilized world, demand that Kolchak be curbed. Control must be transferred to a truly democratic government based upon and recruited from all the parties that have remained true to the principles of the March Revolution (1917), excluding definitely the Bolshe at one extreme and the reactionary monarchists at the other."

Kerensky then began to see red and declared that the British and the French, or at least their agents, were constantly aiding the reactionary elements who surround Kolchak. "The Associated governments cannot hope to save Russia from continuing anarchy unless they agree on a common policy such as we drew up when preparing for the conference at Prinkipo. In that way we would achieve a democratic coalition and stand foursquare against the extremists of all parties. And I must add that owing to the fact that it has no commitments in power politics, the United States alone is in a position to launch such a policy."

Longuet, left-wing editor, and also Cachin, leader of French radicals, are furious at what they consider the attitude of the Allies toward Russia which they say shows open hostility to the People's government. I protest that we are really doing nothing but watching and waiting, and I admit I think this is the wise course to pursue.

Whereupon, yesterday Longuet flounced out of my office with the ultimatum, which I shall not pass on to those more immediately concerned, that "unless the Big Four abandon their criminal design to destroy the Russian Peoples government there will be revolution in France and anarchy in England." Cachin's parting words were: "I am a disillusioned man. If the peace that is being handed out by the Four had been what the President promised the people, there would have been no need for all these vexatious reservations and obscure supplementary guarantees."

I throw no stones, but to my diary I admit that the "acid test" has been too much for us. We are leaving the Russian problem unsettled and certainly unsolved just about as it was dumped on our doorstep months ago. But the problem is not worse than it was then and the people most directly concerned are tackling it—more power, and above all, more common sense to them. It can at least be said that during the long months of "delay and dawdle," as it is called here, we have learned to appreciate the difficulties of the situation and if we do go in later we might act intelligently. In the meantime the strange dark people about whom we hear so much and know so little have a chance to save Mother Russia in their own way. I sincerely hope they will rise to the urgent occasion and that the era of famines and mass murders, of incredible filth and indescribable squalor under the Tsars, of which I saw so much, will never be revived.

November 30, 1919

On November 9, in his speech at the Guild Hall, Lloyd George formally abandoned the Russians. "I do not regret the aid we have given," he announced, "but we cannot continue our intervention in a civil war which seems interminable." Clemenceau said this was a capitulation to the Soviets and he sent an angry letter to House, then back in America. "If this step was in any way permissible," he wrote, "he should have given advance notice to his Allies. The little Welshman is a deserter in the face of the enemy."

With the President incommunicado I do not think that House will answer this letter, at least not in definite terms. The Russian problem remains now as it was in the beginning, the "acid test," and the desired solvent seems to defy all research. House commented: "The conference of ambassadors seems to have succeeded the Supreme War

Council, and whether they know it or not they would seem to be in full charge. I do not envy them their task."

* * * * *

February 24, 1919

Several days ago a *petit mot* came from Iswolsky, whom I had known fairly well in other days when he was the ambassador and again when he directed the foreign affairs of Holy Russia. Today he is a refugee from the Reds and when I called I found him lodged at the Meurice in an attic room, one of the class to which the valets of important visitors were generally assigned. He is recovering from a sharp attack of influenza which has left with him a hacking cough.

Fortunately for me he did not choose to talk about the New Russia. He merely said:

"I am a man without a country. Today Russia is a vacuum, and what I might say about the actual situation would be pure guessing."

He did, however, lift another corner of the veil that has so long shrouded the Secret Treaties. In fact, he revealed another angle of the Sykes-Picot agreement, which even in its simplest form, the only one we are allowed to know, is giving the Conference so many headaches.*

"It is quite forgotten that Russia was a party to that arrangement as much as France and Britain. Yes, in those days," he interjected bitterly, "Russia was a great power and had to be consulted.

"In the first six months of the war we had overrun Galicia; we had rescued Serbia from the Austrians; our war objectives had been achieved and many at home thought why should we not reach a separate peace with the Central Powers unless something further is offered us, another bait?

"And Italy? She was not faring very well; she wanted something more than had been promised by the Treaty of London, which drew her into the war. In these circumstances, in May, 1916, the Sykes-Picot agreement was concluded, arranging an almost complete partition of Turkey in Asia as well as in Europe. France was to take at least the coastal strip of Syria and southeastern Anatolia. Britain was to get southern Mesopotamia and also the ports of Akka and Haifa on the Mediterranean; we were to get most of Turkish Armenia.

* See the next chapter on the Arabs.

"Of course, these arrangements were concealed from the Arabs and from the Italians, to whom conflicting promises had been made previously, but there was a leak somewhere, and the Italians screamed to the high heavens; to placate them, the British, Italian, and French prime ministers met at St. Jean de Maurienne (April, 1917) and the cards were reshuffled. Italy had to be given more to keep her in the war. This was before Caporetto, you see, and we had not begun to appreciate how heavy was the handicap of her assistance. Italy had to be appeased, she wanted 'more' and she demanded and was given, on paper, southwestern Anatolia with the towns of Adalia, Konia, and Smyrna. Practically the whole coast of Asia Minor was in this way earmarked for Italy. But there was a flaw in the arrangement, not through inadvertence, I fear. Britain and France signed the agreement, but as this belated consolation prize for Italy infringed on the Russian sphere at the Dardanelles, it was stipulated that only after the consent of Russia had been secured would the arrangement become effective, and that consent was never given.

"The promised booty was very tempting, but the Italians, doubtless wisely, hesitated to go in alone and take it. And now it would seem that Clemenceau and Lloyd George, and perhaps even Wilson, are urging the Greeks to go ahead and take what was promised to Italy. How confusing it all is, and how shameful. The men of the Soviets are, of course, absolutely without scruples, but at least they refuse to be bound by any of these secret partition treaties."

When I reported to House Iswolsky's revelations, he lifted his hands to heaven and said:

"Perhaps on the day of final judgment we shall learn all the details of the secret treaties, but I greatly fear not before. Sykes-Picot agreement! Well, it was not only the king in Hedjaz who was hoodwinked."

CHAPTER III

The Arabs Plead for Freedom: Emir Faisal, Colonel Lawrence, and Gertrude Bell—The Desert Queen

Paris, January 21, 1919

When the Arabs presented their case and the Emir Faisal,* Colonel Lawrence, and General Nouri Pasha came before the Big Four, they were certainly the most resplendent figures that had ever entered the Quai d'Orsay. Dark and subtle, but with a voice attuned to the great open spaces, Faisal talked right out in meeting and glowered down upon the prime ministers of the Great Powers who sat uneasily at his feet. Clearly he came not as a suppliant but to demand the rights of his people and the observance of solemn agreements which, as the emergency was over, some were inclined to forget. Lawrence was his interpreter and he further emphasized the emphatic words of the desert king.

"The aim of the Arab nationalist movement," insisted Faisal, "is to unite the Arabs eventually into one nation. We believe that our ideal of Arab unity in Asia is justified beyond need of argument. If argument is required, we would point to the general principles ac-

---

* Emir Faisal, third son of Sherif Hussein, was commander in chief of the Arab forces which, with the help of T. E. Lawrence, so materially contributed to English General Allenby's victories in the Near East. He was later (1920) proclaimed King of Syria.

cepted by the Allies when the United States joined them, to our splendid past, to the tenacity with which our race has for six hundred years resisted Turkish attempts to absorb us, and in a lesser degree to what we tried our best to do in this war as one of the Allies.

"My father has a privileged place among Arabs as the head of their greatest family and as Sherif of Mecca. He is convinced of the ultimate triumph of the ideal of unity, if no attempt is made now to thwart it or to hinder it by dividing the area as spoils of war among the Great Powers.

"I came to Europe on behalf of my father and the Arabs of Asia to say that they are expecting the powers at the Conference not to attach undue importance to superficial differences of condition among us and not to consider them only from the low ground of existing European material interests and supposed spheres of influence. They expect the Powers to think of them as one potential people, jealous of their language and liberty, and they ask that no step be taken inconsistent with the prospect of an eventual union of these areas under one sovereign government."

These words, in the light of subsequent events and the habit of loud-speaking which prevails in the world today, do not sound arrogant or even assertive, but they were so regarded at the time when the Western Powers were flushed with victory and the Khaki election campaign of Lloyd George in England with its promise to "hang the Kaiser" and to exact the uttermost farthing in war indemnities had rolled up such tremendous majorities. And it was further thought that the Emir's challenge would quicken controversies which had better be allowed to slumber for a season. So I was asked by one of the Big Four to suggest to Lawrence a change in the tactics rather than in the strategy of his campaign. Might he not soften the impact of some of Faisal's words that were giving offence in influential quarters? Would it not be wise for him to follow the precedent of Professor Mantoux, the official interpreter at the plenary sessions of the Conference, who smoothed out so many rough places in the impassioned appeals of the nationalistic speakers?

"I see the point and I have the greatest respect for this gentleman," answered Lawrence. "Perhaps he is right; but I cannot follow his suggestion. You see, I am an interpreter, I merely translate. The Emir is speaking for the horsemen who carried the Arab flag across the great desert from the holy city of Mecca to the holy city of

Jerusalem and to Damascus beyond. He is speaking for the thousands who died in that long struggle. He is the bearer of their last words. He cannot alter them. I cannot soften them."

February 2, 1919

I have at least one notable advantage over the distinguished delegates to the Conference; over one and all of them without, I believe, a single exception. I enjoyed a slight acquaintance with Lawrence of Arabia before he became the romantic figure of the war in the East. This happy chance came to me in this wise.

Hastening back from the Philippines in February, 1915, I embarked at Hong Kong on the Blue Funnel freighter *Perseus*. I was enticed to this step by the assurance of friends that this fast cargo boat would reach Europe several days before the French mail steamer that was leaving at about the same time. This assurance the *Perseus* lived up to until an untoward incident developed in Suez which for some hours threatened to defeat our plans.

The *Perseus* was bound for Liverpool with a burden of much needed tin from Banka in the Dutch East Indies, but en route she was to call at Genoa (Italy was on the verge but as yet had not entered the war) and there unload two thousand tons of sesame seed. To me this huge item of cargo smacked of *The Arabian Nights*, but the sight of it on the ship's manifest excited other and very suspicious thoughts in the minds of the British shipping controller at Suez. Might not this strange stuff reach the Germans through the Italian port, as undoubtedly so much contraband was doing? and might not those diabolically clever Germans use it in the manufacture of some new and terrible explosive?

This suspicion held us up and promised to greatly delay my arrival. The captain had an even more substantial grievance, as his bonus for the hazardous trip depended entirely upon the date of his arrival in England. The manifest revealed that the seed was consigned to the syndicate of Lucca Olive Oil, producers, and frantic telegrams went forward to them asking for explanations. Unfortunately these appeals had to take their turn after the official and war news cables with which the wires were burdened, so it was natural that a delay should occur. Indeed, twenty-four hours elapsed before the syndicate "came clean" with a very damaging confession to them—although it released us. Their frank if reluctant admission was that this year's crop of olives around Lucca had been a complete failure and so as not to disappoint their customers the syndicate was bringing the sesame seed from western China "because it is the best substitute for our world-famed product." The explanation concluded with a touching appeal, "Do not delay the ship, the olive-oil cupboard of Europe is bare and our customers are thirsting for it."

During the hours of delay a young English archaeologist by the name of Lawrence came aboard and advised us as to the best method to protect with sandbags the bridge and the ship's engines, for at the time the Germans and Turks were within shooting range of the canal. He was serving as a subordinate officer of the Arab bureau of the Egyptian government awaiting the arrival of a little steamer which was to take him down the coast to Akaba. He brightened the long hours with his information as to how things were going in the Middle East; he was helpful in expediting our departure when the word of explanation came and waved his *bon voyage* to us as we started to enter the canal that was no joy ride in those days. It was due to this chance meeting and to the fact that, as he said, my name smacked of Derbyshire, that Lawrence came to call within a few hours of his arrival in Paris (January 19) and wrote for me his first account of the great march of the Arabs from Hejaz to Damascus.

January 23, 1919

Lawrence gave me the pleasure of a long visit on Tuesday and filed with me a *précis* of the Arab demands. He then asked of me what he called a favor which I was only too glad to grant. It seems that his hand-written account of his campaign in Arabia, the triumphal march from Medinah to Damascus that he gave me several days ago, was the first he had written; that Hankey, Secretary of the British Empire delegation, wanted a copy for his files. I let him have it and got it back in twenty-four hours, a very precious possession.

Lawrence asked me to read the memorandum he had brought with him, to make suggestions, and then to accompany him to Faisal for further questioning. It was not a bad statement, shorter and clearer than many with which we are deluged, but in my talk with the Emir this afternoon I think he put his case in a better light.

"To begin with," said Faisal, "I hope you will try to disabuse the minds of many of our Allies that we Arabs are an uncivilized people. I venture to point out that much of our culture has been incorporated into the civilization of the Western World. Not a few of the achievements of our learned men are indeed regarded by some as its principal ornaments. It is true that a few of our tribes were submerged in the days of the great migrations, but the people of Hejaz, my father's kingdom, successfully maintained their independence when, in the fifteenth century, many Christian nations were compelled to bow down before the invaders from Central Asia.

"Coming to the present day, it should not be forgotten that we, together with the Macedonian Turks and the Albanians, had a large share in the overthrow of Abdul Hamid, the Red Sultan. [See Chapter XII.] On that happy day, throughout the Arab lands, committees were formed with the purpose of obtaining the right of self-government which the new constitution guaranteed. But the men of union and progress did not fulfill their promises. Syria and all the Arab lands were deprived of the modicum of freedom they had enjoyed even under the Old Turks, and the promised charter of self-government—that became a scrap of paper. Despite the most cruel persecution we persisted in our agitation, and with the Great War came our opportunity. When the Allies declared that they were fighting for justice against force, for liberty against tyranny, we made common cause with them because our ideals and our objectives were the same. We went into the struggle under the banner of the King, my father, and I had the honor to command his gallant troops who contributed substantially to the victory.

"And here is a point I wish to emphasize. It seems to be generally forgotten. We of the Hejaz were not a submerged people. We had been independent for centuries. Ours was a unique position in the Arab world, but we entered the war to liberate our less fortunate race brothers and it should not be overlooked we entered the war, like America, when the prospect of victory was far from promising. We had the very poorest equipment to wage modern warfare, and the first campaign resulted in the devastation of many of our lands and in the destruction of not a few of our cities. The Turks committed unspeakable atrocities upon our civilian populations, notably at Aouali and in the valley of Yambou. The Turks respected neither the laws of man nor of God and they never will when they have the upper hand. Incredible as it seems they did not even hesitate to despoil and desecrate the Tomb of the Prophet. The horrors of Belgium pale before what happened in Syria. Dr. Bliss of the American college in Beyrouth is here to tell you all about it. It is a conservative estimate, which he will confirm, that counting those who were hanged, those who died before a firing squad, and those who did not survive the deportations to Anatolia, more than three hundred and fifty thousand Syrians perished. In Irak and in Mesopotamia, in the battles of Hilla and at Karbala, at least thirty thousand more fell.

"We swept the Turks out of Hejaz; everywhere they were routed except at Medina. There, despite their artillery, of which we had none, we held them and then with our mobile columns swept north to redeem Syria. With aid and succor now in sight, the Syrians rushed to our camp at Akaba and, aided by Allenby and his gallant men, English and French, we liberated Syria.

"This, in brief, is a statement of the military aid we brought to the Allied cause. But there is another contribution which should not be overlooked. The wily and unscrupulous Turks had declared a Holy War against Christendom, and that was a dangerous weapon. It might have exerted a disturbing influence upon the course of the campaign; indeed, it might have proved disastrous to our cause. Misled, the Moslems of India and in other lands might have joined up with the Turks but for the fact that we, the most ancient of the Moslem peoples and the Guardians of the Tomb, remained steadfast. Our allegiance to the West demonstrated that this was not a war against our religion but a war to safeguard it, and so the Holy War cry of the Turks came to nothing.

"It is upon these real achievements and the justice of our cause that we base our moderate demands today. The mere recognition of the independence of the Hejaz would be a mockery of such outstanding services. Hejaz is and always has been independent. We entered the war, I repeat, not to improve our own position but to liberate our brothers in blood and in religion who have been throughout the centuries less fortunate. Above all else we did not enter the war to have our brothers and their lands apportioned among the Allies, although, of course, we recognize that this new servitude would be quite different from the yoke of the Turks.

"We are not asking for a favored position but merely for justice and the fulfillment of solemn promises. Those who say that we should be discriminated against because we, the Arabs, are a wild, unruly people incapable of self-government and not entitled to benefit by the Wilson doctrine of self-determination, should not be listened to. I am confident that even the least fortunate of our race are as able to assume this task as were the Greeks and the Serbs and the Bulgars but a few decades ago. When liberated, they too had been deprived of the rights of free men for centuries. They knew no more about self-government, in the Western meaning of the word, than we today, and yet they have maintained their independence, and at least two of these little nations have contributed materially to our common victory.

"We demand our rights and a recognition of these facts. Our lands should not be regarded as war booty by the conquerors. Our provinces should not be allocated to this or to that power. We have paid a heavy price for our liberty but we are not exhausted. We are ready to fight on, and I cannot believe that the great rulers here assembled will treat us as did our former oppressors. I think they will act from higher, nobler motives, but—if not—they should remember how badly it has turned out for our former oppressors."

It was a good fighting talk and I liked it. Through it all Nouri Pasha hovered in the background, now and again coming forward to check up on some of Lawrence's interpretations of the Emir's words. He accompanied me to the door and said quite sadly, "When are we going to have our talk about the Barbs and the noble steeds of the Arab strain?" I admitted, sadly too, that the outlook was not promising. "At the Conference only two-footed animals are being trotted out." Then he said, "I abhor mechanized warfare," and so we horse lovers parted in sadness. The day of the centaurs is over, although cavalrymen will not admit it.

*   *   *   *

On January 24 Emir Faisal sent me the following memorandum setting forth the aspirations of his people and the purpose of his presence in Paris. Lawrence brought it, and several days later, together with Gertrude Bell who had now arrived, coming directly from Bagdad, we went over it very carefully. Some changes were made as a result of our consultation and in appreciation of the "local" political situation that was developing. This was a wise course to pursue, I think, but personally I prefer the Arab platform in its original form, which follows:

The country from a line Alexandretta-Persia southward to the Indian Ocean is inhabited by "Arabs," by which we mean people of closely related Semitic stocks, all speaking the one language, Arabic. The non-Arabic-speaking elements in this area do not, I believe, exceed 1 per cent of the whole.

The aim of the Arab nationalist movements (of which my father became the leader in war after combined appeals from the Syrian and Mesopotamian branches reached him) is to unite the Arabs eventually into one nation. As an old member of the Syrian Committee I commanded the Syrian revolt and had under me Syrians, Mesopotamians, and Arabians.

We believe that Syria, an agricultural and industrial area thickly peopled with sedentary classes, is sufficiently advanced politically to manage her own internal affairs. We feel also that foreign technical advice and help will be a most valuable factor in our national growth. We are willing to pay for this help in cash, but we cannot sacrifice for it any part of the freedom we have just won for ourselves by force of arms.

Jezireh and Irak are two large provinces with only three civilized towns separated by large wastes thinly peopled by seminomadic tribes. The world wishes to exploit Mesopotamia rapidly, and we therefore believe that the system of government there will have to be buttressed by the men and material resources of a great foreign power. We ask, however, that the government be Arab in principle and spirit, the selective rather than the elective principle being necessarily followed in the backward and long-neglected districts until time makes the broader basis possible. The main duty of the Arab government there would be to oversee the educational processes, which are to advance the nomad tribes to the moral level of the people of the towns.

The Hejaz is mainly a tribal area, and the government will remain as in the past suited to patriarchal conditions. We appreciate these better than Europe and propose therefore to retain our complete independence there.

The Yemen and Nejd are not likely to submit their cases to the Peace Conference. They look after themselves and adjust their own relations with the Hejaz and elsewhere.

In Palestine the enormous majority of the people are Arabs. The Jews are very close to the Arabs in blood, and there is no conflict of character between the two races. In principles we are absolutely at one. Nevertheless the Arabs cannot risk assuming the responsibility of holding level the scales in the clash of races and religions that have in this one province so often involved the world in difficulties and wars. They would wish for the effective superposition of a great trustee, so long as a representative local administration commended itself by actively promoting the material prosperity of the country.

In discussing our provinces in detail I do not lay claim to superior competence. The Powers will I hope find better means to give fuller effect to the aims of our national movement. In our opinion, if our independence be conceded and our local competence established, the natural influences of race, language, and interest will soon draw us together into one people; but for this the Great Powers will have to ensure us open internal frontiers, common railways and telegraphs, and uniform systems of education. To achieve this they must lay aside all thought of individual profits and their old jealousies. In a word, we ask you not to force your whole civilization upon us but to help us to pick out what serves us from your experience. In return we can offer you little but gratitude and peace.

February 6, 1919

After long delay, Faisal and Lawrence were received today by the President. He told House he was struck by the Emir's noble bearing; but the Arabs are greatly disappointed. Evidently the President was reserved and most certainly noncommittal. Lawrence tells me that the long-delayed interview was a formal conference rather than an exchange of views. "We merely established a ceremonial contact, and that to the Arabs is a great sorrow."

Sir Mark Sykes was one of the strangest and most perplexing figures at the Conference. He was co-author of the Sykes-Picot agreement or protocol, which gave to the French much that Lawrence and Allenby had promised to the Arabs. [*1920.* The Sykes-Picot agreement was drawn up in 1916 for the purpose of harmonizing the conflicting claims of France and Britain to spheres of influence in the Middle East. It subdivided the Arab area and gave Syria to the French. British preponderance in Irak and in Transjordania was recognized. Palestine was given a special status but it was not very clearly drawn. While there are many contested points, in the main the agreement determines the political situation today and is thought by many to be responsible for the existing confusion.]

You get the measure of the man when I tell you that even after this slip Sykes was by no means unpopular with the Arabs. As a matter of fact they held him in high esteem with the reservation, however, that "he hez make one big mistake, but Sir Sykes he work it out all right." And the Armenians and the Zionists also worshipped him. There was no mistake about this; "Sir Sykes" had the gift of popularity.

Sykes was born, like Robinson Crusoe, in Yorkshire, I should say about forty years ago, the only son of a Tory squire with large estates and with other resources which made him quite indifferent to the output of his fields and farms. The squire was a great traveler in out-of-the-way places and on these travels he was generally accompanied by his boy, who seems to have escaped the servitudes of regular and methodical schooling. When the boy was but ten, Father Sykes and son spent a winter with the Druses of the Lebanon, and then the youngster was handed over to some Jesuit fathers who had started a school at Monte Carlo—of all places in the world! Later he was transferred to Brussels and from there to Weimar. He arrived in due course at Cambridge with considerable knowledge of the world and more than a smattering of four or five languages, but his tutors were unanimous in expressing the opinion that he would never be able to stand the varsity examinations that awaited him, not even the "Little Go," which boys from the public schools took in their stride. "But I was saved this disgrace," explained Sykes. "The blessed Boer war came and I joined up."

In many ways Sykes was a companion piece to Lawrence, though the former had fought his way to prominence under the handicap of great wealth and the footsteps of the latter had always been dogged by poverty. They were in disagreement on many questions and particularly as to the panacea for the turbulent Arab world, and Lawrence once in my presence was quite emphatic in his words of rebuke. But Sykes was quite unruffled. "Let us approach the question in a broad-minded way," he said. "Of course I admit I do not always approve of the stand I have taken on a number of subjects or the things I have done in a whole-hearted way. The results of my efforts are often discouraging, but I do insist that my intentions have always been of the best."

As Lawrence admitted, you could not be angry for long with a man who talked like this. But the situation had to be clarified, and this could only be done by bringing Sykes to book to find out how much of his recent activities were backed by instructions and how much was due to his (as many thought) over-heated imagination.

Speaking for himself, and not for the British Foreign Office of which, however, he was the titular head, Balfour admitted frequently that the Arabs had gotten us all into a "jolly mess, but I have told Sykes to be here on the ninth and he will make everything clear. You see, gentlemen, he knows those Arab lands just as I know Aberdeenshire or, say, Kent."

February 11, 1919

I was very much on hand when the morning of the ninth dawned on which the pro-Arab and the pro-Sykes-Picot forces were to meet each other face to face before the Council of Ten in the famous Clock Room. In fact I committed what would have been an indiscretion had I been a person of any importance. I went to the field of battle with Lawrence and there I joined Faisal and Nouri who were flanked by handsome young aides arrayed in robes and tunics of many colors, all of them with flashing, hungry eyes like the hawks of the desert. I could not refrain from saying, "Sir Mark must be a brave man to face that phalanx," and Lawrence answered quietly, "He is a brave man and, worse luck, a stubborn one."

There was a great shuffling of papers and then Balfour mumbled to the serviceable Hankey, "I think we'll put Sykes on now. What?"

"Have just had a message: Sykes has a bad cold. Can't talk."

"Dear, dear. How provoking. I had so hoped we would get on with this business today. Tell him it will go over until the eleventh but he must not fail us then. I suppose we shall have to take up the next item on the agenda. What's that? Oh, yes, those islands in the Baltic. I never can remember their names."

The Arab contingent filed out. They were inclined to think that Sykes was playing possum, but not so Lawrence. "If Sykes admits he's sick I fear he's ill," he said.

On the eleventh we all assembled again. Balfour was as usual quite a little late in arriving; blushing like a bride and with profuse apologies he said to his colleagues of the Ten: "Now we'll get on with it. I'll put Sykes on the stand immediately. Hankey, where is Sykes?"

"His servant has just brought me sad news," said Hankey in a low voice. "Sykes is dead. He died this morning at daybreak—septic pneumonia following on flu."

"Dear, dear," muttered Balfour. "It seems as though we shall never get on with this problem. And now, Hankey, what is the next item on the agenda? And do please see to it that I get the proper papers and that the important paragraphs are flagged. I so hate wading through interminable documents. . . ."

Faisal was a generous foe. Sykes' coffin was returned to Yorkshire covered with a carpet of rare flowers which the Emir placed on it with his own Sheriffian hand. There were services in Aleppo and in

Jerusalem for the soldier who had been withdrawn from the fray so suddenly, and in many other places where his motives were held in higher esteem than were the resulting policies.

February 12, 1919

The postponed meeting which took place one day later was not only interesting because of the confrontation of the Arab sheiks with their former champions, of short memories, but because it gave us an opportunity to fathom Mr. Balfour's extremely shallow knowledge of at least one of the secret treaties which has so frequently figured in international discussions and even in the debates of our own Senate.

Through Colonel Lawrence, Emir Faisal, in language that was but thinly veiled if it can be said it was veiled at all, pointed out the duplicity with which the Arab world had been treated by the Great Powers. He read the original agreements between King Hussein, Lord Kitchener, and General McMahon that brought the Arabs into the war. He dwelt with emphasis on the promises His Majesty's Government had made to the Syrian Covenanters on June 11, 1918.

"And now we are told," he shouted, "that none of these promises can be fulfilled because of the Sykes-Picot pact, an agreement to divide many of the Arab lands between France and England, negotiated months before, in May, 1916. We are told," continued Faisal, with a biting irony which he made no attempt to restrain, "that this secret arrangement cancels the promises that were made to us openly before all the world."

[The date of this secret treaty should be carefully noted. It was signed and sealed eleven months before the day on which, it is asserted by the opposition senators in Washington, that Mr. Balfour was standing in the White House and pleading with President Wilson for an opportunity to unburden his soul and tell the world about the secret misdeeds of Old World diplomacy. And yet in February, 1919, he, Balfour, showed his ignorance of at least one of them and not the least important one. Certainly Mr. Balfour's bearing and attitude at the meeting gives no support to the senatorial indictment.]

It was plain that Mr. Balfour was bewildered and that he only recalled the existence of the Sykes-Picot document in a vague and general way. "That's the treaty that gives Mosul to the French," said one of the bright young men who sat at his elbow. He at least had read some part of the agreement that distributed the lands of the Middle East.

"How extraordinary," commented Mr. Balfour. But unlike his daring chief, Lloyd George, Balfour, minister of foreign affairs, was not inclined to dive into "troubled waters" unless his theologians and geographers were standing by or within hailing distance.

Baffled he may have been, but certainly he was not flustered. As cool as an icicle, Balfour now announced: "Owing to the tragic death of our expert, the review of these complicated negotiations, so generally misunderstood, will have to go over to another day." And so it was ordered, to the relief of many who recognized that Anglo-Saxon diplomacy was in for an unhappy hour. The subsequent proceedings were, wisely, carried out quite.privately.

[*1923.* As long as Balfour was minister of foreign affairs they never "got on" with the Arab problem. Four years later when he had been succeeded by Lord Curzon, who took advice from Winston Churchill and from Lawrence, what appeared to be a fair if temporary settlement was achieved through long negotiations in Cairo and Bagdad.]

February 26, 1919

Emir Faisal has moved from his apartment in the Continental and is more at his ease in a small private hotel he has leased on the Avenue du Bois. At his request I call frequently, about twice a week. Like everyone else he wants something. First and foremost, he wants President Wilson to assume the mandate over Syria and then to appoint him as his lieutenant and deputy. When last week under instructions I told him that there is little or no prospect of this, he piped down with the more modest request to have an American army officer attached to his Mission. I have passed this on to the Colonel and he has sent it on to General Pershing with his approval. Certainly a competent soldier should be selected, at least to accompany the Emir when he visits the battlefields on March 10; otherwise I fear that the important participation of the American army in the Allied victory will escape notice.

In the privacy of his home, which with a few draperies and rugs he has transformed into something like a nomad's tent, Faisal presents quite a different figure from the one he cuts when, flanked by Law-

rence and Nouri Pasha, he addresses and at times browbeats the assembled prime ministers and their advisers on Middle Eastern affairs
in the Clock Room at the Quai d'Orsay. There, with his rakish tur-
ban, his gallant gold-embroidered coat, his very visible scimiter, and
his bejeweled revolver (by no means concealed), he looks what he
doubtless is—a son of Mars, Oriental version.

But in his home, under what seems to be a canopy of silk and embroidered velvet, he presents a very different and as it seems to me a
more sympathetic figure. He wears a black tunic and tight-fitting
black trousers. In his hand there is always a chain of beads, a sort of
rosary. He counts them constantly as though to be certain they are
all there. He is frequently lavish in his praise of the American teacher,
the elder Doctor Bliss who founded the college at Beyrouth. "I wor-
ship him," he says, "as all Arabs do because he was a sage and a
prophet. It was he who foretold the future of our race, and it was
he who by educating our boys made that future possible. In my
army there were some who had been educated by the French fathers
and a few by the English doctors, but those who had studied at the
American college in Beyrouth were the most reliable and efficient."

Yesterday Doctor Bliss the younger, the son of the founder of the
great school, came in while I was with the Emir and we put him
through the third degree—politely, of course. But the younger Bliss
is wary. He would like to see America take over the mandate for
Syria, but he knows the Senate will never consent even if the President does. Perhaps he thinks it unwise to waste time discussing the
question, and he simply said: "I am a bookman, an educationalist, not
a statesman. Not even a politician," he adds with a wry smile. "The
President has asked me for my opinion and I have given it. I have
urged him to send a commission of trained administrators to Syria to
confer with the people, to find out exactly what they want, and then
to decide what it would be just, and also wise, to give them now."
The President is not given to enthusiastic personal appraisements, but
he has a high opinion of Faisal. Last Monday in my hearing he said:
"Listening to the Emir I think to hear the voice of liberty, a strange
and, I fear, a stray voice, coming from Asia." How I wish I could
pass this on to the Arabs—they are so downcast. But I have no right
to do it; most certainly it was said in confidence.

Faisal with his picturesque flankers and adjutants is at once the
charm and the mystery of the Conference. He can speak French

quite well when he wants to and he explodes with laughter when he tells that he, too, has had parliamentary experience:

"It happened in this way. When Abdul Hamid was dethroned, the Committee of Progress that took over issued a call for an assembly, and I was summoned to Constantinople to represent the Hejaz. I worked over my speech, saluting the new freedom, for a month but they would never permit me to deliver it. They kept me under polite arrest, but it was arrest all the same, and it lasted for two years. Then I escaped to the desert; but as I traveled light I did not take my speech with me. It is lost forever."

The French are highly indignant over the favor shown Faisal, generally, and the high esteem in which he is held by the President and the American delegates. Hardly a day passes that "under-cover" men, closely allied to and doubtless subsidized by Paris bankers and concession-seeking syndicates, do not put in appearance and take up much of our time in denouncing the Emir as an adventurer who counts for nothing in the Arab world. "He counts indeed for less than nothing," they insist, "because the noble Arabs know that he is in the pay of English landgrabbers who have formed companies, later to be chartered, which will, under the guise of religion, take over the Arab lands and suck them dry—as they have the rest of the world."

Some day, perhaps, we shall know the truth about all these things, but that day has not dawned yet. In the meantime the French and the British are fully occupied in "interpreting" the innumerable contradictory treaties they made with Arab tribes and factions during the fighting years.

February 27, 1919

Today Lawrence and Gertrude Bell (the "Desert Queen") lunched with me. It was not a gay affair, for we each had a tale of woe to tell. Lawrence, like all paladins, is high strung and has his moments of deep discouragement, and this was one of them. But, even so, in this his hour of depression he did not break out with the angry recriminations against those responsible for the mess in the Arab world, so frequently reported in the press as his views.

"As for myself," he said, "I would like to retire to a little cottage, say in Somerset, and write a book about the rise and fall of the Abbasid Caliphate. It would abound in topical references and I would probably starve to death while doing it, just as so many other more deserving men are starving today."

I admitted that I too wished to retire from the splendor of the Crillon, turn my back on the living world, and, under the guidance of Boissier, confer with Cicero and his friends and, with the charming Gaston as cicerone, explore the ruins of what was once the "glory that was Greece and the grandeur that was Rome."

Miss Bell was disgusted with the French and also, for the moment at least, with her faint-hearted countrymen. Nothing was being done for the Arabs. Even the visiting commission was hanging fire.

"Of course these people are shortsighted and almost incredibly stupid," she insisted, "but I shall fight on."

She certainly did, and a few days later she wrote me the letter of thanks and encouragement which I am glad to insert. It reads:

Monday

Dear Major Bonsal:

I send you a brief note on the Commission [to Syria].

I think it much to be regretted that the Question cannot be settled here without such prolonged delay & I am inclined to believe that with the threat of a Commission hanging over them, the French might prove less intransigeant & that a satisfactory accommodation between them and the Syrian Nationalists could be reached.

As you know it would be possible to give them a free hand in Beyrout & the Lebanon.

I am sending you also an account of our self-determination enquiries in Mesopotamia. If you have time to glance through it you will notice that the salient characteristic of my people is that they have no settled conviction as to what they want. Their one wish is that they should be given time to make up their minds. No Commission, I feel convinced, will be in a better, or indeed in as advantageous a position for finding out their real opinion as we were, for the Oriental does not speak freely to people whom he does not know. And the net result is that there is no real opinion.

Thank you so much for your help and sympathy.

Yours sincerely,

GERTRUDE BELL

Major Bonsal,
American Delegation.

The above letter is part of the official correspondence of the Paris Peace Conference.

February 28, 1919

The Arabs had many friends at the Conference, but none more unswerving in allegiance to their just cause than this honest, gray-eyed, North Country English girl. In a sense, as is so often the case, her letter, if read without due attention to the circumstances existing at the time it was written, is misleading. She did not mean to say that the Arabs did not know what they wanted; they wanted an independent state and they did not want the French to stay in Syria. But as between a mandate by Britain, with her special imperial interests in the Near and Middle East, and that of far-away America, they were in doubt, and no one knew it better than Gertrude Bell. Britain had special interests which at any moment might seem vital, and if America received the mandate, she was so far away that she might forget all about her distant wards. Gertrude had studied the problem quite closely and, not entirely without reason, she was inclined to think that our legislators in Washington often forgot their responsibility for our wards in the Philippines.

March 29, 1919

This afternoon Faisal and Lawrence came for what is probably a farewell call, as the Emir says he expects to return to Syria in a few days. Faisal was more self-contained, certainly less obstreperous, than he was the day he stormed and thundered before the Council of Ten. He read to House the protocol of the promises the British made to his father, King Hussein, on October 24, 1915. Clearly it promised recognition of Arab independence, outside of Bagdad and Basra, if the Arabs joined up with the Allies. Then he read the Sykes-Picot agreement of May, 1916, providing for a very different and a very definite partition of the Arab lands. Of course these contradictory promises were made under the stress of a disturbing military situation, but all the same no white man could listen to them without deep regret.

"Now it seems I shall have to return to my people empty-handed, and I am at a loss to explain why. I have come to ask you again what chance is there of America taking a mandate over our country and our people? In this way the danger of the present friction between England and France that may result in war would be avoided and my people would feel assured of ultimate independence."

House said that he could not make any definite promises. The President was interested and would use his good offices toward a favorable solution, but the Arab lands were far from the American sphere and acceptance of responsibility in Asia would be quite a departure from American tradition. Suddenly Faisal's face, hitherto so placid, became distorted and the long-covered fires blazed into view. "We Arabs would rather die than accept the supremacy of the French—although it be sugar-coated as a mandate subject to the control of the League."

When Lawrence had quieted him down Faisal put another equally awkward question: "What will America do to save what is left of Armenia?"

House could only answer that the question was under advisement and study; that "if the advice and consent of the Senate could be secured, the President would accept a mandate over those unfortunate people."

House then said the President had determined to send a commission to Syria to investigate and report back. "What do you think of it?"

"I think well of it," answered Faisal, "but the French will leave nothing undone in the way of hampering the work of the commission. The American commissioners will have to be sturdy fellows."

[A few days later, President Wilson nominated Dr. King of Oberlin College and Charles R. Crane, a well-known sympathizer in the Arab cause, as the American members of what he thought was to be an international commission. The French declined to nominate a member and the British failed to do so. In the following summer the Americans visited most of the disturbed Arab provinces and reported that a French mandate was unacceptable to the people and would result in war. Little attention was paid to the report in America and it was ignored in Europe. Recognizing that all the war promises had become dead letters, a few months later Faisal made the best bargain he could with Clemenceau. He was given Damascus and the interior of Syria, but in April, 1920, the Supreme War Council, without authority, it seemed to many, gave to France a mandate over Syria, whereupon the Clemenceau-Faisal agreement was torn up by M. Millerand. "Inshallah! I shall remain in Damascus," declared Faisal, and it is a fact that it required the heavy artillery of Generals Gouraud and Sarrail to blow him out of the oldest living city in the world.]

April 29, 1919

Ten days ago the Syrian kettle came to a boil again. The commission shows more and more reluctance to "shove off." House told Clemenceau that the delay was scandalous and that he must intervene. "It is a scandal, I agree," answered Clemenceau; "Lloyd George on all fours has crawled away from the position he took up so valiantly three months ago; but what have I to do with this mediaeval matter? What has the Tiger to do with a *politique des Curés* [church polity]?"

Hoping for a settlement or at least light on the problem, House brought about a meeting between Clemenceau and Faisal, escorted by Lawrence, in the Presidence (the Tiger's lair—really the Ministry of the Interior).

"We must have the French flag over Damascus," shouted the Tiger before his visitors were seated. "No," answered Faisal, for once in a loud voice.

"I insist—we must have the French flag over Damascus," roared the Tiger. "Never," answered Faisal with eyes flashing, and the interview came to an end without the usual formalities.

A few days after his disappointing interview with the Tiger, Faisal left for Rome where he is reported to be coquetting with the Pope in regard to the French Protectorate over the Catholics in the Near East. Curiously enough it is the radical and godless Boulevard sheets which are most indignant over this reported course of action—or lack of it.

Charming Lawrence came in to thank us for our good offices which, it must be confessed, have achieved anything but substantial results. He admitted that personally he was in a quandary. With relief and satisfaction he was more than ready to abandon the political world and return to his first love, archaeology. "But," he lamented, "here is the rub. Syria is the most promising land to dig in; but there I'm compromised by the stand I have taken, and if I go there now there will be a row. So I shall return to Oxford and vegetate—worse luck!"

Before he left me, Lawrence dropped a bit of information which is more enlightening as to the Arab problem than many volumes of Blue Books or White Papers. "The main trouble is," he said, "there have been too many cooks out there and between them they have certainly spoiled the broth. From the beginning of the war and down

to the present time, the Intelligence section of the Indian government
has been paying the Wahabite Emir (Ibn Saud) one thousand pounds
a month to make war on King Hussein of Mecca, our ally; and at the
same time our War Office has been paying Hussein about the same
sum to harass the Wahabites [that is, the Saudi Arabs, now top dogs
in the Arab world]. I wonder if the French are prepared to continue
these subsidies? It really doesn't make much difference; in any case
there will be hell to pay, and that will continue until we get together
and honor our war-time pledges. Mind you, I don't say we have deceived them intentionally, but we have reached the same result by not
letting our right hand know what the left hand was doing."

[Three years later I saw Lawrence for the last time. "I have
fought a dog fight in Downing Street for three years," he explained,
"and justice has been done as far as it is possible at this late day." I
thought he had done wonders. He had at least brought two Arab
kingdoms into being and he had made many Englishmen and a few
Frenchmen blush for shame. "What the outcome will be of course
I do not know," were the last words I heard from the lips of this pala-
din, "but I am determined it shall never be said that I drew profit from
the part I played in the war or the transactions that followed upon it.
I have declined to enter the colonial or any other service. I would
rather starve—and probably shall."]

CHAPTER IV

The Zionists and Ben Israel

Paris, January (undated)

On Tuesday the Zionist delegates appeared before the Council of Ten. They had their day in court and each spoke his piece. The Paris press, certainly not unfavorable to the Jewish claims, is not enthusiastic over the showing that was made and *Débats*, the great journal which is reputed to be owned by international Jewish bankers, is particularly severe in its criticism of the delegates and of the tentative plans they presented. It is pointed out by the critical editors that the spokesmen held divergent views—as if that did not happen whenever a delegation comes to the court of the Great Assizes.

Three delegates appeared and I could not see that they were far apart, although in matters of detail they were certainly not of one mind. Mr. Weizmann appeared for the Anglo-Saxon Jewish communities, M. Sokolof for those of Eastern Europe, and M. Sylvain Levi represented the Jews of Western Europe. Each and every one of them demanded a Jewish national home in Palestine, but they differed as to ways and means to secure it and as to the form the new state, if it is to be a state, should take. The real problem is one that no one faces squarely, it seems to me. How can a national home for the eleven million Jews who are scattered throughout the world be launched in Palestine, a poor country, supporting with difficulty its present population of less than a million, the great majority of whom are not Jews?

M. Levi of the French Zionists, speaking for himself and for many French Zionists, said he was not asking for an independent Zionist state. He called attention to the undoubted fact, so generally ignored, that even Mr. Balfour in his declaration says that the present non-Jewish inhabitants are not to be removed or even in a political sense "crowded." What he and his organization want, he asserted, was the right to settle Jewish communities in Palestine with the same privileges and the same responsibilities as the neighboring communities of Moslems and Christians. Sokolof and Weizmann listened to this moderate statement with evident displeasure. They too were not in complete agreement, but they both envisaged an independent state to occupy not only Palestine but all of southern Syria from Haifa to Akaba. At first, they admit, they would not object to leading strings for the new-born state. They would accept a provisional and short-termed mandate to be exercised by a nation selected by the Council of the League of Nations as soon as it is constituted.

If the views of the advanced Zionists prevail there is trouble ahead. Many, very many, intelligent and informed Jews admit this. It is conceded that the present inhabitants of Palestine have occupied their lands for centuries; indeed, some of the Syrian communities claim descent from the Hittites who were in possession at the dawn of history. Be this as it may, all who know the situation from actual contact and not merely from propaganda leaflets admit that these people have dwelt in their present homes for two thousand years, that the occupancy of the Jews does not go back to immemorial times, and that their sojourn before the Dispersion was brief. Why should these "old settlers" be expelled, they ask, to make room for newcomers who are ill informed as to the way of life that would be imposed upon them in the promised land of dreams, which in actual experience would prove a great disappointment?

Auguste Gauvin of *Débats* has constituted himself the spokesman for this group of moderate Zionists and has expressed his views to the Colonel at least twice; and he hopes to see the President before he is committed to what Gauvin calls "an impossible project." He insists that no one, least of all Mr. Balfour, had in mind a national state such as seems to be contemplated in the new demands, or rather interpretations of it, now being made. He quotes the original declaration of Balfour under date of November 2, 1917, which reads:

"The British government would regard favorably the establishment in Palestine of the Jewish people and will do what it can to facilitate it, under the reserve, however, that none of the civil or religious rights of the non-Jewish communities already settled in the country should be impaired."

"Not a word in that justifies the demand for a national home in a political sense," adds Gauvin.

The French attitude was expressed by M. Pichon in these words: "There is complete understanding between the French and the British governments in regard to a Jewish establishment in Palestine." That certainly would not seem to contemplate the erection of a national political state. Indeed, he adds, there are only the indiscreet words of Sir Robert Cecil which justify the demand, and they were spoken informally at a Zionist meeting and are not contained in any official document. Sir Robert, then Under Secretary of Foreign Affairs, did say at a meeting in London's Exeter Hall: "We want the Arabs to have the Arab lands; we want the Armenians to have Armenia and the Jews, Judea."

"But they are all scrambled together," maintains Gauvin. "Can the Conference unscramble them? I doubt it."

Naturally I have talked to Emir Faisal and to Lawrence on the subject. They admit that the Arabs are involved in the situation, but for the present they wish to keep out of the discussions. They hope that the Big Four will not further complicate a situation that is already most difficult.

"Room could be made for perhaps a million Jews in Palestine," said Faisal, "if the same number of Christians and of Moslems were deported. That is what the Turks did in Armenia and elsewhere under the stress of war. Will Christendom follow their example in time of peace? I trust not."

Gauvin sees at least one silver lining in the dark clouds overhanging Palestine. "Very few Jews want to go to their Holy Land and ours, and also unfortunately the sanctuary of the Arabs, except as tourists or to make a religious pilgrimage. Perhaps the whole question could be solved if it was placed in the hands of a competent tourist agency."

I fear Gauvin is mistaken; the situation is more serious than he thinks. Many Jews, seeing the complete overthrow of the predatory and Jew-baiting powers, are inclined to believe that the moment is opportune for the Conference to settle their age-old problem along with all the others that are coming before it.

In addition to the racial and religious antagonism between the con-

testants for this long-coveted territory there is also an economic conflict which should not be overlooked. Speaking in terms familiar to
Americans, the Arabs are sheepmen and the Jews for the most part
are small fruitgrowers. Most of us know what happened in many of
our western states when these economies clashed at a time when some
of our territories were as undeveloped as is Palestine today.

A few hours after the formal hearing Dr. Weizmann called on the
Colonel and asked for an opportunity to restate his views. I was
called in and I drew up the following memo, which the Doctor read
and pronounced correct. It seems, at least to me, to differ quite radi-
cally from his formal statement. It reads:

I and many others think it would be unjust, indeed most unjust, for us
to ask of the Conference the founding at this moment of an immediate
Jewish state (in Palestine). It is for us, we think, to ask in the first place
for recognition by the Great Powers of the fact that Palestine was the land
of the Jews in the past and should in the future become the home of the
Jews. Our first pressing need, and this we ask insistently, is for opportunities and favoring conditions to enable us to bring the Jews back to
Palestine. If these requests are granted obstacles now in our path would
be cleared away and it would then depend on the Jews themselves to build
up the Jewish commonwealth. To begin our new status we would need
a trustee and we are united in the belief that Great Britain should be
nominated for this post. We admit that the land problem should not be
ignored at the same time the vision of the delegates should not be obscured
by the misleading information which here abounds. There is we claim
ample elbow room for all; there are only seventy inhabitants today to the
square mile of territory which could comfortably carry from three hundred and fifty to four hundred and without in the least encroaching on
the rights of the Arab peasants.

How the Colonel and all the other delegates wish that this were
true! Faisal and all the Arabs deny it *in toto*. In fact they are in
agreement that the present meager Jewish population (small indeed in
proportion to the colonists the Zionists wish to bring in) would starve
to death, certainly could not become self-supporting, but for the subsidies that come for them from various philanthropic committees in
Paris, London, and above all New York. Mr. Balfour with the best
intentions has launched an ugly problem.

* * * *

Two days later Lawrence came in with a rough tentative sketch of
the memorandum which the Emir is determined to file with the dele-

gates. I urged him not to be precipitate, above all not to let the Emir
assume a position which might be regarded as final and irrevocable.
Lawrence agreed with me but asked me to submit the views, which
he says the Arabs without exception hold, to Colonel House with a
request for advice and above all guidance. This I have done, but
down to the present the only reaction from the Colonel was a low
whistle and the remark that "Balfour with the best intentions in the
world has certainly rocked the boat that was already sailing on anything but an even keel."

Briefly, the sketch of the memorandum which Faisal is soon to file
with us, unless happily he should be dissuaded, is about as follows:

If the views of the radical Zionists, as presented to the Ten, should prevail, the result will be ferment, chronic unrest, and sooner or later civil
war in Palestine. But I hope I will not be misunderstood. I assert that
we Arabs have none of the racial or religious animosity against the Jews
which unfortunately prevail in many other regions of the world. I assert
that with the Jews who have been seated for some generations in Palestine
our relations are excellent. But the new arrivals exhibit very different
qualities from those "old settlers," as we call them, with whom we have
been able to live and even co-operate on friendly terms. For want of a
better word I must say that the new colonists almost without exception
have come in an imperialistic spirit. They say that too long we have
been in control of their homeland taken from them by brute force in the
dark ages, but that now under the new world order we must clear out;
and if we are wise we should do so peaceably without making any resistance to what is the fiat of the civilized world.

This was bad but by no means unexpected news. I was not prepared, though, for the new factor which Lawrence now injected
into the problem of what is to be done with the "much-promised
land." He went on to say: "The Zionists, and also Mr. Balfour, have
overlooked the fact that in Syria and in Palestine there are about one
hundred and twenty thousand Christian Arabs who, unlike the Moslem Arabs, have anything but friendly feelings for the Jews, whether
they be new or old settlers. They claim to descend from the hard-
hitting Hittites of whom we read in the Old Testament, and they
claim to be the original inhabitants or at least the earliest settlers in the
disputed land. Certainly these people have claims based on the undoubted fact that they were "occupants" before the Arabs came or
even the Jews put in their appearance. What is the Conference going
to do about this new angle of the thorny situation?

I told Lawrence I had not the remotest idea, but I hoped it would be something intelligent. Hopefully I suggested, "It will be turned over to the League like so many of these problems that cannot be adjusted while the war psychosis prevails. Only then will solutions be found for these innumerable racial and religious conflicts."

Time and again Lawrence repeated, "These new Jews are coming in a very militant spirit. Of course I admit that in view of the way in which they have been treated in many regions of the Western World this is natural enough; but still most regrettable." I agreed. The outlook for peace in Palestine is anything but bright.

March 10, 1919

Knowing as I do only too well the close watch that the delegates keep on the visitors to other delegations and the extreme vigilance with which what might be called our "frequentations" are observed, I was not, and certainly had no reason to be, surprised when my good friend Nouri al Said, Emir Faisal's closest adviser, came in this morning to introduce to me a learned Fuki or talib, one of the doctors of the famous university mosque of Al Azhar in Cairo, undoubtedly the most influential institution of learning in the Moslem world. Curiously enough this center of religious and racial propaganda operates under the eyes and apparently with the tacit approval of the British Protectorate.

After presenting him, Nouri said as he withdrew, "This learned man wishes to enlighten the American delegation as to the dangers and the great difficulties which the ill-considered words of Mr. Balfour have created in Palestine, indeed throughout the Middle East." Fortunately the learned man spoke English not only well but with much distinction, and so for once at least my desk was not a diminutive Tower of Babel.

"Our land is not empty," he began after compliments, "and it is not waste land. Despite anything that Mr. Balfour may say to the contrary, we have developed it to the very fullest extent of its capacity and we have developed it as our national home for thirteen hundred years. From it we Arabs have drawn our sustenance and prospered as it has been God's will that we should. Our people do not receive pensions or draw remittances from rich co-religionists in other lands as do the wandering Jews who the international bankers wish to remove from their flourishing cities. Even our less fortunate brethren receive blessings from on high, and the One God gives his approval to their laborious days. We shift for ourselves and not a piastre comes to our communities from Mecca. Indeed we the faithful in all lands tighten our belts and yearly send our contributions to the keepers of the shrines and to the guardians of the Thrice Blessed Tomb.

"And Jerusalem that these wanderers falsely claim is ours. She is one of the four cities of Paradise. Supreme she stands with her sister shrines, with Mecca, with Medina, and with Damascus. These are the earthly reward that Allah bestowed upon the faithful. In these consecrated places we are nearest to Heaven, indeed, there we are neighbors of God. And yet, incredible as it would seem, there are those who in defiance of the will of God would take them away from us.

"These Jewish intruders are being brought to our land by men who for the most part do not know the evil thing they are doing, although of course it is clear that the motive of some of them is to get rid of these drones who sap the vitality of their communities. And there are a few who have the effrontery to say that our dear land is destined to be by the will of God their national home from which, they lament, they were driven centuries ago when might was right, but that today when right prevails over might it must be returned to them. They are careful not to say that by ruthless violence the Jews established themselves in our land but could only maintain themselves there for a short period, that they were the first to draw the sword the sharp edge of which they were to feel later, and indeed may again if the nations permit them to continue their absurd pretensions.

"The Jews are strangers in the land they seek to annex and from which they would expel us; they belong in Chaldea, and their place of origin is on the banks of the Euphrates. If men would only listen, the falsity of their claims would be convincing. Even Abraham to whom they often appeal in support of their faulty title deeds recognized formally and officially that he and his people were intruders in the land of Canaan."

"When was that?" I ventured to inquire, and so revealed my lack of knowledge of the Scriptures.

"Do you not recall that he did not want his son, his beloved Isaac, to marry a stranger woman and that he sent an envoy into the Chal-

dean lands to secure a suitable woman of his own tribe to perpetuate
his line?"

I here interpolated the statement, as so often before, that the American delegation had decided in our attempts to right ancient wrongs to
go no farther back than the Treaty of Westphalia, but the learned
Fuki now with something like fire in his eyes brushed this statute of
limitations aside.

"In your Bible, which you revere and which we respect, is the story
of the cruelties practiced by these covetous people in their conquest
of Canaan. Fortunately their ruthless arrogance carried with it its
cure; the little tribal kinglets got to fighting among themselves, and
so it was not difficult for us to expel them from the lands they had
stolen. They held it but for a very few unhappy years, but we reconquered it and have held it, until now unchallenged, for centuries.
Our right of conquest was as valid as theirs, and we have maintained
it until now unchallenged for thirteen hundred years.

"These wanderers with forged documents and lying chronicles are
seeking to expel us from the shrine which to us has always been the
most august sanctuary. It was from the Dome of the Rock that our
Prophet ascended into Heaven on his famous god-given steed. After
the turmoil of the Herodian and the Roman wars it was on the un-
shakeable foundation of the Rock that the Emir Omar, the Sherifian
Conqueror began to build the great Mosque which these homeless
faithless men seek to pollute. The Emir Omar had spent his energies
in holy works, and so it happened that long life was not vouchsafed
him, and so it was that the magnificent shrine was completed by his
noble successor, the Emir Abdul Malek. To build this splendid offering to the One God, he collected monies throughout the Moslem
world, and you can read in the Arab chronicles that 'seven times the
revenues of Egypt were expended in furnishing our shrine.'

"Until now our right to the holy places has never been contested.
Even when the misguided Crusaders came in their might from all over
Christendom and seized the Holy City and held it for a few years
after 1229, they recognized our rights and by the treaty between war-
riors, which was always religiously observed, the Haram and all the
sacred area remained in our hands, and so it has been by uncontested
right until the present day.

"But do not mistake me. We Arabs are not an imperialistic people;

unlike these vagrants and troublemakers we have no wish to start another world war which we fear, and not without reason, would destroy what of civilization now remains. Look, we do not claim the return of Andalusia, although there we developed a brilliant civilization and founded seats of learning to which all Christendom came seeking instruction and light. On the other hand we admit frankly that what we hold today, even if it was won by the sword, by the grace of the sword we shall continue to hold it. We are a virile people and the Jews are not. What Jews have bled to reconquer the land they claim? Where are their martyrs? Nowhere! But we, during the great war to save civilization, we have fought shoulder to shoulder and boot to boot with our British and our French allies, and they have most solemnly promised that for us the prize of victory would be a great Arab state, that all the tribes, even those who have been long submerged, would be freed. And now, at least so the Jews maintain, they have pledged themselves to dispossess us and give our lands to aliens. We do not believe such infamy is possible; but if it comes, we will again place our trust in our swords and in the justice of the One God. We shall remain the masters of our ancient home even if it becomes a graveyard. Of course we should prefer to live in peace with all the world; but if there is no other defense, we shall declare a Holy War against the Unbelievers."

It too was a good fighting speech. I found it impressive. These words are being heard by millions throughout the Moslem lands. I am sorry for all the world and its children who yearn for peace. Wise old Bacon said the most baleful vicissitude of mankind is that of sect. What a pity that after years of pitiless warfare, with undoubtedly the best and the noblest motives in the world, Mr. Balfour should have opened wide this Pandora box of racial and religious hatreds!

April 18, 1919

Mr. Balfour is growing increasingly sensitive at the criticism of the declaration he made to the House of Commons on November 2, 1917, which at least the Zionists have interpreted as the promise of a Jewish state, a national home for the long homeless people. It is undoubtedly unfortunate, and certainly Balfour failed to appreciate the fact, that Jerusalem is esteemed holy not only by the Jews but by the Christians and the Mohammedans as well.

To House yesterday Balfour voiced this complaint and with it his explanation. "My declaration was not inspired by sentiment, although I am free to admit I think we owe the Jews something substantial for the way, in all quarters of the world and on many battle fronts, they have rallied to the support of the Allies. Not the least of my grievances is the fact that neither my critics nor my friends have really read my declaration, which I can assure you had been carefully weighed and long pondered over. Indeed, even the Zionists who are most vitally concerned seem quite unfamiliar with its contents. I came out for a Jewish homeland in Palestine in so far as it could be established without infringing on the rights of the Arab communities, nomad as well as sedentary. Indeed I thought that in the terms of my declaration the rights of the Arabs were safeguarded as never before."

Then Balfour's pale face grew flushed. Evidently he was angry all through. "I should think any person would see that my pronouncement was not dictated by sentiment but was a war measure. I thought that our war aim was to give equal rights and even-handed justice to all the oppressed. May I not say that was our rallying cry and that it reverberated throughout the world? In a word it was what you call in the States our 'slogan.' It was, I thought, merely a happy coincidence that this belated act of justice to the Jews would establish their national home at the Eurasian crossroads and would prove a protection to the wasp waist of our empire, Suez."

House assured Balfour that even his critics appreciated the noble purpose of his proposal, but he admitted he saw difficulties ahead if the project were ever to be realized.

[1924. The fighting in Jerusalem and in Jaffa in 1920 and 1921, some of which I witnessed, and the resulting ferment among the Arabs, showed only too clearly that these misgivings were well founded. Indeed, in the last-mentioned year, well-meaning Mr. Balfour, while visiting in Palestine, only escaped from the hands of the rioters by the most opportune arrival of a British war vessel which carried him speedily out of harm's way. The problem that the declaration raised still defies solution. On the other hand, it has proved of great help to the German propaganda among the Arabs who, justly displeased with their treatment at Versailles, are inclined to think that their claims in Asia, as well as in Africa, would receive more intelligent and generous treatment in Berlin.]

*   *   *   *

In the foregoing paragraphs I tell the official story of how it fared with the Zionists at the Conference. They are fragmentary, but at least they reveal all I know officially about the subject which was one of the most hush-hush of the problems that were discussed and so often sidetracked at the Conference. Certainly the problem remains unsolved and the Balfour Declaration, in my judgment at least, does not rate high as a peace panacea. It has alarmed fifty million Arabs in or living adjacent to the areas where the religious clashes have occurred for centuries and also at least two hundred million of their co-religionists who, scattered throughout the world, are adjusting their tribal differences and seeking to form a Moslem bloc which all agree would not be helpful to world peace. I say nothing about the conflicting views which are advanced every Sabbath as to the disposition of this much promised land of Palestine, from the pulpits of the discordant Christian churches.

There was, however, one man who came to the Conference who was confident that the problem, nearly as old as time, had been finally adjusted and that now the peace that was once in Jerusalem would spread all over the troubled, war-racked areas. He was an octogenarian Jew from Cracow, the duly accredited agent of his synagogue in what was before the war Austrian Poland. Through his forbears he had been a refugee in many lands, a stranger in all of them, ever since the Dispersion. Part of his name, all that I could well remember, was Ben Israel. He came to see me frequently, mainly, I fear, because no one else would see him. I told the yeomen of our guard that I was always at home to Ben Israel and that if I was in conference he was to be asked to wait.

The fact of the matter is that I enjoyed his company because he was the only man within a radius of a thousand miles of the Hotel Crillon who was convinced that the Conference had settled any of its problems; to him the fiat of Mr. Balfour was stronger than the Holy Writ that had been ignored by men of all sects for hundreds of years. Ben Israel was presenting us with a *res adjudicata*, the only one in sight of the squabbling delegates. Who was I, a mere subordinate, that I should scrutinize the matter more closely? To this waif, this refugee on the seas of intolerance and persecution, I could not bring myself to play the role of a kill-joy. Perhaps the old man may die before the hour of rude awakening strikes, I thought. Whatever my purpose may have been, I never by word or gesture revealed the doubts that assailed me when he said (it was his word of greeting as well as his parting salutation), "Next year in Jerusalem we shall meet. Oh, happy, happy day when the dog-brothers no longer shall swagger about the Holy Places!"

Ben Israel was a charming talker in all the many languages which he commanded, and he had a persuasive way with him which I found impossible to resist. Indeed, in our second talk, without the slightest effort, with but a few well-chosen words, he swept into the discard all my defenses against reopening any problem that antedated the Westphalian treaties, and soon I found myself listening with rapt attention to his versions of ancient wars in Judea and the campaigns of the Crusaders. While he admitted with a certain pride that he had been born in a windowless room and had often slept on the doorsteps of his more fortunate brethren, he was scrupulously neat in his long-worn clothes. The little curlywigs of hair that clustered about his ears were not greasy, as is so often the case with the East Jews, and his long-drawn parchment features would have delighted any sculptor.

He had many novel ideas, and one at least was rather disconcerting to one who views, as we all are beginning to do, the discord and the bickerings that are developing in the councils of the so recently victorious Allies. "With us," he asserted, "discord has only come with defeat. Alas, in the days since the Dispersion we have become divided into sects and we have lost the strength that comes with unity, battling over absurd trifles. We might well have been redeemed from the political slavery that has been ours for centuries throughout the world had we remained united, but despite the injunctions of the prophets, that was not to be. Today we wail at the Wailing Wall, but we do not wail together; even in sackcloth and ashes we stand apart.

"So today a son of the Akénazim, however versed in Talmudic lore, will not marry into a Sephardim family or take a wife from among my people who, though proscribed and banished by Isabella, still speak her language in all the lands of their exile. Twenty years ago a Jewish lord who had prospered mightily in banking sought to put an end to this unhappy schism by offering a bonus of ten pounds to each of those who, by marrying outside of their narrow sect, would rise superior to this ancient and most unworthy prejudice. The result? There have not taken place any of these mixed marriages. The dowry money is still rusting in the great man's coffers."

Ben Israel was so distressed over this tribal exclusiveness that I thought to cheer him by admitting that we Christians too were kept apart by very trivial differences. "Behold the Czechs and the Slovaks," I said. "They are blood brothers; doubtless both are West Slavs. They have been held apart, but now they are free to unite and enjoy their freedom and independence together. But they can't get together. The new state would be fine, they admit, but the Czechs want to write it Czechoslovakia, while the Slovaks insist upon having their distinct nationality capitalized as is here written, *Czecho-Slovakia*."

My revelation brought little comfort to the envoy from Cracow. "With us it has been worse, much worse than that," he insisted. "Our people will not pray together. They will not live together. They will not eat together, and many a man and woman has died of starvation rather that accept a crust from a member of the antagonistic sect. Millions of people have been involved in this uncharitableness—and do you know how it came about? It sounds incredible, but is nevertheless as true as the Old Testament. The elders of that far-distant day disagreed as to the way chickens should be dressed for the kitchen. For centuries millions have suffered because of this most trivial difference of opinion."

April 22, 1919

When I returned ten days ago from my foray into Southeastern Europe, under the auspices of General Smuts, one of my first inquiries was of Ben Israel. The bo'sun said he had not been around for some time; that when last he called he had a hacking cough, "and I gave him some lozenges." I felt I ought to look him up. In fact, only my sudden departure for Vienna had prevented me from making the call upon which he seemed to set great store and which indeed I had promised to make at the first opportunity. Although the decision had been reached (of that he was confident), Ben Israel wished to show me certain documents in Hebrew which would remove any doubt as to the validity of the Zionist claim to the Holy, the much promised, City. I now looked up his address and started to make good on my promise—and more, to refresh my soul with contact with the only man I had met in Paris who believed that his problem had been solved.

I came at last after many wanderings to the large tenement in a dark narrow canyon street which ran out from the rue Pigalle. It was indeed a human hive as I stood at the entrance, wondering where I should begin my inquiries; men black and white and yellow emerged from the dingy portal. I could not locate the *loge* for a time, but finally a little child with one shoe on and one shoe off kindly led me to it by a back stair. The door on which we knocked was evidently barricaded against complaining tenants, but when I mentioned Ben Israel, the stern face of the guardian of the gate relaxed. Here was a tenant who had left a pleasant farewell. "He is gone, the poor gentleman," explained Madame la Concierge with a sigh. "He died two weeks ago.

"I had not seen him for days," she went on, "and unlike so many others he had always been punctual with his rent. I banged on his door, and when there came no answer I called in the passing *sergot* and he broke in. We found the kind old man, who never made a complaint about anything, lying on the floor with his head pillowed on a pile of manuscripts. I thought he was asleep, but when the police doctor came he pronounced him dead; said indeed he had been dead for several days.

"Another Jew tenant told us what to do and in a few hours a number of his co-religionists appeared, in long black gabardine coats just like the one he always wore and had died in, and they prepared him for burial. I must tell you the Alliance, I think they called it, gave the old man a very *chic* funeral the very next day. They carried him down from his dark room with a black-bearded cantor leading the way with a voice that shook the building—but pretty it was not. When they brought him out on the street, I followed, of course, to show my respect to a good tenant who always paid his rent while there was life in his body, and I could not believe my eyes. There, awaiting the poor man who had never ridden even in a *sapin* in his lifetime, was *un magnifique corbillard*, a splendid hearse, all covered with a cloth encrusted with silver and gold.

"But one thing they had cheapened on," now admitted the concierge, although she evidently hated to point out the sun spots in this picture of unexpected splendor, "and that was his coffin. In fact, it wasn't a real coffin at all; they had bundled him into four rough planks, unpainted, unplaned, and knotted, held together not by nails but by rough wooden skillets."

When I explained that this was the proper ritual according to the law and the prophets, the concierge was greatly relieved. "They were good people," she admitted, "those black-bearded men of the Alliance. They paid me the rent for four more weeks—the time they thought it would take them to assort those parchment papers he studied day and night by candlelight, for his was a windowless room—all he said he could pay for. And that was *chic,* don't you think so?" I agreed.

I did not grieve unduly for Ben Israel, although I shall miss him.

CHAPTER V

King Nicholas of Montenegro and Essad Pasha of Albania: The Black Mountain Folk vs. the Sons of the Eagle

December 4, 1918

Of the many suitors and suppliants who, awaiting their critical hour at the bar of the Great Assizes, are gathered here, King Nicholas of Montenegro and Essad Pasha, who represents many of the Albanian tribes and perhaps all who are Moslems, while not the most important, are certainly the most picturesque. I visited both their mountain fastnesses years ago, and today I find them sympathetic and extremely interesting. They are both men of magnificent thews and sinews, and of the visiting monarchs of the West, only the gallant King Albert of Belgium need not fear physical confrontation with their stately figures.

They come as suppliants, it is true, but not on bended knee. In fact they are quite stiff-kneed, and perhaps that is why I like them so much. (Here are so many who crawl and creep around, falling on all fours whenever obsequiousness would seem to further their plans.) I do not play favorites as between these stalwart champions, but I must admit that my Colonel has frequently chided me for the strong preference I show for their company—a preference I have never sought to conceal because I know by unfailing signs that my chief shares my sentiments and would like to see more of them.

Nicholas has maintained his sovereignty over the Black Mountain country and fought for the Cross in the benighted Balkans for six decades, although from his fresh appearance and upstanding figure you would never suspect that he had passed the half-century mark. He is well aware that he is in danger of being deposed by enemies assembled here more versed in intrigue than in open battle in which they were always worsted. Essad too, under the Crescent, has taken a leading part in many of the long and pitiless campaigns that have been waged by the discordant races and the militant churches of the dark peninsula. He now aspires to lord it legally, quite legally he insists—that is according to the Law of the Mountains—over that gaunt pile of rocks that juts out from the east coast of the Adriatic, the aerie nest of the sturdy Albanians who have defended it against all invaders and would-be conquerors back to the days of the Greeks and the Romans.

Unfortunately today the Neo-Roman Imperialists regard this rock-bound coast as necessary to the security of their homeland and their budding empire. In any event they claim it as at least a token reward for their services to the Allies (services not held in high esteem here) during the World War. [See Chapter IV.]

More recently these champions of ancient feuds faced each other in mortal combat under the battlements of Scutari. Nicholas conquered and Essad capitulated, but not to the Black Mountain men, at least that is his claim. "I surrendered," says Essad, "to the great ships of the comity of nations that most unjustly were allied against me, and they were more numerous than the gulls of the Adriatic. To them and to them only I surrendered, so that I might live to fight another day. And that will be a dark day for Nicholas."

Almost suffocated by the miasmas of intrigue that flourish so rankly in Paris, and confronted by the false faces that are seen here in every quarter, I find it refreshing and most cleansing to note the fierce hatred which blazes in the eyes of these champions whenever the name of the other is mentioned. This is real primeval stuff! These men fight and hate each other in the old style, much as did the Homeric heroes on the "ringing plains of windy Troy."

All those in attendance at the conference, whether delegates or observers, who are totally ignorant of Balkan conditions (and their name is legion), are talking continually of a confederation as the unfailing panacea for the situation in the Balkan Peninsula which has provoked so many wars and promises more in the immediate future. The economic advantages of a confederation and a customs union are obvious to everybody except the people immediately concerned, who seem to delight in little wars that have the unfortunate habit of spreading to other regions and setting Europe in flame. If argument on the subject could be maintained, the economist would only have to say the word *Sarajevo*.

Of course, there are many circumstances and cogent reasons which explain the warlike proclivities of these unfortunate people, some of which unwisely I voiced not knowing what they would lead to. I explained didactically, as one will who has spent some years in the disturbed and disturbing regions, that *Balkan* is an old Turkish word which means mountains or very high land. Then getting into my stride I explained that a great geographer of the Gotha School had asserted that the turbulence of peoples corresponds to, and is in proportion to, what he termed the "rugosity," of the lands in which they dwelt. The people in flat lands are peaceful by nature, while those who dwell in regions that are "wrinkled or corrugated" are inclined to fight at the drop of a hat. I described at some length the failures of many movements for confederation and a better understanding among the people of Southeastern Europe, some of which I had witnessed. These admirable plans had always failed, although they had been eloquently and very ably advocated by men who should have been accepted as leaders.

"In the war-racked peninsula," I continued, "we are confronted with racial and cultural differences and above all by religious animosities and rivalries, and as Bacon said long ago in his book on the vicissitudes that afflict humanity: 'The greatest of these is the vicissitude of sects.' The Bulgars still dream of the day of the great Czar Simeon, the Serbs hark back to the spacious empire of Stephen Dushan, and the Albanians are quite confident that the blueprints of Scanderbeg are not outmoded. Unfortunately also the churches are not very helpful to the peace-talker, although, of course, their intentions are of the best. The members of the Greek Church look to the Patriarch in Stamboul, the Bulgars are beholden to their Exarch, while the Croats and the Slovenes look to Rome for spiritual guidance; and this, as it filters through to the mountain folk, is not always of a conciliatory character."

Unfortunately for me, my expert knowledge proved impressive, and well before I knew it I was given the unwelcome task of bringing some of the fiery chieftains together and of talking to them convincingly. Reluctantly I began with the chieftains of the two smallest warlike tribes: King Nicholas of the Black Mountain folk and Essad Pasha, representing a number of the eagle clans who have been squabbling for years over the possession of a few barren foothills that lie between their respective territories.

As I had visited both these Balkan chiefs on their native crags, I was urged to bring them as near as possible to the spirit of conciliation which it was thought should prevail at the Conference. I lunched them and I dined them—separately. My dream was, of course, to bring them together, to have them break bread at my table, drink plum brandy, and smoke the pipe of peace. My talking point was the frequent reunions in our happy land of the gallant men who wore the blue and the gray, who had fought each other for four long years and yet were now meeting so frequently on the very fields where the bloody battles had been lost and won. "After four years of fratricidal war, today they meet as brothers should. Why not you?"

"But we have been fighting those godless Albanians for four hundred years," demurred Nicholas. "That makes a difference." Indeed it does.

Then I tackled Essad. "Break bread with Nicholas? or any of the Black Mountain folk? Impossible—that would be against the law of the mountains which we are all pledged to respect."

Essad had the dangerous gift of picturesque language and not seldom he gave it loose rein. He had served as minister of war to the Prince of Wied during the short and hectic sojourn of that German princeling in Albania.

[Prince William of Wied, cousin of the German Kaiser, was offered the crown of the newly autonomous Albania by the Western Powers after the First Balkan War and the crisis of 1913. Internal unrest and the outbreak of the World War forced him from his throne a year later. At this time (1918) Albania was occupied mainly by the Italians, but also by the French and the Yugoslavs. Its capital, Scutari, was under an interallied administration.]

"At the London Conference" [1913], Essad related, "the machinery of the new state was well set up, but the choice of the resident engineer was unfortunate. It soon became evident that the real purpose of the Prince was to weaken our people so that we might, without further resistance, drop into the lap of Austria and so cease blocking the march of the Germans to the sea. Soon we drifted apart, our relations became much less cordial, and I, though his minister of war, had to summon guards to protect my life against the machinations of my sovereign.

"The Prince surrounded himself with Austrian engineers who had come ostensibly to modernize the old palace on the coast where we, the members of the government, were living. But they really came to 'remove' Essad Pasha from the scene; of course, in such a way that murder would not be suspected. This the Prince thought would be more easily accomplished down on the coast far from the atmosphere of freedom on the hills which is the birthright of my people. All day these alien intruders would be busy with their ostensible occupation, but at night they would prowl about the palace, and I soon saw that their sinister purpose was to learn where I and my wife were accustomed to sleep. When the veil of friendship was cast aside and the Austrian fleet bombarded the palace, a shell, which fortunately did not explode, landed in my official bedroom where, however, I was most careful never to sleep."

Essad if possible was still more critical of the behavior of the Italians in the last days of their first sojourn on the Albanian shore. [The Italians, *et al.*, fled before the Austro-Bulgarian seizure in 1916.] "I was out on the hills," he related, "ostensibly shooting woodcock, but really I was getting in touch with my mountain folk and seeking a plan by which we might escape the foul plottings of our enemies. At home and abroad I told them: 'We Albanians number five million, all with national consciousness, all hoping to retain our independence, yet we are given to tribal warfare and family vendettas, and it would be wise to ask for a dual protectorate, say of America and of England, until we have learned the difficult art of self-government and also have acquired a taste for peace.'

"This was my hope when suddenly the bombardment began and the Italian garrison in Durazzo dropped their rifles and fell on their knees. 'Santa Madonna! Santa Madonna!' they implored, but as no help came from Heaven or elsewhere they ran away like hares, only faster.

"There was a French colonel there heading the French Mission

(Colardet), and I said to him, 'Let me defend the bridge with my men and I can assure you the Austrians will never get across!'' But he said, 'No, I can better trust these battalions of rabbits than your band of wolves.'

"You see, those Europeans were very unfriendly to one another, but most of all they feared my gallant tribesmen. Then the cowardly Italians sneaked down to the port and made for the boats; but before they went they had thought of their bellies and they cut the throats of my two magnificent chargers which I had bought in England at a cost of half-a-million francs. They were magnificent animals, completely war broken; and those miserable rabbits took their noble carcasses along with them to serve as meat rations on their ignominious flight."

December 5, 1918

At a lunch with him last week, to which he invited me in a formal manner, Essad honored me with a commission that showed that he was broader-minded in religious matters than many, including myself, had supposed. It was a strange repast. We were quite alone, because, as he said, he had an important communication to make, one which if it prospered would exert a benign influence upon the turbulent conditions that prevail in the Balkans. Behind his chair and also behind mine stood heavily armed servingmen, their blue tunics bulging out with pistols and their gorgeous belts bristling with yataghans. They stood to guard us only, and the food was served by the Parisian waiters of the tourist hotel who tried, not quite successfully, to ignore the strangeness of the scene in which they were involved.

Now and again, vexed by a tough morsel on his plate, Essad would drop his ineffective fork and, picking up the hunk with his fingers, would throw it disdainfully over his shoulder. The servingman never failed to catch it in his mouth and seemed to enjoy his share of the feast. The spectacle carried me back to experiences in Prisrend and Prishtina and even in more civilized Usküb on the Vardar years ago.* Then I too had in this manner thrown tidbits to my servingman; but

* See Albanian chapter in the author's *Heyday in a Vanished World* (W. W. Norton, New York and London, 1937).

today I was out of practice, so when the repast was over I simply slipped a twenty-franc note to the guardian behind my chair and he seemed to be perfectly satisfied. Evidently Paris had corrupted him as it has so many others.

Over the coffee, which was brewed in the slow, deliberate Macedonian way, Essad broached the subject that had evidently been on his mind for some time.

"An Albanian friend who has lived long in Boston brought me last week an item of disquieting news," he began. "He says your honored President is an Elder of a church which some consider, doubtless unfairly, as narrowly sectarian. Whether this be true or false, this rumor has decided me to reveal what may be regarded as my religious outlook. While my people are divided as to churches—a division which the Tsar * in Stamboul, until I helped to dethrone him, and the Emperor in Vienna always fostered—you must have seen how very liberal and catholic my people are when left to their own devices. You surely have noticed during your visits to Albania that when our peasants prepare to sow their crops they not only ask the Moslem mullah to bless their fields and their labors, but also the good will of the Christian priest was asked and paid for by them if they could afford it. I think your President should be advised of the situation in my land and of my personal attitude which, you can assure him, I would never allow to become a barrier to the happiness of my people.

"To begin with, I want you to explain what happened in our country after Kossovo [1349] and the tragic battle that was fought there. The Turks with their green banners and their horsetail standards overran our lands killing all who would not praise the one God and his prophet Mahomet. We had always been Christians; in my family many had suffered martyrdom, and my forbears would gladly have accepted the fate which the fortune of war imposed if only their lives and their property had been at stake. But this was not the case. The lives and the property of the Albanian people were in the balance, and my ancestors did what I have always considered was the proper thing for them to do. They bowed down before the green banners. They admitted the truth of the proverb, 'Where the sword

* The Albanians and many of the Balkan peoples often, to the confusion of the Westerling, referred to the Sultan as Tsar.

is there also is the Faith,' and by so doing they saved their people and their land from utter destruction."

In an aside Essad now drew a parallel which he thought was devastating to the forebears of the hated Nicholas. "How stupid those Montenegrin bishops were," he commented. "Instead of admitting that there are many roads to Heaven and that no church has the exclusive control of the entrance gate, they fled to the mountains and took refuge in the caves. They saved their faith, it is true, but they lost their civilization. They sank to the lowest level of the human race. Even your Nicholas, who has been presented at many courts, is under his gorgeous trappings but a boor."

And now came the definite proposition. "My fathers saved our people and we served the Ottoman Turks faithfully until the moment came to overthrow their sultan, which we gladly seized. Today if my religion, which was imposed or at least accepted only under duress and to save our people, is an obstacle to our return to the Christian fold, I—we—would all recant as did our forebears, and to save our people accept once again the creed of long ago."

I told Essad I would not fail to advise Colonel House and other delegates of his patriotic reasonableness, and I did so. But, doubtless wisely, our commission refused to have anything to do with the Albanian settlement. Like so many other problems it is allowed to drift along, and a deluge of blood will be the result.

[At this time, doubtless under instructions from Rome, Signor Nobile Chiesa, aviation expert of the Italian delegation, made a terrific attack in the French and Italian papers upon the stalwart Essad. He said that, while Essad was quite ignorant of any civilized language, he was very familiar with all European currencies and would accept bribes in any one of them. In the matter of language, at least, Chiesa is quite mistaken. Essad spoke a baffling French although apparently he wrote it with distinction, but he had a good knowledge of Italian, with which we eked out our conversation. Certainly it was not the *lingua Toscana*, but his meaning was always unmistakable. How he hated the Italians and how he loved to vilify them in their own language!

In his mountain tongue, though, Essad sums up with a song his feelings on this subject: "What is it that sports feathers but is not a bird? That carries a rifle but is not a soldier? That wears trousers but is not a man—the Italian Bersagliere!"]

December 6, 1918

One of the dreams I cherished in the first hopeful days of the Conference (as mentioned in a previous entry) was to bring Nicholas, the undoubted champion of Balkan Christendom, and Essad, the Saladin of these modern crusades, together at my table; not, of course, at the Crillon where we would be exposed to the Argus-eyed gaze of the press, but in some remote restaurant, well out of the path of the conferees. The denouement of the plot was to tip my Colonel off and have him drop in casually at the place of meeting in his rôle of apostle of peace, and have him once again pronounce his familiar lines, so often effective: "All men are brothers. There are but few points of friction between us, and with but a little patience and good will, these can be ironed out."

However, the Colonel soon ruled out as unthinkable all thought of a formal meeting with these champions of the Balkans. He said it was not permissible under the Protocol, but I could see that he toyed with the idea of a chance or clandestine meeting.

Once he admitted: "I always get along best with mountain men. We seem to understand each other right away. My anteroom is crowded with lowlanders talking about dollars and cents, debts and trade privileges, and I confess they bore me. I envy you your contacts with the highlanders. How I would enjoy sharing them with you! But of course it is impossible. And you must not tempt me. From what you tell me I picture the hard-bitten Nicholas as a John Sevier who with 'over-the-mountain men' walloped the Red Coats in the Carolinas; and Essad I picture as a ringer for Big Foot Wallace of the Pecos country, who would ride for a week in the tropical sun if only at the end of the journey there was a chance of a gun battle. I should like to meet them, but, of course, it is impossible for the present."

Clearly my Colonel was weakening.

Another reason why I was never able to pull off what might well have been a confrontation of incalculable consequences in the Balkan situation was the increasing reluctance of Essad to leave his comfortable quarters in a Champs Elysées tourist hotel generally patronized by cosmopolitans. Adored and even idolized as he was by at least half the Albanian tribesmen, the Pasha was cordially hated by many others. He went out as little as possible, and when he did he was surrounded by heavily armed followers and he himself carried with him quite a battery of Brownings.

[Despite these precautions, within a few months Essad Pasha was dead. In June, 1920, the National Assembly, in which most of the Albanian clans were represented, recognized the position of their delegate to the Conference in Paris and proclaimed him king. On the thirteenth of that same month, as he was about to leave to be crowned in Tirana, he was assassinated in front of the Hotel Continental in Paris by a certain Averni Rustam, a fellow countryman whose clan had waged a blood feud with Essad's tribe for decades and who could not tolerate Essad as his monarch.

In the person of his favorite nephew, Zog, however, Essad reached the uneasy throne of the Albanian Eagles. In 1924 Zog became president of Albania and four years later, with a Napoleonic gesture, crowned himself king in Tirana, the forty-fourth successor to Scanderbeg, the legendary ruler of the Eagles.]

December 18, 1918

Today I feel that in all fairness I must put on record a more detailed account of my relations with Nicholas, his Royal Highness, King of Montenegro, which has been long withheld even from these confidential files. I must admit that these relations have not escaped misrepresentation in some quarters. They go back twenty-five years, and perhaps a few more, and I have for him such a deep admiration that when the problem which his future presented to the Supreme War Council came up, I felt it was only right that I should reveal to the Colonel, my chief, the ties of ancient friendship that bound us; and also to confess that on this subject my judgment might be colored by the admiration I had long felt for the "alone-standing, stalwart fighter" of the Balkans. This frank confession earned me a compliment that I cherish. "That is just like you," said the Colonel. "You have put your cards on the table. I shall of course be glad to discuss with you the Montenegrin problem, but when it comes to a decision I shall have to go it alone." And then the Colonel made the only ill-natured remark that I ever heard fall from his lips. "You are different from X; whenever he tips away to lunch at the Hotel Eduard VII where, as is well known, the Italians set a magnificent table, I feel in my heart that the Yugoslavs will lose another island."

"I never broke bread with King Nicholas," I protested; but weakening under the Colonel's scrutiny I confessed, "I had a few slivoviches with him, and once or twice, after the heat of the day was over, we pledged our respective countries in raki."

"That rules you out," decided the Colonel; "you must see that you cannot sit as a member of the jury before which the King comes as a suppliant." As I was excluded from the jury, I felt that I could go the limit as an advocate. "As a passing stranger, I sat with the King as an assessor or coadjutor on his bed of justice in Cetinje years ago, and what I saw justified me in maintaining that Nicholas is a great and good man as well as a stalwart fighter. Yes, I sat with him and saw him, as did Ulysses of old, 'deal unequal laws unto a savage race.' While it was certainly rough and ready justice, strictly according to the Law of the Mountain, in only one instance can I recall a verdict perhaps not in strict accordance with the evidence. The King did close an eye to help an old soldier who had stood by his side in one of the many battles for the coveted port of Scutari. A magnificent-looking fellow he was, who fed his flocks on the mountaintops in summer, in the valleys in winter, and who was ready to fight the Turks, or anyone else, whenever the signal fires on Lovčen blazed."

"In that I see no basis for your exclusion," said the Colonel. "We all love the soldier, but I fear you are holding back the gravamen of the charge."

"Give me time," I stuttered. "It was this way. A lowlander, a villager, a measly looking fellow who sat quite still in the days when brave men were arming, now declared that this mountaineer soldier had herded into his flocks sheep and goats that did not belong to him.

" " 'Tis a lie—an atrocious lie!' answered the mountain man. 'Had I been in want of sheep or even goats, I had only to tell my Gospodar, my King, and he would have helped his soldier in need.'

" 'True, true,' said the King, 'that is the course I would have pursued.'

"Then the King argued with the accusing villager. 'May you not be mistaken?' he suggested. 'Wise indeed is the shepherd who knows his own sheep. And then, of course, if they are there, your sheep may have forced their way into Petko's flock without the least inducement from him.'

"The King now lit a fat cigarette and with a dark look at the villager announced, amid applause from the many who had gathered under the great tree where the bed of justice was held: 'The case is dismissed; I cannot convict an old soldier on evidence as flimsy as this.'

" 'But my sheep! my goats!' screamed the villager. 'My brand marks on them are perfectly plain.'

" 'Well! well!' said the King, 'it may be so. Yet perhaps your goats forced their way into Petko's flocks of their own volition. Bring me the evidence on this point set out in writing by the Elders of the village this day fortnight when, God willing, I shall once again dispense justice.' "

The Colonel grew thoughtful. He was evidently interested now in the monarch of the Black Mountain. "I must meet King Nicholas. Clearly that is my duty," he mused.

December 28, 1918

It had been a long week of economic discussions and plans for reparations and plump indemnities that were no more substantial than fairy tales, as the Colonel sorrowfully admitted. I had plagued him so constantly that at last he consented to visit the King of Montenegro, who had now moved into town from his suburban residence and was residing so conveniently down the rue de Rivoli at the Meurice.

"Let's take a car," the Colonel suddenly agreed. "I am bursting with impatience." Then a shadow of care swept over his face which, in anticipation of the long-desired but often postponed meeting, had been so sunny. "But you don't think he will ask for a loan?"

"Not a chance," I reply gaily. "All he asks for is a passport to return to Lovčen—for the rest he will manage himself."

I must say that on this occasion, so important from every point of view, the King did not demonstrate the subtle qualities for which he has been long famous throughout the Near East. The moment after bidding us welcome and ordering Danilo, his heir (with a sturdy frame but a decidedly weak face), to go for coffee and sweets, he danced over to a lacquer cabinet and produced a number of ribbons and rosettes and crosses with yellow metal attachments that glittered and may have been gold.

"You are my true friends, or you would not be visiting a dethroned king. I beg of you to honor me and our friendship by wearing these tokens of my high esteem and my admiration." With that he tried to attach what was, I believe, the highest class of the Order of Danilo the Great upon the Colonel's coat, and upon me he thrust an order almost as high. The Colonel drew back and we both, gracefully I trust, waved away the temptation. We had by this time a regular form refusal for compromising gifts or decorations of any kind.

"We cannot accept," said the Colonel, with a pained expression on his face which did honor to his Thespian ability, "because our government is not in a position to reciprocate with a corresponding honor." And then the Colonel went on: "But for this barrier, the temptation to accept these signal honors from your Majesty's hand would be irresistible, but even so, would it be wise? Would not our desire to serve you be handicapped? Would it not be said that, after having been showered with the highest honors, is it possible for these American gentlemen to maintain the judicial attitude they should when Balkan questions come before the Conference?"

King Nicholas was not slow to see the force of this remark, and soon the decorations were safely housed again in the lacquer cabinet. After a few sips of most excellent coffee, the real business of the meeting got under way.

"My Colonel," began the King, "it distresses me that the fate of my land and that of my line is causing you anxiety. Permit me to say it should not. Lend me but for a few weeks your commandant here as a symbol of American sympathy; secure for me the passports so long denied which will permit me to reach the frontier of my native land, which your commandant knows and also loves, and the Montenegrin problem will vanish as does the snow on Lovčen when the sirocco blows. I am an exile and a man under an unholy ban, but once I cross the border the soldiers of my son-in-law and of my grandson would flee and I—I would not deign to pursue them."

Having settled in this summary manner the diplomatic and military features of the problem, the King now took a lighter and a more personal view of the situation.

"Let your commandant go with me as your plenipotentiary and as the representative of liberty-loving America. What a time we shall have," and the King in anticipation roared with laughter. "We shall go shooting in the mountains, in my beloved mountains; we will bring down chamois and mountain goats and bear and wolves, particularly the wolves which have become a pest to our peasants because the Swabs * who have overrun the low land are afraid to follow them to their lairs as we do." Then turning to me and rather leaving the Colonel out of the shooting symposium, the King went on: "I promise you a great big bag of *jarebica*, the most beautiful bird that flies. It is larger than the partridge, has red legs and a red bill, and I can tell you we shall have to climb the highest peaks to get a crack at him."

"But what about your mission of pacification?"—this from the Colonel, who, it seemed to me, was not a little nettled at being left out of the shooting party.

"That will be accomplished in a moment," said Nicholas. "When my people hear the crack of our rifles on the mountain peaks they will rejoice, and down in the valleys there will be peace and joy-dancing. . . ."

A few minutes later a change came over the spirit of our host; the sturdy old king who had survived sixty years of constant warfare fell into a reminiscent and indeed a somewhat bitter mood.

"Our national life which we preserved from our enemies is now threatened by our friends. All the battles we fought are forgotten. It is little remembered that we served as the bulwark of Christendom against the infidel Horde for centuries, and little help came to us from the people we shielded; only Russia helped us, and she, being far away, could help but little. By persistent fighting we recovered the lands that belonged to us and we liberated our Serb brothers of the plains who had been overrun and submerged. We did not rest until we secured our seaboard towns—our windows on the world of the West, where men were happier because we had protected them—and we raised the cross once again over Antovari and Dulcigno. The world then hailed us publicly as gallant fighters for the true Faith, but they whispered that we were savages and that indeed few of us could read or write.

"And in a narrow sense that was true; I admit it. The school of the Montenegrin boy, and girl too, had been from the day the Horde arrived in Europe unrelenting mountain warfare. We had no need to write down the story of our race—that our boys and girls imbibed with their mother's milk, and they sang it as they defended the mountain crags that were at once our home and our refuge. Yes, we did become illiterate because we had to fight day and night for

---

* A term the Montenegrins and other South Slavs use when they wish to speak disrespectfully of the Germans—and that is generally their wish.

our creed, our independence, our faith, our man- and our woman-hood. But before the Horde came, mine had been an enlightened people loving the ways of peace. In those days Obod, today a battle-scarred village, was the Athens of Southeastern Europe and from there the records of our faith and our civilization were communicated in our tongue to the outside world still in darkness." *

Suddenly the old King sobbed aloud. "It is forgotten now," he said, "even by our own people, but it is God's truth that those leaden types of Obod were melted down to make bullets with which we stopped the enemies of our creed, and the precious manuscripts which revealed the glories of our race were used as wadding for the guns that saved Christendom. Had we not made those sacrifices, there might well have been no printing in Western Europe today. It might have become there a lost art, as it has with us; and the spoken language in the West might well have become Turkish. History reveals that some nations have short memories, but today in our hour of need it seems incredible that these services should be completely forgotten."

"That shall never be," said the Colonel, who was deeply moved. "In some way which we do not see plainly at present Montenegro will be restored to her ancient glory."

* * * *

Back at the Crillon I slipped to the Colonel Tennyson's great sonnet and he read it and read it again.

> O! smallest among people, rough rock throne
> Of Freedom, warriors beating back the swarm
> Of Turkish Islam for five hundred years,
> Great Tzernagora, never since thine own
> Black ridges drew the clouds and broke the storm
> Has breathed a mightier race of mountaineers.

"We must leave nothing undone to help these gallant people and their noble king. If the Powers fail us, I shall ask Texas to take Montenegro under her wing," concluded the Colonel.

* The British Museum possessed, before the Blitz at least, a book from the Obod Press printed in 1493—the year after the discovery of America! And there are said to be many other books bearing this imprint in the monasteries of Ryllo, but I have never seen them.

December 21, 1918

Today Andrew Radovich, the former prime minister of Montenegro and at present the bitter enemy of King Nicholas, tracked me down to a restaurant in the Passage des Princes where I often take refuge from my ethnic factors. He brought with him a young fellow countryman just liberated from an internment camp through the intercession of King Alfonso of Spain. This hard-bitten youngster is a nephew of King Nicholas' queen and so by marriage is related to the House of Savoy.* The royalties are evidently standing by each other, and unless I misread the signs of the times it is none too soon for them to be doing so.

Radovich had often delighted me with his stories of the Black Mountain boys who had taken to the high hills and harassed the Austrians, but his obvious purpose today was to convince me that King Nicholas had during the World War abandoned organized resistance much too soon and that for all his stalwart appearance he is really a tricky fellow who would bear watching. In the course of one of their disagreements, the King, according to Radovich, had yanked him from the premiership and with shackles on his limbs had thrown him into prison.

"The shameless fellow then visited me and with no idle purpose," said Radovich dramatically. "He had tears in his eyes, and he added he would not be happy as long as I was in chains and I—well, I told him: 'Bishop-King, my arms and legs are in chains but my soul goes free, as it never did in the days when I served you and tried to follow your serpentine path.' "

Apparently the Serbians when they rushed into the Black Mountain country liberated the former premier and, as some maintain, sent him to Paris to make all the trouble he could for King Nicholas. One of his talking points is to the effect that Montenegro could have held back the Austro-German armies for years, as they had held back the Turkish horde for centuries, but for the perfidy of the King.

"If we had only fought shoulder to shoulder with the Serbians, the Germans would never have been able to pollute our soil or

* King Nicholas attained international connections through his daughters: he married one daughter to the King of Serbia; two others were wives of Russian grand dukes, and Helen, his fourth, became the wife of Victor Emanuel III, and Queen of Italy, in 1900.

devastate our fields and villages. For fifty years he kept the Serbs and our Black Mountain folk apart, and now you see the result: no railroads, no communications, no modern weapons; only our stout hearts against modern artillery, and, inevitably, the result was defeat." So runs the story of Radovich.

I turned from politics and listened to young Djourovitch, who had an interesting tale to tell. He was a law student, and when the Austrian invasion came he went to the hills where he was soon joined by many other fearless spirits. At least half of them, he said, were Montenegrins from America who had worked in the mines and the lumber camps of our Northwest until the tocsin sounded that brought them home.

"We were splendidly equipped," he maintained, "in very short order. We drew our rations and our guns from the Austrian transport trains. Soon wandering Polaks and Czechs joined us and we led a merry life. Often in Austrian uniforms we would descend into the garrisoned villages and, with false information, send the invaders into the mountains on wild-goose chases. Then we would kill the officers and men who remained behind and we would also kill the very few of our countrymen who were so traitorous as to do business with the invaders and make profits out of our misfortunes. Not many, but some of the women had been so shameless as to consort with the Austrians; in one village we found nine of these. These we marked for life, that is, we cut off their noses."

The young bloodhound was particularly bitter against Serbs; indeed, he thought well of the Albanians who had harassed the retreat of the shattered Serbian forces on their march to the sea. "The worst of it is," he continued, "the fact that many of them [Serbs] are our blood brothers. Take the Mirdites, for instance, that infamous Albanian clan; they are really Serbs or Bosniaks who flinched and fled to the highlands while we held our ground against the Turks.

"When I return home I shall devote my life to exterminating these robbers and murderers who disgrace the Serb blood that flows in their veins. They are men who will kill their blood brothers for a pair of shoes."

I left the young barbarian with gloomy forebodings as to the nature of the peace we are bringing to the Balkans. There the melting pot will boil over with gore before the hostile tribesmen settle down again to the workaday world that awaits them—if any of them survive.

January 6, 1919

King Nicholas has filed with the Secretary General of the Conference his protest against the situation in Montenegro for which he holds, with some justification, the Allied Powers responsible. It is but little toned down from the advance copy he gave me some days ago. It is a sweeping indictment of the Serbian authorities and their armies that surged into the Black Mountain country to replace the occupying Austrians during the last days of October, 1918. He says that at least four thousand of his men and several hundred women are now in prison and have been or are shortly to be brought before military courts, "because they oppose the annexation of their country to Serbia." [King Nicholas himself had bitterly opposed annexation with Serbia (his son-in-law, Peter, was King of Serbia) during most of his reign (1860–1918).]

"All of these men are patriots," the King insists, "and at least eight of them were ministers in my government when, without a moment's delay and without asking for guarantees of any kind, we threw down the gage of battle to the Central Empires, although we well knew that owing to our geographical position immediate help from the Western Allies was impossible.

"Furthermore, among these men arbitrarily held under most uncivilized and unsanitary conditions there are many priests and civilians who at great risk to their lives and property opposed and greatly harassed the Austrian invaders. As a matter of fact, to these gallant men and women the Serbian army of today owes its very existence. These are the people who in 1915 saved the Serbian forces from annihilation or ignominious captivity when, driven from their own territory by overpowering numbers, they undertook the march over the mountains to the sea.

"The only charge that can be brought against these patriotic people is that they have protested against the annexation of their homeland, secretly ordered by the Belgrade government, and that they have opposed, sometimes with arms, the way in which the invaders who claim to be 'blood brothers' take possession of their villages, devastate their fields, and steal their flocks. It is said that some of these bandits have been murdered. This charge is true; my people admit it; but such acts are not reprehensible. This is the attitude my gallant people have always maintained against those who sought to despoil our country. Not a few of my people, with the recklessness characteristic of men who have always been free and are determined to remain so, have refused to submit to this treatment and many, very many have been shot down lightheartedly as though they were rabbits when they attempted to escape from the wired concentration camps.

"Last month when the French government, speaking for the Allies and the Supreme War Council, requested me not to return to my beloved country until conditions were more stable, I acceded to this most unwelcome delay because the government of the republic gave to me and to my people the most solemn assurance that the 'Allied troops' would respect the sovereignty of our state and the liberties of my children. 'Allied troops,' as it developed later, were only Serbian bandits and marauders. While at first these assurances were only given verbally (to save time, I was told) they were formally confirmed by M. Pichon, the French Minister of Foreign Affairs, in a letter dated November 4, and later, if possible even more authoritatively, in a letter from His Excellency, M. Poincaré, the President of the French Republic." The King then showed me both the letters, and they are textually exactly as he has represented them to be.

"Despite these solemn promises," continued the King, "the Serbs, in the name of and apparently with the authority of the Allies, continued to dragoon my people and enforce their authority by what is called by some observers an 'Asiatic terror,' although we are bound to admit that the outrages of the Turks in the old days were milk-and-water affairs in comparison to what we are now undergoing at the hands of our 'blood brothers.' "

January 22, 1919

My repeated arguments to the effect that the Serb, Pasitch,* and

* Nikola Pasitch, called "the Old Fox of the Balkans," was a wily, violent, ex-radical who, after a youth spent in being condemned to death and banished for his anti-royalist plots, served as premier of Serbia and its successor state, Yugoslavia, 1906–1926.

the Belgrade government are ignoring Point II of the famous Fourteen [freedom of the seas], and that the present actual invasion of the Black Mountain country by the Serbians is even less defensible than the former onslaught of the Austro-German forces, at last carried conviction, and when the matter was brought before him President Wilson took his first affirmative action since his arrival in France. He approved of the memorandum which I had drawn up, and what was more, he secured for it the approval of all the great men assembled in the second session of the World Assizes. It declared that all the Serbian troops, irregulars as well as regulars, who were overrunning Montenegro and dragooning its people must be immediately withdrawn. If an army of occupation proved necessary to maintain law and order and to prepare the country for the American panacea of a "free and fair election," the troops of a neutral power should be substituted for the Serbian forces.

To accompany this decision, I had drawn up for King Nicholas to sign an appeal to his people which I was quite hopeful would aid in the pacification of the disturbed districts. In it, the King called upon all loyal Montenegrins to refrain from hostilities and return to their homes to avoid armed conflicts whatever the provocation; and it concluded with his hope expressed in these words: "I am confident that in accordance with President Wilson's noble program, now ratified by all the powers, the people of Montenegro will be given a full and early opportunity to decide upon the form of government they may desire."

I had great difficulty in inducing the King to sign this appeal, but as this was a part and a most important part of the bargain, I had to insist upon it.

It is difficult to say exactly what happened to this manifesto of the Powers and the appeal of the King that went with it. Both were radioed from the American, the British, and other naval vessels that were patrolling the Adriatic, but the French and the Italian ships, which were far more numerous in these waters than ours, showed little zeal in bringing the news of the peace policy to the distracted country. Even the English, apparently out of homage to Belgrade, showed little energy in passing on the good news. At least this was the information that reached us through American naval channels. However, some steps toward pacification were taken. Several brigades of Serbian troops were withdrawn and the assembly at Podgoritza which had been upheld by Serbian bayonets and which had declared the deposition of King Nicholas collapsed. The call of the King addressed to his people to return to their homes and refrain from active hostilities secured in some mysterious way a much wider circulation than did the assurance of the Powers that the harassed mountaineers would be given an early opportunity to decide for themselves what form of government they preferred—and that was most unfortunate.

I am compelled to admit that my plan was not a great success and that, while crediting me with the best possible motives, the King regretted he had followed my advice. A few days later he told me (he was in "grape-vine" communication with his partisans at home throughout the Conference) that many misleading versions of his appeal had been placed in circulation and that by not a few it was considered a complete surrender and even a suggestion that the people should make the best possible terms with Belgrade.

"And of course that was the very last thing I wanted them to do," protested the King. "The very last thing I wanted them to do was to lay down their arms. I am a fighter, they are fighters. I wanted them to fight for the freedom of the Black Mountain to the last man."

March 12, 1919

Today I must note in my locked diary one of the most "hush-hush" of the many graveyard secrets, to use the Colonel's expression, that it contains. Ten days ago King Nicholas showed me the original of a cable which he received from President Wilson in the summer of 1918. It appears that his agent in Washington at this time had approached the White House with the request that recognition and encouragement be afforded the struggling Black Mountain folk who, by their guerilla tactics, were harassing the Austrian forces of occupation quite as effectively as have the Poles and the Czechs—indeed all the oppressed and overrun peoples in their respective territories. The cable apparently resulting from this *démarche* is dated July 12, 1918, and on the face of it certainly confirms the position which the President took in enunciating the eleventh of the Fourteen Points [guaranteeing Balkan states free access to the sea], the world-wide Magna Charta of all the at-present submerged peoples. The cable reads:

I am confident that neither you nor the noble people of Montenegro will allow yourselves to be cast down by the present untoward situation but that on the contrary you will have implicit confidence in the firm determination of the United States government and people that in the final, certain and assured victory, the integrity and the rights of Montenegro will be recognized and safeguarded.

WOODROW WILSON.

Of course the cable may be a forgery; if it is, I am confident that the King is its victim and not the perpetrator of it. My Colonel has of course tried to elucidate the matter, but down to the present without success. In the files that the President brought with him from Washington there is no copy of the cable, much less the original record, and the King frankly admits that a confirmation of the cable by mail, as would have been the usual practice, never reached him. President Wilson recalls an interview with the Montenegrin envoy at about this time and also that he spoke encouraging words to him; but he has no recollection of having sent the cable, although he is not willing to deny that he sent it. This may be another instance of a typewriter near at hand and a dislike of secretarial assistance having resulted in embarrassment for our chief magistrate. The failure of a mail copy to authenticate the cable is not remarkable. At this time King Nicholas had taken refuge in Italy, and mail to the Allies, owing to the activities of the U-boats, was most uncertain and precarious.

The King is determined to show the cable to President Wilson and is insistently demanding an opportunity to do so. And nothing could be more understandable. The Italians are withdrawing the slender support they at first gave to the father of their Queen, and unless help, indeed real assistance, comes from Wilson, the King's chance of returning to his battle-scarred kingdom is slight indeed.

This change of policy in Rome is not an enigma to those who believe that the teachings of Machiavelli are still honored and practiced at the Consulta. To them it is clear that Italy wishes to further weaken the by-no-means harmonious confederation of the Serbs, Croats, and Slovenes by the addition of the Montenegrins who, they are confident, will soon be in chronic insurrection and so, indirectly at least, will aid Rome to control the Adriatic sphere. This I believe is a correct assumption. I am confident that a great majority of the Black Mountain people want to maintain their political independence of Belgrade whatever the economic disadvantages may be, and that they are willing and eager to fight for it.

March 24, 1919

My admiration for King Nicholas (which some denounce as blind partiality) has caused many of the Serbs to make statements which in my judgment do not tally with the facts; some indeed are laughable. This morning de Giulli and two of the other Belgrade propagandists came into my room and announced that in examining the Holy Scriptures of St. Cyril and St. Methodius they find that the deposition of Nicholas was therein decreed and sanctioned by these good men centuries ago. Their attitude induces me to think that the world is going mad and perhaps that I am getting "nutty" myself. They brought with them a Bible in Old Slavonic and began to read from it.

"In these holy writings," they insisted, "we find authority and justification for the course we are determined to pursue. Here is a sign and a portent which must be heeded if our people are to be saved. The Armistice came into effect at the eleventh hour of the eleventh day of the eleventh month. Clearly that is not an accident; it is an indication for our guidance, and following it what do we find? Listen, in the eleventh verse of the eleventh chapter of the eleventh book of the Old Testament we find these words: *And because he was a bad king his kingdom shall be taken away from him and he shall be despoiled.*

For a moment I was tongue-tied, but soon I rallied. "You quote from a schismatic bible," I answered, "and from a text which I cannot accept. If the Conference is to be guided by the Scriptures, and as yet there is no agreement on that point, we shall insist on the King James' version." They left me very much disgruntled but announced the coming visit of Ante Trumbitch, their leading delegate, with data greatly to the disadvantage of King Nicholas—and much more up to date.

There are, of course, many stories in circulation very unfavorable to the course the Black Mountain monarch has pursued in the years of confusion and tumult. They carry weight with those who unlike myself have not been immersed in Balkan miasmas for years and are, as I am, consequently inclined to disbelieve any story that comes from that quarter, especially if it is plausible. Many of the lesser Belgrade people assert that Nicholas, so far from having been, as I and many others claim he was, "an alone-standing, stalwart fighter for freedom," from the very beginning of the World War was at pains to be on friendly, indeed intriguing, terms with both camps. "And then he was always a subsidized mercenary of the Tsar," they assert.

I confess this last blow below the belt robbed me of my diplomatic composure and I answered it in a wholly unseemly manner. "Just as you are, no more and no less, the mercenaries of Uncle Sam. He provides the money, the food, and the ammunition. And you? You provide the secret treaties which make the world unsafe for democracy!"

After explosions such as this, we disarm and shake hands and try to talk sensibly. I must say, however, that old Pasitch, knowing as he does better than anyone else how vulnerable is his own record, lends little or no official countenance to these scandalous stories. He bases his demand for the deposition of the King and the union of the two Serb states upon higher ground. "Montenegro is too small and too poor to survive in this troubled world. For the last three decades she only made both ends meet by the subsidies which came from Russia." He then added: "I do not suggest there was anything dishonoring in the acceptance of this assistance. Far from it. That money was earned by the brave Black Mountain boys on many a bloody battlefield with the Turks. But today Russia has vanished from the scene and the great White Tsar is no more. We must welcome back into the Serbian fold our brave brothers of the Black Mountain"; so says Pasitch.

But to avoid the charge of partisanship, if that is possible, I must not entirely ignore the other accusations against the King that are in circulation here, even if that circulation is due, as it is almost entirely, to high-powered propaganda. You hear in many quarters that the King quit fighting too soon and that before he sought refuge in Italy under the wing of his daughter, the Queen, he was not as helpful as he might have been to the Serbians, greatly harassed as they were by Albanian bandits on their desperate retreat to the sea. Judgment on these and kindred matters, to be worthy of consideration, requires intimate knowledge of conditions in this sector of the Balkans at this time, which few of the King's critics possess.

It should be recalled that for years a party had existed in Old Serbia, a by-no-means insignificant party, strongly in favor of the annexation of the Black Mountain principality to the kingdom. While the plan was often sugar-coated under the slogan of "union of all the Serbs," it always aimed at the deposition of the hard-fighting Nicholas. The result of this agitation was unfortunate. The brotherly feeling that should have existed between the two branches of the Serb family was seriously impaired. When Belgrade was bombarded by the Austrians, and the politicians who had for years plotted his downfall were in flight, I rather think that Nicholas accepted this with Christian resignation. But it is quite certain that he never joined with the hired bands of the Central Empire and the local Albanian bandits in harassing the heroic retreat of the Serbs across the snow mountains to the sea. Indeed, he helped them all he could.

Those who are determined to place the more unfavorable construction upon the King's activities throughout the war, and particularly during the darkest moments of it, exhibit what purports to be a letter from the King to the Emperor Francis Joseph offering peace and the assistance that Montenegro could still furnish, if he were assured the possession of whatever Serbian lands might remain after Austria had appropriated what she might consider necessary to safeguard her road to the Aegean. I never saw the original of this letter (although I asked for it, it was never forthcoming), but how any Serbians, after their quite recent experience with the Viennese forgery factory, as disclosed in the Friedjung treason trial,* could credit its authenticity for a moment passes my comprehension. And of course they did not; it was merely another bit of mud with which they hoped to plaster the heroic figure of the man who stood and still stands in the way of their selfish plans. Perhaps the letter should only be taken into consideration as indicating the low level to which the war psychosis had reduced some members of the Belgrade gang of character assassins.

It is, however, an awkward fact that throughout the war and down to his death in October, 1918, Prince Mirko, the second son of the King, was in Vienna. Upon this fact the accusation that King Nicholas maintained a footing in both camps is based. It is further alleged

---

* Dr. Heinrich Friedjung was an historian of some standing in Austria who in the Viennese press published a series of articles charging a number of Serbo-Croat politicians with treasonable practices. He was sued for libel by fifty-two of these aggrieved statesmen. In the course of the trial it was proved that the unfortunate historian had received most of the documents upon which his charges were based from the Austrian Foreign Office and also that two thirds of them were bare-faced forgeries.

that Mirko was authorized by his father to make proposals to the Central Powers whenever a favorable moment presented, and that these proposals were far from being in accord with the public pledges of the Montenegrin government. I took this charge up with the King and, far from being offended at my frankness, he seemed to welcome the opportunity to deny the accusation.

"My boy, Mirko," he said, "on the urgent advice of his doctor, took his wife to Vienna for treatment in June, 1914, and unfortunately was there when war came. The Austrians immediately placed them under guard, but I must say that at first and for many months they were both treated with some consideration, and that fact is the foundation for the story that they were on friendly terms with the enemies of our country and of the Entente Powers. Of course the Austrians later, under threat of placing the unfortunate young couple in a concentration camp, did try to make Mirko pronounce in favor of the Austrian Balkan policy, but he remained steadfast. Toward the end of the war the attitude of the authorities was much less considerate, and this circumstance, and the anxiety which he suffered because of the health of his wife and the uncertain future of our country, brought about his untimely end.

"But if my boy made any mistakes it was because he heeded my advice. I soon established a secret channel of communication with him and I made it quite plain that his duty now was above all else to survive. I urged him to listen to whatever propositions the Ball-Platz would care to make to him, and this he did. In this way very valuable information reached me, and through the Rome foreign office I passed it on to the Allies who found it useful. I even told Mirko, and I am not ashamed of it, in the last analysis to consent to any steps, to any change of attitude the Austrians might insist upon. 'Once again in freedom you cannot be held to engagements you were forced to make while in captivity'—but I am bound to say it never came to that, and it may be said that on the whole my children were treated fairly well by the Austrians. Through Mirko they thought to exert considerable influence upon me. But the death of my boy thwarted whatever hopes they had in this direction."

[Full corroboration of this sad story came to me in 1935 in a surprising way. Under the guidance of "Steve" Stevovich, a Montenegrin guide with headquarters in Ragusa, I had the good fortune to make a number of motor-car excursions into the Balkan countries with which I had been familiar in the slow-moving horseback and Paietan riding days. "Steve" had not the most remote idea of my interest in King Nicholas, and I only advised him of my friendship after he had told me the following story.

"I was and had been for four years, ever since my return from America," he related, "the personal chauffeur of the King. In June, 1914, he summoned me and told me that the wife of Prince Mirko was very ill and that I was to take them to Vienna. In view of the condition of the roads in those days, I thought he wished me to drive them to railhead, to Skoplje, or to Nisch at farthest. But no, he meant exactly what he said, and when we got under way I saw the reason of his injunction. After suffering from a nervous breakdown, Princess Mirko was out of her mind more than half the time, and travel on the railway would have attracted public attention to her unhappy condition. More than once we had to place the unfortunate lady in a strait jacket with which the doctor had provided us before we left Cetinje. After five anxious days I delivered the unfortunate couple at the sanitarium in the city that poor Mirko was not to leave alive, and I only got back into Serbia the day war was declared." So the old King told the plain unvarnished truth although with natural delicacy he held back some of the more distressing details of the unfortunate incident.]

April 26, 1919

Slowly but irrevocably, I fear, the Montenegro problem has faded from the picture. Sympathy for King Nicholas is frequently expressed, and in some quarters it is sincere; but the consensus is that nothing can be done about it or for the sturdy King, out of tune with the times.

After Wilson's illness early in April *—and how serious it was we are only beginning to appreciate—the President naturally, indeed inevitably, concentrated his energies upon main objectives: the Peace Treaty with Germany; the acceptance of the League and the Covenant by all nations. Strangely enough the active, the very active influence exerted against the little principality came from the officials of the foreign office of the land whose Queen [Elena] is the daughter of the king they seek to depose.

* See Chapter XVII, "The Conference Runs into Heavy Weather."

April 28, 1920

Through other channels, when Queen Elena became passive, King Nicholas, her father, continued his efforts to obtain authorization to return to the Black Mountain country. His requests were never definitely refused; he was always put off with the plea that he must wait still a little while, until the situation had "cleared up." Months later and still in exile, the sturdy Nicholas died, and although it was one of the Fourteen Points nearest to President Wilson's heart, the restoration of Montenegro to its former independent status was never achieved.

But it can be said, nevertheless, that the fate of the Petrovich family was more fortunate than that of the Romanoffs, their constant allies and unfailing protectors. Alexander, the grandson of King Nicholas, ascended the throne of what was planned to be the federated monarchy of the Serbs, the Croats, and the Slovenes [Yugoslavia], while Nicholas the Second, the son of the great White Tsar who had proclaimed the lord of the Black Mountain as "his only loyal friend," was butchered in the dark Ekaterinburg cellar to make a Communist holiday. And with him died the little Tsarevitch I had first seen on that memorable day in Tsarskoe Selo (1907) when, with pomp and circumstance and much barbaric splendor, he was proclaimed Grand Hetman of all the Cossacks and heir to the empire extending from the Baltic to the Pacific. And with him perished his sisters, the charming grand duchesses I had so admired as I saw them tenderly nursing the wounded soldiers in the overflowing hospitals of St. Petersburg in that war winter of 1916 when the dark shadows began to lengthen over what was then still called Holy Russia.

And this is by no means a complete list of the misfortunes that have overtaken the "anointed" of the Lord, who until quite recently by some were considered immune from the changes and chances of fortune that beset lesser folk. Kaiser "Bill" is an unwelcome refugee in misty Holland, and Emperor Karl vegetates in Lausanne. The Sultan of Turkey, whatever his name may be (no one bothers to recall it today), is a lonely sojourner on an Aegean island. And Ferdinand "the felon," as he is rightly called, who, by cunning and duplicity, from an intruder in Roumelia worked his way up to become the Tsar of all the Bulgars, haunts the antique shops of Weimar and Coburg bent on completing his collection of ancient Greek coins. And speaking of coin, yesterday a Hungarian magnate, whom I knew in happier days, came in and touched me for five dollars. "What a world it is," he soliloquized; "Until 1868 we, the E's, *frappéd* our own money."

When you call the roll of those who in the last few months have suffered the "slings and arrows of outrageous fortune," the lot of Nicholas Petrovich is not a particularly unhappy one; but this, I am compelled to admit, he would never concede. When on my last visit, I talked to the King in this strain, he nodded his great lion-like head, but his words showed that he did not acquiesce in my philosophy.

"I shall write no more notes of remonstrance to the powers who are unworthy to receive them," he said, "but I will write and rewrite the songs of my people, and these songs will hearten and sustain them until once again the light of freedom and of liberty shines down upon them from the summit of Lovčen."

January 3, 1924

King Nicholas, still in exile, died on March 1, 1921. Even at the last, when life was ebbing, he refused to abdicate in favor of his grandson, Alexander, and it was because of this that he was not allowed to return to his beloved Lovčen. I understand, however, that his ashes have now been interred in the soil which he loved and so gallantly defended.

CHAPTER VI

Fiume and Italy's Passion Week

Note: The row over whether the Adriatic port of Fiume should be given to Italy or to the newly formed Yugoslav state was a complex and important one. The Italian claims to the city were set forth in a memorandum to the Conference dated February 7, 1919, which demanded possession of Fiume on the basis of the request made by "the Italian majority" (following the plebiscite conducted by the poet-filibusterer, d'Annunzio) for Italian annexation. Other arguments advanced by Italy's delegates included: The Treaty of London, which some assumed assured Italian domination of the Adriatic and the Dalmatian coast; the necessity of a bulwark against Germany and Austria above that supplied by the Serbs, Croats, and Slovenes (Yugoslavia); and the fear that Orlando's ministry and the good will of the Italian people would disintegrate unless Fiume were included in Wilson's promise (Ninth Point) of "the rectification of the Italian frontiers on clearly recognized national lines."

November 18, 1918

Di Martino, Permanent Under Secretary of the Italian Foreign Office, came this morning by appointment, but as the Colonel was under the weather he was turned over to me. He is a dapper little man with a sharp, shrewd fox face. He told me he came at the wish of Sidney Sonnino, his chief, the Minister of Foreign Affairs who was still detained in Rome, and that he had been ordered to place his cards on the table face up. He certainly did so.

What struck me most about the little man was the way in which he ignored all the shibboleths and the slogans which are resounding through the world today. When I mentioned the Fourteen Points he seemed to regard them as literature. As to the "compass of righteousness" with which we had all agreed to steer a new and better course, any reference to this provoked a pitying smile.

Di Martino was still living in a world of power politics, of key positions, of strongholds heavily fortified, of spheres of "legitimate" influence. "This is not an ideal world and it never will be," he asserted repeatedly, "and we must face the facts, however ugly they may seem." He was not slow in getting down to brass tacks.

"The outstanding fact of the situation," he went on, "at least as viewed from Rome, is that the Serbs of the Kingdom and the Yugoslavs of the outlying regions are not united, are not homogeneous, and I doubt very much if they will ever become so. For instance, you must know the Serbs and the Croats are culturally miles apart. A peasant Croat is intellectually superior to the average statesman of Belgrade, and he will never consent to the domination of a people whom he regards as a band of ragged, illiterate ruffians. It seems to us that what your President, who we all revere, has in mind is to place these two fighting wild cats in a bag and expect them to behave like good kittens." (While of course I did not admit it, to my diary I may confess that my recent Yugoslav contacts furnished some corroboration to this Italian's point of view.)

Getting his second wind, Di Martino continued: "Whatever becomes of the German Austrians, whether they try to stand alone or are permitted to throw in their lot with the North Germans or with the Bavarians, it is quite certain that if the Croats are to survive economically they will be drawn into the German orbit. And then? I admit no one knows what will happen, but I do know we must prepare for quite possible eventualities. We must adopt precautionary measures, and I am directed to place an outline of these before Colonel House. Unfortunately for Italy, the keys to her national integrity, under one version of the new doctrine of self-determination [that Fiume was always a Croatian port], will be placed in the hands of people we cannot regard, in the light of recent experiences, as either friendly or reliable. To achieve such a result was not our purpose in entering the war. For this we did not sacrifice a million men and assume a staggering war debt. We recognize that self-determination is applicable to many regions but not to the shores of the Adriatic, and we can never consent to placing the strategic positions indispensable to our safety in the hands of strangers who have often been our enemies and who are even now acting in a hostile manner.

"If this policy is persisted in, let me tell you what the result, the inevitable result, will be. Very lightly the Croats and the Slovenes will be brushed aside. Over the weak rampart of Yugoslavia, a 'poor house' divided against itself, the Germans will reach the Brenner and the Adriatic, and after all our expenditure of blood and treasure we will be face to face with a Germany stronger and better equipped for battle than she was when in 1915 we joined in the struggle." [In retrospect I see that Di Martino was not the least of the minor prophets—thus 1938.] When I placed the memo of this conversation before the Colonel he said, "A dark portent of the things to come, discouraging but enlightening."

January 6, 1919

Here is what really happened on the Dalmatian front in October as related by one who saw it all—with unbelieving eyes, I should add. A young naval lieutenant has just arrived from the Adriatic with dispatches for Admiral Benson, which our senior naval officer immediately communicated to House. He was on a ship of the so-called blockading squadron which did not stop d'Annunzio's filibustering expedition.* The lieutenant's conversation is more illuminating than the dispatches and I record some of it here.

The poet-politician claims that he is handling a difficult situation according to Wilsonian precepts; that on October 27 he held what he insisted was "a free and fair election" in the American style. He announced that his party was the *Unione Nazonale*, but that all were eligible to vote. However, all but men of the Unione were driven from the polls. The booths were placarded, calling upon all to vote as patriots and "shoot down the traitors." The representatives of the world press who arrived from all quarters of the globe were not allowed to enter the "liberated city." To their petitions the poet answered: "You men have always described me as a notorious publicity hound, so I have decided that the only account of this important event will be written by me and placed in the confidential files of the government in Rome."

* Italian possession of Fiume came to symbolize to this wildly romantic radical the conflict between Italy's aspirations and the more restricted benefits the Allies wished to impose. A year later, in September, 1919, he marched into Fiume and for fifteen months defied his own government and indeed the whole of Europe. Ousted finally in January, 1921, he became an ardent Fascist and was titled a prince in 1924. On March 1, 1938, he died.

The Susak bridge was closed, but still a few Croats or Dalmatians did get across, and despite the formidable barrier of bayonets around the booths two hundred did vote, but of course their ballots were not counted. On the following day, d'Annunzio announced that seven thousand votes had been polled and that all confirmed his declaration of May 18 that Fiume was an Italian city, had always been so, and as long as he lived would remain as such. "I will hold this pearl of the Adriatic coast against a world in arms," he announced. He then mentioned Gorizia and a number of other important cities and sites that would have to be liberated. "If we do not hold for civilization these key positions, the flood of barbarian Slavs will surge up to the walls of Trieste," he announced.

On the following day, continued the lieutenant, the poet thumbed his nose at the Supreme Council. "This historic movement is written in the best, the noblest, blood of Italy," he proclaimed, "and it cannot be hindered, much less stopped, by Paris." Then he concluded with his favorite phrase: "The old world is no more."

Well, the Supreme Council greeted this defiance with silence. Of course they asked Rome to enforce their decrees, and then nothing happened.

"Encouraged by this weak-kneed policy," said the disgusted lieutenant, "the poet rabble-rouser landed in Zara, which he claimed was another *Italianisimo* port, at the head of six hundred of his Arditi. On his return to Fiume he announced that he would soon take possession of Spalato and most of Istria and that out of his conquests (he called them reconquests, however) he would form an independent Italian state.

"The English admiral told us to go slow; that the Arditi were quite out of hand, and that they were about to attack Montenegro and take a slice of the Black Mountain. But if he ever planned it, d'Annunzio did not follow it up. He probably knew that if he did he would be coming up against something more formidable than the decrees of the Supreme Council. When I left," concluded the young lieutenant, "the Italian admiral who had two ships on the coast joined the filibusterers, so now the poet has a naval force. Just as I left, the new Italian premier, Tittoni, went on the air and announced that Fiume was always an Italian city and reproached the Allies for not understanding the situation. Again the Supreme Council by silence consented to this high-handed proceeding."

I heard one of our delegates say today, and not the least important of them, "*e finita la commedia*." But I do not think so. Flaunted in this way, the decrees of the Supreme War Council are not worth the paper they are printed on, and this inaction will open the floodgates to many other and much more important revolutionary movements. The new public law of Europe may be more respectable than the old, but I fear it is not more effective. Of course, as many argue, Fiume is not very important, but the principle is vital to the New Order.

April 16, 1919

I told the Colonel today that further talks with the Italians, with Orlando, with Di Cellere and Company, were a pure waste of time. When pushed, and certainly we have pushed them at times diplomatically and at others somewhat forcibly, they always come back to the ninth of the Fourteen Points, which authorizes for Italy a readjustment of frontiers along clearly recognizable lines of nationality. We can recognize them, geographers and ethnologists can recognize them, but apparently no Italian can. At this vital point of the discussion they simply "go blind."

Orlando, the smooth and silky Sicilian, is at once obliging, courteous, and impossible. First off, he accepts with grateful enthusiasm House's proposal that Wilson should act as a mediating umpire between Italy and new-born Yugoslavia. Then suddenly his sunny countenance darkens and he whimpers that we shall live to regret the day we brought into the world the "new-born Yugoslavia, the unhappy mixture of Serbs, Croats, and Slovenes."

I tell him we had nothing to do with it; that on October 28, 1918, they proclaimed themselves a happy band of brothers and launched their ship upon the angry waters of Europe as a sovereign state—a sovereignty won through much suffering. Then the brow of the Sicilian Premier lightens and he says: "We are fighting side by side with your President. He is our sword and buckler." Then he quotes the oft-repeated creed of his foreign minister, Baron Sidney Sonnino: "Although always acting in full and complete conformity with the fundamental principles of President Wilson, Italy must uphold her territorial claims based on the conventions that govern and regulate our participation in the war." (He refers, of course, to the bribe, the bait that brought the Italians into the conflict, the Treaty of London, April, 1915, which promised Italy much territory on the Adriatic, but not Fiume.

April 23, 1919

This has been Fiume week; the air is filled with rumors and with counter rumors; an explosion is expected any hour. There is nothing in sight that suggests a settlement, and yet, with but a little good will on both sides, it should not be difficult. Gallovresi, one of Orlando's secretaries, has just been in and he has, I think, spilled the beans. He says in view of what d'Annunzio is shouting throughout the length and breadth of Italy, Orlando is quite convinced that unless he secures the coveted port Italy will go Bolshevik and, while the Prime Minister does not stress this point, that he will then be out of a job.

When House saw Clemenceau this afternoon he took up the matter, although it is one on which the Tiger does not talk with his usual frankness. He did say, however, that in the stress of war his predecessor and the English statesmen had promised Italy practically the earth, but not Fiume. "I told Orlando last week that he thought I was the sainted King Stanislas of Poland who, when he was bitten by a dog, not only pardoned the animal but gave him a chunk of cheese in addition. Well, my name is Georges, not Stanislas. I am not giving cheese to the boys who scampered away from Caporetto. I shall live up to our treaty pledge, and in addition I shall convey a frank expression of my profound contempt. But I shall give no extras.

"In his Fourteen Points Wilson promised to Italy 'a rectification of her frontiers according to the recognized lines of nationality'; but unfortunately these lines are far from clear." Reflecting, Clemenceau continued:

"Have you ever thought, my dear House, how absurdly patient the poor hoodwinked people are? Rarely, very rarely, do they hang a diplomat. And I beg you to view what Italian diplomacy is doing now. These absurd disciples of Machiavelli are replacing the traditional enemy, the white-coated Austrians whom we have destroyed for their benefit, with the valiant Serbs. It's an exchange they will live to regret. But our hands are tied. If they insist upon sticking fiery barbs into the proud flesh of the Serbs, Croats, and Slovenes there is nothing we can do about it; we are bound by the terms of our bond. Of course, I have dropped and shall continue to drop words of warning into the big ears of Orlando. I tell him he is making a poor exchange; that the South Slavs are valiant fighters; that if they are provoked they will prove a very different enemy from the motley Austro-Hungarian conglomeration we have just put out of existence. But he, poor simpleton, only listens to the mobs in the piazzas who shout: 'We want Fiume—*evviva Italia irredenta.*' "

As a matter of fact, the Tiger is bored and at times quite appalled by the outlook. Yesterday he said to me: "Perhaps you recall that in 1917 I said: 'Those Austrian statesmen have putrid consciences.' I was right; but there are many others whose consciences deserve to be classed in the same category. How I would like to retire into the Vendée and write a sequel to my philosophy of history *(Le Grand Pan)*—that would be a hair-raiser. That would make the dust fly. But just because '*je faisais la guerre,*' they tell me I must make the peace. I hope we shall be successful, but it is going to be difficult, most difficult."

As a matter of fact, the Adriatic problem is more complicated than it appears even from the Tiger's presentation of it. By the Eleventh Point Wilson promised Serbia free access to the sea—at least a port on the Adriatic—and the Serbs and many others assert that Fiume is the only port half-way suitable. But then, in Point Nine, he boldly guaranteed "a readjustment of Italy's frontiers along clearly recognizable lines of nationality." Here a head-on collision between the Italian claims of "nationality" and the promise of the President is only too apparent.

It may be true, as Sonnino asserts, that during the armistice negotiations he, Sonnino, made a reservation on the Ninth Point, but although present I did not hear him, and certainly the record is far from clear. Nobody apparently heard him; perhaps because no one was paying attention to Italy at the moment (we were dealing with Germany). Yet here is developing a rift in the foundation wall which may bring down the whole peace edifice. I have again suggested to House that the disputed city be placed under the sponsorship of the League with a fixed date for a plebiscite ten or fifteen years hence. To us looking at it from a distance and disregarding the undoubted fact that Fiume has become a symbol of victory (or defeat) to the excited people of Italy, it seems an excellent arrangement; but it is certain neither of the contenders will like it. House told the President last week that in his judgment the only way to keep Italy out of

Fiume was "a military occupation or perhaps a naval demonstration. In this neither Britain nor France will take part. Do we want to do it alone?" he asked.

The President remained silent; so did House, but clearly he thinks we should do it—or shut up.

April 20, 1919

Wilson had a sharp encounter with Sonnino today. The Italian seems to be fighting not only for more of Dalmatia but for other strong positions that would give his country supremacy in the Balkans.

"There is the gravest danger in that quarter," Sonnino said. "No one can foresee what will happen down there in the next five years or even in the next twelve months. Placing the control of all or any part of this region in the hands of a League of Nations that is not made powerful with an adequate military force is an absurdity; more, it is a criminal action. These are a reckless, warlike people, very able in the use and in the manufacture of forged documents."

Here Wilson interrupted: "How can we promulgate an entirely different set of principles for our treaties with Austria, Bulgaria, and Turkey from those we insist upon in our treaty with Germany? There must be a single, and I hope I shall not have to say it again, an honorable standard for all these treaties. We are pledged to establish a new basic principle, a new international morality, one that has been so often ignored in the last century. Never has a greater or a more vital question been presented than the one with which we are now confronted. I do not know whether France and Britain consider that the Treaty of London conforms to the principles upon which the Armistice was offered and accepted [that is, the Fourteen Points] and upon which in my view the Treaty of Peace is to be written. But I can and I do say that I do not think so. You are placing a great burden upon me; but I shall not shirk the responsibility you impose. If you insist, I shall have to state openly to the world the basic reasons of my objections. I cannot accept for myself or for the United States responsibility for principles which are in direct contradiction to those for the maintenance of which we entered the war."

It was after this passage in arms that the three prime ministers requested Orlando to withdraw his Foreign Minister (Sonnino) from the sessions. He was told that his presence was *"incomodo"* (incon-venient).

[*1938.* In the at times acrimonious verbal clashes in the course of the negotiations between Mr. Wilson and Signor Orlando, the Italian Prime Minister, as to the possession of Fiume, there was one which even today has an almost topical significance. "Mr. Wilson," shouted the usually urbane Sicilian, "there are at least thirty thousand Italians in that most Italian of cities. We cannot abandon them to the by no means tender mercies of the Yugoslavs—treaty or no treaty." (Orlan-do's figures were of course greatly exaggerated.) "Signor Orlando," countered the President, "there are at least a million Italians in New York, but I trust that you will not on this score claim our Empire City as Italian territory."]

April 26, 1919

The attitude of the President in the Fiume imbroglio is being hotly discussed and has given rise to many interpretations—not all of which can be correct. Some assert that what they call his "mulish stubborn-ness" is due to his regret (at times they call it his "remorse") at hav-ing conceded the Brenner and the three hundred thousand bed-rock Germans who live in the South Tyrol to the grasping Romans. As to why he made this disastrous concession, I at least am not informed. Some say he acted on a sudden impulse; others that he was beguiled to take this unfortunate step by one of his advisers on geographical matters who loves to dine at the Hotel Edouard VII, where undoubt-edly the Italians set an excellent table. But whatever may be his rea-sons, it is evident that the President, as far as Fiume is concerned, has returned to his original principles embodied in the Fourteen Points, and which, as he at least insists, were frankly accepted by Orlando during the armistice negotiations.

Tardieu puts in appearance daily, almost hourly in fact. He begs the Colonel to persuade the President to take a realistic view of the situation, which he asserts is endangering the none-too-friendly rela-tions between Rome and Paris. His argument is this: "The good will of Italy is more important to the peace of the world than the ultimate disposition of a miserable Dalmatian fishing village." And he adds: "I fear that the Italians, unless they are 'sweetened,' will turn pro-German."

Under instructions from the President, House has talked repeatedly with Lloyd George and with Clemenceau and also with those of their experts to whom the prime ministers are inclined to listen. All agree that their sympathies are with Wilson, but unfortunately they are bound by a treaty which they cannot ignore. When told that Fiume is expressly excluded from the Italian domain and given to the Croats by the secret treaty, they say nevertheless that Italy must be kept happy or Orlando will not sign, and then our united front against the barbarians is broken.

In his report on the negotiations as of today, House told the President: "The situation is perfectly clear. Orlando will not give up Fiume because he is convinced that if he does his ministry will fall, and Page * wires from Rome that the Sicilian's conclusion is perfectly correct. He asserts that no ministry that signed the treaty without Fiume as part of the booty would survive." He (House) then went on to say to the President:

"In our insistence on giving Fiume to the Yugoslavs we stand alone and unsupported, except for a few expressions of platonic sympathy. What is the wisest course? We can keep Italy out by force of arms, perhaps even by merely sending a few warships to the Adriatic port; but then the united front would be broken and Germany and Russia would rejoice—and not without reason."

The President listened with interest but said nothing. He had, it seemed to me, embarked upon his course without exploring the dangers that lurk ahead. In my judgment, the Colonel is against military measures to keep the Italians out of the disputed port. He thinks that would be an armed intervention in the affairs of Europe, which neither the Congress nor the people of the United States would approve unless they had been consulted in advance. I think, though he does not say so, that the Colonel is in favor of a policy of postponement, of procrastination; of bringing pressure to bear upon both Belgrade and Rome not to fight, and so, after a cooling-off period, to have the problem certified to the Council of the League as one threatening the peace of the world, which under the Covenant it is empowered to face and should solve.

May 4, 1919

After half a dozen interminable conferences, now with Trumbitch

* Thomas Nelson Page, American Ambassador to Italy.

and Korosec for Yugoslavia and then with Chiesa and di Cellere for Italy, the Adriatic problem failed to yield to our diplomatic treatment. The Colonel grew weary of listening to complaints not all of which were well founded. And I? Certainly I was quite fagged out by my interpreting duties. And then an idea occurred to me. As the sequel proves not a very brilliant idea, perhaps it should be regarded merely as a lazy man's effort to escape continuing responsibility and increasing boredom. I cannot claim that my idea was even novel, because the same plan was being pursued in the Saar dispute.

The hope of a reasonable settlement under my plan was based on the conversations I had had with leading Italians and above all with prominent Croats before victory came and pretensions began to sprout. I knew that both parties to the dispute were claiming more territory than belonged to them either by historic rights or by the doctrine of self-determination. And both parties to the dispute knew that I knew this. I also knew there were areas for which probably each of the disputants would fight and that there were others which they claimed merely for trading purposes. I talked in confidence with most of the delegates, many of whom had sat with me at the Congress of Submerged Nationalities (Paris, September, 1918), and I also took counsel with Professor Salvemini, who was active for Italy's legitimate claims, among which he did not include Fiume. Seton-Watson, pupil of Supillo and an eloquent advocate of the Slav claims that would bear scrutiny, helped me to draw up a boundary line between the two nationalities which was much nearer the truth than the frontier that was drawn in the Treaty of London.

In this way we tossed about free cities and played ducks and drakes with not a few islands, and we certainly whittled down the territory which both countries claimed and insisted, it being a vital interest, much as they preferred peace, that for this they would have to fight. I made a "graph" and a map showing what we had accomplished. There was the city of Fiume and the port of Susak and a little of the adjacent territory. All the rest was assigned. "But this area, Colonel," I explained, "we shall call *Disputanta*, and we shall place it under the administration of the League of Nations for the period of fifteen years. Then we shall end up with a free and fair election, a plebiscite, Uncle Sam perhaps presiding over the ballot boxes." The Colonel was enchanted with what he called "a magical solution of all our troubles." He ordered a number of copies of my map made and he distributed it widely. In a few days it got into the papers, and to the anger of the Colonel it was ticketed, we shall say, as the Smith-Jones plan, names far better known than mine.

So far as I know the plan was mine, but it was so simple and indeed so obvious that it might well have occurred to other observers. Then, to tell the truth, on closer contact with the *dramatis personae* I was not infatuated with it nor was I confident of its success, as perhaps I had been in the first blush of authorship. I was even willing to concede it was not the most perfect instrument that ever sprang from the brain of man. I also had come to the conclusion that the only way to keep Italy out of Fiume, which by rank propaganda had been accepted by millions of her deluded people as a national symbol, was by military force, and I was convinced that none of the powers wanted to make the effort, least of all Uncle Sam.

I succeeded in letting the plan go into history as the Smith-Jones plan and very, very soon it was relegated to the dead files. Hunter Miller put the document in perfect legal shape and then both sides dropped it.

* * * *

I find these memos in my daybook:

April 14th. The President told Orlando he would consent to giving Fiume the status of an international port with full measure of local autonomy. Orlando's answer was a sibilant Sicilian "No."

April 19th. The President made what he regarded as a further concession. He was willing to place the disputed port and a rim of surrounding country under League administration somewhat like the Saar, with the promise of a plebiscite at some future and more tranquil day. This seems to be a revival of my plan, endorsed by House but long since lost in the general shuffle. It has at least one virtue. Neither of the contenders would suffer immediate defeat. They could both hope for victory at the polls at some not too distant day and then perhaps, as Tardieu remarks (he is enthusiastic for the plan), "No one would care whether he was saddled with the miserable fishing village or not." I do not agree because I know how important this sea front is to the Yugoslavs; but it was not necessary for me to express an opinion, for in half an hour Orlando had answered with a rotund "No" rather than his usual Papal "*non possumus.*"

April 28, 1919

Even for those who were present and heard the uproar and witnessed the resulting disorganization in the ranks of the peacemakers, it is hard to understand and consequently most difficult to describe what has happened in Paris during what the Italians call the "Passion Week of 1919." It is certain, however, that President Wilson, in publishing to the world, although it was addressed to the Italian people, his views on the Adriatic problem that denied the right of Italy to claim Fiume, set off a time bomb the course and explosive qualities of which should not have been difficult to foresee. Even before the extremely unfavorable reception of the document in Rome was apparent, there were not a few who announced that Wilson had smashed the Peace Conference and that the Americans had better go home. The storm of fury that broke upon the President's head evidently surprised him, although Colonel House, who had sensed the high explosives which the document contained, had urged him to start his campaign by first reading the manifesto to Clemenceau and to Lloyd George. This he had apparently done at an official meeting, and, in the judgment of the President, they had both concurred in the statements made and fully approved of the views expressed.

Indeed, according to the President, Lloyd George went even farther. He (George) spoke of a memorandum which at his suggestion Balfour had drawn up in which the Italian pretensions to Fiume were combatted, even more vigorously than in the Wilsonian text. The President had understood Lloyd George to say that he would publish this memorandum within a few hours with a statement demonstrating his complete approval of the President's position. His (the President's) impression was that M. Clemenceau had concurred in the views expressed but had made no announcement as to what action he would take.

In view of the fact that no formal records of the words exchanged, much less of the agreement reached, were kept, it is not surprising that the recollections of the distinguished participants in the conference are widely divergent. Mr. Wilson was impressed with M. Clemenceau's desire to keep in the background for reasons which he understood and respected. He had stated several times to the President that by the act of his predecessor France was a party to the Pact of London, providing for the division of spoils in anticipation of that victory which admittedly hung fire until America entered the war. The Tiger on several occasions had shown a reluctance to discuss the problem, but he had made it quite clear that Italy alone could release France from her given word. On the other hand, the President was quite certain that Lloyd George had pledged himself and his government to back up the American view and to hold the Adriatic bridge with him.

The President's argument was as follows: He insisted that the events of the last few months had completely transformed the Adriatic problem and that it should now be settled in the new spirit that was abroad in Europe, in fact in the world. He pointed out that the once powerful Austro-Hungarian monarchy had disappeared. He argued consequently that the Treaty of London, drawn up in the stress of a dark period in the war and designed as a protective bulwark for the submerged nationalities against a predatory power, then powerful and rampant but now destroyed, should be canceled. He suggested that the proposal of cancellation might best come from Italy, but as this was not the case, he made the suggestion himself.

Orlando, quite sincerely no doubt, chose to regard the manifesto as a direct appeal to the Italian people over his head. He told House that it was an invitation to the electorate in his country to repudiate their representatives in Paris and the government that had sent them there. All the Italian newspaper correspondents in Paris, with whom hitherto he had not been a favorite, rallied to his support when he stated that the manifesto was a challenge to his authority and that his position was: "The Italian people must choose between my leadership and that of Wilson."

It was not long before the first extremely sensational newspaper dispatches from Rome were confirmed by our official advices. Apparently, the Italian people had reached an immediate decision, and it was wholly unfavorable to our President; many of the avenues and streets in Italy which had so recently been given the name of Wilson, the Liberator, were "de-baptized" in short order. And suddenly, overnight, Orlando and even his colleague, Sonnino, so generally disliked both at home and abroad, became immensely popular; civic crowns were voted them by many municipalities, and the cities awarded them the palms which are only given to those who have deserved well of their country. When Orlando, having walked out on the Conference [he returned May 6], arrived in Rome seeking a re-

newal of his mandate, he tasted for him the unusual sweets of unbounded popularity. While it is true he made the effort, he could
not divest the ovations which he received of a distinctly anti-Wilson
character.

The President was distressed at the uproar. But he was not the
man to bow his head to the storm nor to seek to explain away the
charges of insolent interference in matters which did not directly concern him. In fact, he stood by his guns and told our newspapermen
and all others who were entitled to hear his views (although he stated
he deplored further newspaper controversy at such a delicate moment) that a vital factor in the peace settlement was in the balance;
that the future peace of Europe, and hence of America, was at stake;
that he would fight with the weapons of diplomacy for the only
proper settlement of the Adriatic problem just as stoutly as he had
fought for it with men and ships and money before the Armistice was
declared.

Isolated as he now found himself, Mr. Wilson was naturally most
anxious to learn what had happened to the British co-operation that
was pledged and the unqualified support of the Balfour memorandum
that had been announced and, as he thought, promised. Many steps
were taken to clear up this mystery, and some of them are doubtless
unknown to me; I can, therefore, only relate with confidence those
that were taken by me under instructions from Colonel House. Lloyd
George was absent when I called at his residence, but all, or nearly
all, of his secretaries were on hand. They seemed to have been mobilized in large numbers to meet the emergency. As they understood
the agreement—or understanding—between Lloyd George and Wilson, the latter's manifesto was to have been released for publication
in the morning papers of April 24 (as to the exact date, I am, as were
they, not quite certain). Unhappily, they stated, the document had
been sent out by the American press bureau so early on the afternoon
of the day previous to the agreed date for release that it had been
published in almost all the evening papers of Europe on that day. I
had to admit that this was unfortunately true; that someone had been
careless. "But," I said, "which is the press bureau that has not been
guilty of similar acts of inconsiderate haste? And after all, what of
it? Could not the Prime Minister of England endorse a manifesto
which through the impetuosity of one of Wilson's subordinates had
been published something like ten hours ahead of schedule?"

Now, as always, my colleagues of the British mission were frank and aboveboard, and they agreed that even after this trifling *contre-temps* (mischance) the Prime Minister could co-operate; but, as a matter of fact, orders had been received from him which canceled all previous instructions on the matter. "Our slate is wiped clean and we can't do a thing until we hear from him again. He has gone to the country and we do not expect to hear from him very soon."

"Indeed," said one of these merry wights, "the last word we had was to the effect that we are not likely to hear from him for some time."

This concluded our business interview, but we then, as often before, resolved ourselves into a "common council" of the younger and, as we thought, more intelligent set and began to speculate as to the motives behind the enigmatic moves of the great men with whom we were associated. One of these charming fellows said:

"My guess is L. G. decided it would not be dignified to come steaming along in Wilson's wake a day or so late; perhaps he will barge in, however, when the atmosphere has cleared up a bit; when he learns that you fellows were not trying to steal a march on him."

Then another of the bright boys chuckled: "You see, we got the roar from Rome early in the evening, long before we had said 'good-night' to London, and perhaps L. G. thought it was no use for him to rush in among the brickbats, and so he told us to lay off, but later on, of course . . ."

May 3, 1919

If Aldovrandi, the secretary of Orlando, is to be believed, and I have always found him hitherto reliable, my previous entries with regard to this delicate subject are incomplete and certainly do less than justice to Lloyd George. He apparently did make an attempt to straighten things out, or at least smooth them over, to prevent the open "break" which is now apparent to all. In these words Aldovrandi describes the interview between Lloyd George and Orlando which he says took place on the afternoon of April 24.

"I ought to know what was said," he asserts, "as I acted as their interpreter."

Apparently Lloyd George insisted upon the meeting which Orlando wished to avoid, and when he appeared at the Hotel Edouard

VII he (George) was nervous and quite pale. "I am taking this unusual step," he began, "because I wish to call your attention to the
fact that the situation with which we are confronted is grave, very
grave. It is not only critical for Italy, it is critical for all of us. All
Europe needs America. Without America Europe cannot continue
to live. I have come to tell you that Wilson, as always obstinate, is
greatly irritated now. In this unfortunate state of mind he has drawn
up a manifesto to the people of Italy which is really addressed to the
people of the world, and he has requested M. Clemenceau and myself
to sign it or in some way signify our approval. We have begged him
to delay publication for at least forty-eight hours, and that is the reason why I am here. I hope to make its publication, which cannot fail
to have unpleasant consequences for all of us, unnecessary. Cannot
we smooth things over? I do not have to tell you the scandal that
will follow upon its publication or how the Germans and our other
enemies will rejoice. The unhappy division that exists in the council
of the Allies will then be apparent to all the world. Let us see if we
cannot stave off this catastrophe."

A few minutes after these words were spoken, Lloyd George left
and while the Italian delegation was deliberating as to how the situation was to be met, one of the secretaries came in with a copy of the
Temps of that evening. In it the manifesto of Wilson was published
and Orlando said: "There is nothing left for us to do but to pack up
and leave for Rome."

So, Aldovrandi.

April 29, 1919

This morning the President gave House a brief account of what
happened at the last-minute meeting designed to pacify Orlando, or
at least to keep him from "running out" on the conference. It was
engineered by Lloyd George and took place in his private apartment
in the rue Nitot. "I regret you were not present," explained the
President, "for while completely unsuccessful it was illuminating."

Apparently before the President appeared Lloyd George had tried
to calm down the now angry Sicilian. Above everything he begged
him to be "careful." "Remember," he said (this from Aldovrandi),
"Wilson is not only an obstinate man, he is also a vindictive one.
We must humor him. If he left us in the lurch, Europe would be in
a sad plight indeed."

Orlando's reply was, "Yes, everybody is generous—including Wilson. Yes, even he promises me everything but what is necessary, absolutely necessary, to save my position as head of the government."

Wilson (still according to Aldovrandi) was very affectionate with the Tiger, who was not in his usual good humor. Wilson addressed him as "my dear friend," and the Tiger's *riposte* was, "I am all of a tremble when you address me with those endearing words." Then Wilson bridled and said, "I will then call you 'my illustrious colleague.'" With this out of the way, Wilson, Lloyd George, and Clemenceau vied with one another in assuring the Sicilian how fond they were of him, how they would miss him, how delightful in many respects their talks had been. Orlando replied, "You may be still fonder of me next week when you may well be confronted with d'Annunzio in my place."

Apparently coming to the conclusion that the Italian situation was hopeless, Lloyd George darted off to the Antipodes and took up the cudgels for little Hughes of Australia, who hates the ground that Wilson walks on, a feeling that is reciprocated in a generous measure. "Hughes is very bitter, Mr. President. He says that great America suffered fewer casualties in the war than little Australia, yet you oppose all her just claims and seek to shape the peace alone, excluding all others."

Again and not unnaturally Wilson lost his temper. "Do you mean to minimize our contribution or to deny that through our assistance the war was brought to a successful conclusion?"

"Of course not, of course not," repeated Lloyd George. "However, we are so far apart as to many problems, let us not pursue this prickly question further."

Then Clemenceau put in his oar. "I made war, but now I want to make peace. I hope you will help me. And mark what I say. I am not going to allow incompetent generals and bellicose civilians to spoil it—not if I can help it."

House laughed quietly as he put away the notes that came to him from an undisclosed source. "What luck we had in not being at that party," was his only comment.

April 29, 1919

I was now told by House to take up the matter with Clemenceau and did so that evening. This was not difficult. For many weeks my visits to the Tiger were a matter of almost daily, or rather nightly, routine. For while the Prime Minister of France had resumed his attendance at the conference of the Big Four, Colonel House had held that this intimate channel of communication after the day's work was done, which had been initiated after Clemenceau was shot [February 19, 1919], was still valuable and that in certain emergencies it might prove even more so. Thus my visits were maintained.

The incident I am about to describe was certainly interesting, but as my mission was far from successful, I must sacrifice my reputation as a negotiator to the drama of the after-midnight scene. When I was shown in by Albert, I found the Tiger in his small study, installed in his large armchair where, half reclining, he could, because of the wound still troubling him, rest and even sleep more comfortably than in his bed. He was wearing the old wrapper and the famous slippers, and on his head was the cap which he called his "day and night cap." As I came in I found him grumbling about the inherent cussedness of books, for like most men with a large and disordered library he could never find the volume he wanted.

"C'est agaçant," he grunted. "In the morning, as usual, I shall have to send to the publisher for another copy and doubtless he'll say, 'Out of print,' as most good books are. 'You must apply at the Bibliothèque Nationale.'"

As I got down to the purpose of my visit, the Tiger listened very attentively. At my recital of the rôle, which in the light of the facts, as far as we knew them, Lloyd George had played, he grunted again. And then:

"I certainly concurred in every statement that Mr. Wilson made, but it was the spokesman of the great associated Power who was speaking. The spokesman of one of the Allied Powers could not speak in that independent way, and I never dreamt for a moment that Mr. Wilson thought that we could. If we did, the whole fabric of the alliance which had at last brought us through the furnace of the World War would have crashed. I won't say I wasn't tempted. I was. Wilson's attitude was straightforward, honest, and true. Yes, for a moment I was tempted to cut my cables, to cast off the old shackles and with him plunge into the unknown. But, no, the thing was impossible. We had fought to uphold the sanctity of treaties and we were trying to erect a barrier against future wars. I saw clearly what it would mean if I went back on my pledges and seconded Wilson. Well, in the first place, it would mean that before I said a word I would have to send at least four divisions of troops to the Italian frontier. Things are very ticklish there today, to say the least, and I should think that the dangerous situation in Europe would be patent even to hopeful American eyes. The Spartacists in Germany, who are trying to overthrow the Weimar Republic, are openly working for an alliance with Soviet Russia against Western Europe. Many think they have already achieved it; the outbreak of war between the victors in the great conflict is by no means an impossibility, and that would indeed be a sad conclusion to our battle to end war.

"Let me illustrate the situation by reminding you of an incident that occurred some ten days ago, which for obvious reasons we have not stressed. One of our most irresponsible boulevard sheets published a canard to the effect that I was opposing Italian war aims. When the rumor reached Italy, even though it was immediately and officially denied and although Orlando announced that he had no cause of complaint against me, anti-French riots broke out in many Italian towns. In Leghorn a mob attacked a small detachment of our soldiers, the very men who had been sent to Italy after the Caporetto disaster to save them. Some of our men were killed and a large number were wounded before order was restored. No, things are ticklish. It is touch and go; we must move very cautiously. From the beginning, I wished Wilson success, but I could not participate in his adventure. And now that the failure of his well-meant move is notorious, the only way I can help is to stand by, not jump overboard with Wilson, but talk quietly with Orlando, reason with him as best I can, and that I shall do."

Paris, July, 1925

The acute stage of the Adriatic problem soon passed, or rather, I should say, it was passed over. Although unsolved, it was displaced on the agenda by the more urgent, although not more important, questions of the future of the Saar, Belgian priority in reparations, and then Shantung. I never asked M. Clemenceau for his permission to publish any of the revealing statements in regard to Fiume that he made to me in the course of these confidential conversations, which were intended exclusively for the information of my chief, and of course I never published them or in any way indicated that such statements had been made. It was his pleasure and his wish that all these matters should be regarded as confidential. Frankly, I admit that, concerning this conversation, I pestered him many times for permission to print, but he would always dart off on some amusing tangent and permission was never forthcoming. Like most "old newspapermen," he had a horror of the modern hair-trigger reporter and a great distrust of amateur news gatherers.

Clemenceau gave me unstinted praise for respecting his confidence in this and several other matters that if published at the time would have proved world sensations. While amused at my persistence now he remained firm in his refusal to let me make public what I thought was the important lesson to be drawn from his decision to stand aside at the time of the Italian crisis. In 1925, when I stayed with him for some days in the Vendée, I returned to the attack and we had what he called a *battle royal* on the subject. I told him that my conscience troubled me, that I thought the deduction that could and undoubtedly should be drawn from his action at this time would strengthen the League of Nations and by the spread of understanding would help along the cause of peace. It would demonstrate, I argued, that the world needed the United States in the League, not because she was so rich and powerful or so "good," but because, owing to her happy geographical position, she was the only great power that could insist upon the truth as she saw it without being forced to move armies to her frontiers.

"Well, you can tell it when I'm gone from this vale of tears—but not now. You will not have to wait long. You are terribly insistent and hopeful, just like that heavy artilleryman who during the war was always clamoring for the manufacture, intensive, extensive, and oh, so expensive, of heavy guns, which never could be brought up to where they were needed by any power that was available. I fear it will be equally difficult now to get the League into anything like effective action, since your good people in America abandoned it on the doorstep of Europe."

Then he rehearsed what was said at our midnight conference, which, as I thought, if made public, would help in the pacification of a distracted world.

"Yes, you wanted me to second something that Wilson, a free-lance in European affairs, had said about the Adriatic problem. I agreed that what Wilson said was true and even wise, but I added that I was bound to a different course by a treaty as solemn as any France ever entered upon. It was in anticipation of the fulfillment of this treaty, you must remember, that brought the Italians into the war on our side, and you may remember at the time we assumed this would be helpful to our just cause. How different was the position of Wilson! He was merely associated with our general war purposes, but as far as this treaty was concerned, of which officially he was ignorant, he was as free as air. And I did tell you that I was tempted, only I saw very clearly that before I joined in on this adventure I would have to talk with Weygand about how many army divisions we could send to the Italian frontier. That, you must admit, would not have been a pleasing conclusion to our peace powwow.

"I admit that your memory of what I said further at this time is correct. Wilson was right; the disappearance of the Austro-Hungarian Empire had put an entirely new face upon the European situation, certainly upon the Adriatic problem, and I hoped that Italy would release us from the obligation, which in a critical moment of great stress we had assumed. I talked to Orlando in that sense, not once, but several times. But I could not ignore the fact that this treaty carried with it the signature of France, duly authenticated, and that only Italy could release us from its provisions.

"When later we talked over the fiasco, and fiasco it certainly was, I comforted Wilson with the thought that the question could be taken up at an early meeting of the League, under Article 19 of the Covenant, which provides for a reconsideration of treaties which with the passage of time and the change in conditions have failed of their purpose, or, as is clearly the case in this instance, have developed into a menace to peace. And he told me that this was his purpose. Then you abandoned Wilson, and later on, as it seems to me, you abandoned Europe. I was disappointed, but, I confess, not surprised. Just as I was compelled to look at the Adriatic problem from the standpoint of our national responsibilities and pledges, so you were forced to look at the European scene, later on, from your traditional transatlantic standpoint of aloofness.

"Had Wilson said to me, as he seems to have said to Lloyd George and most certainly did not say to me, 'Clemenceau, will you make common cause with me?' I would have been compelled to answer, 'Mr. President, most certainly not, but from the bottom of my heart I wish you luck.' And I am afraid that is the attitude and the feeling of the great majority of Americans as they view the turmoil in Europe today."

CHAPTER VII

Among the Many Poles: Paderewski and Dmowski

January 5, 1919

For days now we have been simply deluged with Polish delegations. They have come in ever-increasing numbers not only from Cracow and Chicago, where Poles thrive, but they have come from all the four corners of the earth. Each claims to be the only simonpure committee duly authorized to represent *Polonia Restituta*.

The Polish National Committee, seated here in a palace of one of the great territorial lords long in exile but not in want, has been formally recognized by the French government, but unfortunately Pilsudski [later (1920) elected chief of state and first marshal of Poland] is in control in Warsaw and in many other districts. He fought the Allied liberating forces of democracy for the first years of the war until his eyes were opened, and then his former friends, the German-Austrians, threw him into prison. He does not seem to be on good terms with the National Committee. As a matter of fact, I should say he is on the worst possible terms with its members—in fact everybody is on bad terms with everyone else. All apparently are exercising the *liberum veto* which brought low the Polish state in the olden days. As I sit and listen to the uproar, I recall an old German saying I heard so often in my student days. It is to the effect that wherever four Poles are gathered together, at least five opinions are held and loudly expressed. I am forced to admit that this is a true word.

When I say, as ingratiatingly as possible, to the visiting Poles: "Of course, you must bear in mind that the Supreme War Council has decided that Poland, like Rumania and Czechoslovakia, powers with special interests, can only be represented by two delegates," they say, "Of course, we understand. While we are all delegates we shall not expect, not all of us, to sit at the Round Table; many of us will be content to act as historians, as theologians, and as advisers to the delegation."

But when we get down to details, the result is a riot. Every delegation demands precedence and priority—the credentials to sustain these claims would fill, and probably by dead weight sink, an ocean steamer. The Allies acclaim Paderewski, and he is the choice of the National Committee here; but in Poland, those who have survived the devastating years of war seem to be enamored of Pilsudski. One of his delegates is a doctor from Zacopane in the High Tatra, and he is very tired. In coming here he has traveled for twelve long days in a small railway carriage meant for six but filled with his advisers to the number of ten.

"Twelve long days we traveled packed like sardines," he says. And then as an afterthought he adds: "Twelve long days, each day with its respective night." A graphic phrase that has traveled in conference circles like wildfire and enriched our vocabulary.

And the little doctor has another grievance. In almost every hour of these long days and nights, so he says, the slow-moving and wandering train from Poland was held up and sidetracked to make way for gala trains, festooned with floral wreathes and crowded, but not overcrowded, with Red Cross girls and nurses. He says they were lolling back in armchairs and drinking beer out of foaming beakers. I did my best for the girls, describing how hard they had worked; and he finally agreed, did the little doctor from Zacopane, that they deserved a holiday and he did not grudge it to them.

From afar the Colonel surveyed this counterfeit presentment of what the Polish Parliament had been in the olden days, and then he reached a decision which unfortunately involved me. "This is a situation that must be handled sternly but with soft gloves, if you can. All the Poles must be summoned to come to my office tomorrow morning. I will not be there; you must take my place. This is the ultimatum that you must deliver to them: 'Poland will be allotted two delegates—no more.' They must fight it out among themselves as to the choice, but no one will be admitted unless all the delegates agree to his selection. There must be no more of the *liberum veto* which, as all historians agree, killed independent Poland in other days. If an agreement cannot be reached, then Poland cannot be represented in the Council of Nations, which would be too bad."

Of course the strategy was the Colonel's. Only the tactics by which it was to be executed were entrusted to my clumsy hands. The Poles came at the appointed hour to the number of thirty and, after a little speech, I led them to the smaller conference *salle* on the third floor designated for the meeting. Unfortunately, the dignity of the proceedings was marred by a little incident for which our inexperienced room clerk, a hard-boiled quartermaster captain, was entirely responsible. What a man he was for giving you wrong numbers!

"It's room 360," he said tersely. But when we got there, the door was locked and while I knocked and knocked the long line of far from harmonious Poles waited with growing impatience. At last, in response to my increasingly angry calls, the door was opened and there stood before us a man who had just sprung from a disheveled bed. But no one had eyes for the bed; the man who opened the door was simply clothed in a union suit of flamingo red. He wanted to know what we meant by waking him up at ten in the morning. He had been up all night straightening out the telephone situation. He was, he admitted, Colonel Carty, known from coast to coast as the "Telephone Wizard."

Another appeal to the military room clerk who did not keep his books up-to-date finally straightened things out. We located the conference room and into it I shoved the innumerable delegates. But I did not lock the door—escape must be possible. And, of course, I recognized I might have to rush in at any moment with a police squad. Then I made a little speech, clothing the Colonel's brilliant idea with my drab words. They must get together. They must all agree upon the choice of two delegates—or else . . . and then I went.

I came back in an hour. The hubbub in the conference room was terrible. I did not even knock. I listened for a moment outside and went away. An hour later I came back. The uproar was still deafening. When I came back at the end of the third hour, a holy calm seemed to have settled over the place. At first I thought they were all dead. Timidly I opened the door and heard these words:

"We have reached complete agreement," they said in chorus. "St. Michael and all the angels have guided us. By common accord, we have chosen Paderewski and Dmowski as our delegates. All the Poles will stand behind these distinguished men; we are grateful to Colonel House for showing us the way to agreement."

It seemed to me that we had reached a happy and almost miraculous settlement, but Colonel Carty was never reconciled to it. We suspected him of jangling our telephone service throughout the following months. He was particularly bitter against me. He never forgave me for presenting him to the Polish delegates while wearing a flamingo-red union suit; at least that was the way in which he described the incident.

[During the war years Paderewski kept in close contact with President Wilson and Colonel House. It is generally believed that the President's announcement on January 22, 1917, that "a united, independent, and autonomous Poland was a democratic war aim and necessary to world peace" was inspired by him. Immediately after the Armistice Paderewski visited London and Paris and then proceeded to Poland via Danzig where he arrived on December 24, 1918. After a narrow escape from assassination he formed a coalition ministry and as prime minister also held the portfolio of Foreign Affairs. As such he was able to secure the official recognition of the new republic, and on April 6, 1919, he returned to Paris to sit in the Peace Conference. He was not entirely successful in harmonizing the several political groups among his countrymen, and his failure to adjust matters with Soviet Russia and his want of success in the problem of Silesia weakened his position. In November, 1919, he resigned and the Pilsudski groups came into full control. He continued, however, to represent his country before the Council of Ambassadors and the League of Nations until 1921, when he returned to the United States and, as the world's greatest pianist, succeeded in paying off the huge debts he had assumed in his many campaigns to secure the liberation of his people inside and outside his native land. Unfortunately this gallant and most gifted of men survived to witness the destruction (1940) of the Poland of which he was the outstanding founding father.]

January 24, 1919

Roman Dmowski came to lunch today and we had an interesting

hour talking about our previous meetings in this turbulent world. First in Tokyo (1904), later (1906) in the city of the Tsars, that protean capital that has changed its name so often in the last decade. But Dmowski has sojourned in what we "old Russians" must now learn to call Leningrad through all its evolutions and transformations. He speaks Russian so well that he could easily pass as a simon-pure Russki, but I have much reason to believe that he would kill me if he knew I confided this truthful statement even to the pages of my locked diary.

Our first contact was in Japan while the war which upset the balance of power in the Far East was raging. He came ostensibly as an agent of the Polish Red Cross. He was flanked by two priests, and the announced purpose of their mission was to give spiritual and physical comfort to the very numerous prisoners the Japanese had taken. As a matter of fact (of course the Tokyo government had not the slightest objection to this), he and his priestly colleagues did everything they could to sap the loyalty of the Poles and to prevent them from returning to their Russian regiments—except perhaps for the purpose of spreading "dangerous thoughts."

Our next meeting was in St. Petersburg in 1906, during the stormy sessions of the Second Duma. Dmowski was the chairman of the bloc that represented Poland in this motley assembly. He was rarely given a chance to speak his mind, not merely because he was a Pole but because of his well-known anti-Russian activities in Japan. But underground Dmowski was busy, very busy indeed.

After the *séance* in which by shirtsleeved diplomacy of the most outrageous description I reduced the Polish National Committees of thirty to a modest delegation of two, I am rather timid in approaching the Poles who were left out of the conference. But the two who were chosen, Paderewski and Dmowski, are my very good friends. Like all Poles I have met down to the present, Dmowski foams at the mouth when you mention the Soviets, but unlike most of his compatriots he knows what he is talking about because he was in Russia writing articles for a Cracow paper when the Red Dawn came. During these exciting days he had many amusing contacts with what he calls very fairly the "sub-leaders" of the Revolution, who were in it for what it might be worth to them, and today he told me of a conversation with one of them, which Dmowski thinks is very significant.

"You who know," he had asked, "take me by the hand and tell me what is the objective of the Social Revolution? And further tell me what this stagnant and shabby old world will look like when you have realized your purpose?"

The "sub-leader" was stumped for a moment. "It is difficult to explain to those whose eyes have not been opened," he stammered; then suddenly he became voluble. "You see that man over there smothered in sables, sneaking down that side street with apologetic steps?" "Yes." "Well, he is a bourgeois and I am a proletarian. But when we have achieved our purpose I will wear a sable coat and look like a bourgeois. With three good meals a day my belly will expand enormously and it will take a lot of sable skins to cover it. And—then I shall look like a bourgeois." "And the man now wearing the sables, who is sneaking down the side street?" "Well, if he survives he will be a proletarian. And if he works hard he may wear a cotton tunic."

I may be mistaken, but if Dmowski fashions the new Poland which is coming into the world with so many birth pains today a lot of people will be wearing cotton tunics, summer and winter. It seems to me that the nation he envisages is the old Poland with its manor farms stretching from the Baltic to the Black Sea—owned by gallant knights and beautiful ladies who travel to Cannes in winter and to Baden-Baden in summer. Who have expensive tastes that make it necessary for their serfs at home to work hard—very hard indeed.

January 3, 1919

Today, not for the first time, the Colonel turned Dmowski over to me for a talk on the tangled affairs of Poland. He stayed with me over an hour, and I trust the words he poured out and the facts that I extracted from him will prove helpful. He speaks equally well in French or English, as I learned when last year Smulski, the Chicago Polish leader, brought him to see me at the War College (Washington). Dmowski is regarded by many as in large measure responsible for the anti-Jewish feeling so noticeable among the great majority of the Poles, and indeed it was upon this subject I was told to "feel" him out.

Dmowski took it very well and, so it seemed to me at least, talked quite rationally upon the thorny subject. It is to be hoped that when he achieves power [he became minister of foreign affairs briefly in 1923] he will act in the same reasonable way. He points out, however, that there are distinctive features in the Jewish problem of Poland which are not met with in other countries. To begin with he asserts that the Ostjuden (Eastern Jews) are a peculiar, a most peculiar, clan and that their activities and characteristics are very trying to those who must live in daily contact with them. "We have in Poland more than one quarter of all the Jews of the world. They form 10 per cent of our population, and in my judgment this is at least 8 per cent too much. When there is only a small group of Jews in our villages, even when they are grasping storekeepers or avaricious money lenders, as they often are, everything moves along smoothly; but when more come, and they generally do come, there is trouble and at times small pogroms.

"We have too many Jews, and those who will be allowed to remain with us must change their habits; and of course I recognize that this will be difficult and will take time. The Jew must produce and not remain devoted exclusively to what we regard as parasitical pursuits. Unless restrictions are imposed upon them soon, all our lawyers, doctors, and small merchants will be Jews. They must turn to agriculture, and they must at least share small business and retail stores with their Polish neighbors. I readily admit that there is some basis in the Jewish contention that in days past it was difficult for them to own land or even to work the fields of others as tenants; that they were often compelled by circumstances beyond their control to gain their livelihood in ways which are hurtful to Polish economy. Under our new constitution all this will be changed, and for their own good I hope the Jews will avail themselves of their new opportunities. I say this in their own interest as well as in the interest of restored Poland. Now, and I fear for decades to come, Poland will be too poor to permit one tenth of its population to engage in pursuits which to say the least are not productive."

I was struck with the great similarity between the views of the Polish leader and those which Count Tolstoi expressed to me during the Russian revolution of 1905–1906 on the occasion of my visit to Yasnaya Poliana. The subject came up in my answer to the philosopher's many questions as to how our "melting pot" was working in the great urban centers of America. Quoting a newspaper article, I mentioned that in New York alone there were nearly a million Jews (at this time—1906), and Tolstoi made no effort to conceal his surprise but changed the subject. On the following morning, however, he returned to the problem which it was clear interested him enormously. "You must not assume from my silence yesterday that I cherish anti-Semitic views. The contrary is the case. I do think, however, that it is unfortunate for a community to number in its population more than 2 per cent of Jews."

I reported Dmowski's views verbally to the Colonel and at his request I put them in writing. His comment was, "I am sure the Poles will try to do the fair thing, but it will be a long time before these religious and racial animosities subside. I agree with the President that before the Poles receive the charter of their independence they must make an iron-clad pledge to give fair and equal treatment to religious as well as racial minorities."

My Colonel is a constant reader and, with some reserves, a great admirer of Francis Bacon, the statesman-philosopher. In his library in Texas he has scores of volumes that this wise man of the world wrote and several hundred dealing with the discussions which he provoked. He would not have us follow in Bacon's footsteps, but when in doubt and perplexity, he says he finds consolation and encouragement in this reading.

"Bacon furnishes a yardstick by which we can measure the progress this old world, so often disappointing, has made. In his study of the 'Vicissitudes of Things,' as he calls it, he wrote: 'And the greatest vicissitude amongst men is the vicissitude of sects and religions.' If Dmowski is truly representative of his people, Bacon's words apply to Poland-about-to-be-redeemed as truly as they did to the world in which Bacon lived. But how encouraging, how refreshing to us—yes, the world does move—is the incident that happened in Brest last week."

I certainly had not forgotten it, as the incident, telephonically at least, had disturbed and delayed my desk work for several days. It developed down there that Bishop Brent, the chief of the corps of chaplains, had been advised by some troublemaker that a large American army unit at the French naval base, while 90 per cent Protestants and 10 per cent Jews with only two Roman Catholics in their midst, was having souls cared for by a Roman Catholic priest. He transferred this priest to a Romish congregation and selected a Protestant sky pilot to take his place. Then the riot broke loose.

The doughboys were indignant and they demonstrated their indignation in a way that would have been regarded as mutinous were we still on a war footing. They marched in serried columns to their colonel, shouting the while, Protestant and Jew alike, "We want our Padre. We must have him back. We do not want any sky pilot but him."

The Colonel had all the papers dealing with the incident on his desk— "and I am going to keep them there. Dmowski is coming to lunch on Monday and I shall show them to him. I think I have the right, indeed the duty, to do this because in the list of the soldiers who signed the demand for the return of the beloved Padre are at least twenty whose names are distinctly Polish. They had lived in America. They, at least, were 'redeemed.' "

May 10, 1919

Yesterday another problem, long regarded as of but little importance, has raised its ugly head. It concerns Silesia or Upper Silesia and what its sovereignty is to be in the New Europe. Both Clemenceau and Tardieu were in this morning and had a long talk with my Colonel at which I assisted.

"Our generals have convinced me," said the Tiger, "that the German grab of Silesia is the first move in the rearmament of Germany, and that another invasion of France will come in five or ten years, perhaps a little sooner, perhaps a little later, but come it will. Our experts and most of the others are in agreement that the disputed territory belongs to Poland despite the fact that large colonies of Germans have been brought in and by strong-armed methods given possession of perhaps most of the small farms. Important as this is, more important still is the fact that if Berlin is given control of these ore regions the rearmament of our truculent enemy will be greatly facilitated."

Here Tardieu interpolated with: "General Weygand says we can with but little difficulty, keep a wary eye on the Ruhr, that near-by industrial and potential rearmament center, but it is a far cry to Silesia, and out there it would not be difficult to veil preparations for a renewal of the war, and there unfortunately is to be found everything necessary to the rearmament of the Barbarians we have only brought to heel after four years of costly war."

When they had left, Colonel House told me that in this matter Lloyd George is making difficulties. He insists upon a plebiscite, at least in Upper Silesia, where even the Poles admit that the German settlers who have been planted there are probably in a majority. House went on to say, "Lloyd George told me only three days ago that he was informed on the best authority that the Germans would not sign the Treaty unless as in other disputed provinces sovereignty had been decided by a plebiscite. If this injustice is done the Germans, we too may not see our way to accepting the Treaty or at best we may be compelled to show our dissent with a formal reservation."

House is greatly worried over this problem and has debated it quite frequently with the "Governor," as he calls the President. Confronted as he is with this decision, he fears that Wilson will accept the plebiscite. "He recognizes as clearly as I do that he may be making a considerable sacrifice, but he feels he must resign himself to it to save the Covenant, for of course if Britain draws back all will be lost. I hope the Governor is right in his belief that once the war psychosis is abated the Covenant will work the wonders that are beyond its powers today." Then with a sigh he added, "Britain does not want a France too strong or a Germany too weak. That is the lesson of the balance-of-power policy; but I question the wisdom of this concession. Out of the ore fields of Silesia may be fashioned the weapons of the next world war."

May 4, 1919

In our walk today through the Tuileries gardens Colonel House said the Big Four are as far apart as the poles on the knotty question of what to do with Upper Silesia. Then he added, "I want you to tell me more fully your thought on this question."

I told him that as far as Upper Silesia was concerned I had little personal experience but I had secured a great deal regarding the efforts and the methods of the Berlin government, acting under the instigation of the great territorial lords, to Germanize Posen, West Prussia, and other districts where it was desired to get rid of large Polish populations. During 1889, and again in the following year, I had visited many of these districts as a special correspondent of the New York *Herald* and had reported fairly and fully what I saw. Large sums were voted by the Reichstag to swing the forced sales of farms long held by Poles and to launch land banks whose only business was to bring in German settlers from other districts, at great expense to the imperial treasury, and above all to expel the unfortunate Poles, bag and baggage.

"Of course the Great Four know little or nothing of those high-handed proceedings," I argued, "or of those ruthless mass expulsions; and being ignorant of the antecedent circumstances, the idea of a plebiscite may appeal to them; but as a matter of fact if put into effect in the districts where the German land-robbers have been successful, it would give the sanction of law and a general amnesty to as high-handed an act of oppression as was ever enforced by a supposedly civilized people." I did not conceal the fact that there was at least one pleasant feature in the ugly episode, and that is that in many districts the Poles have held fast. The German settlers, brought in at great expense, have proved shiftless, with the result that the imperial treasury is in the red for at least one hundred million dollars and the Prussian treasury even more—the only lasting result of this inhuman crusade that failed.

The Colonel asked me to draw up a memo to be submitted to the President setting forth what I had actually seen in the contested districts; also copies of the legislation under which the Disconto Bank of Berlin and its local agencies acted. This I was able to do the following day.

I was indeed glad to have had an opportunity to testify to what I am sure from personal observation is the true situation. Lloyd George, however, still insists upon the plebiscite and Clemenceau opposes it. Mr. Wilson would as always like to see justice done, but he does not want the Conference to come to grief over the Polish problem, important as it is. Clemenceau demands that Paderewski and Dmowski be heard on this vital question. They certainly should be.

[Some days later Paderewski and Dmowski were heard but not listened to, and subsequently the plebiscite was agreed to. Many months elapsed before the Supreme War Council ventured to carry out the plan in view of the disturbed conditions that prevailed, for which the Germans were almost exclusively responsible. In some districts the Poles were successful and in others the Germans. In many districts where the latter were successful it was the new settlers brought in in the manner I have described who carried the day.

These districts of mixed population presented undoubtedly a very thorny problem, but in this instance the ends of justice were most certainly not attained.]

May 13, 1919

This is a black day for the Poles; for France; perhaps for all of us. Most reluctantly, it is true, but all the same the President is about to yield to the demand of Lloyd George that a plebiscite be held to settle the Upper Silesia dispute. Both Clemenceau and Tardieu have frankly admitted to House that as a result of the way in which for the last thirty years the Germans have planted colonists in the disputed region they would not be surprised if the vote revealed a German majority. Clemenceau adds with his usual emphasis: "If the plebiscite turns out this way you will be giving legal sanction to a ruthless crime." He has frequently pointed out that it would not be difficult for France to keep an eye upon what the Germans may do to prepare for their war of *revanche*—in the Ruhr at least. But not in faraway Silesia, "that is beyond our ken and yet that contains all the ores that our aggressive neighbors would need for rearmament. If the Germans cannot abide Polish sovereignty, they should be returned to the regions from which they came."

These are the arguments Lloyd George advances in favor of the vote: the Germans will not sign the Treaty unless the doctrine of self-determination is honored in Silesia, as elsewhere, and he adds that if in this matter the Germans are discriminated against there will be an uproar in Parliament and perhaps he could only sign with reservations.

To save the Treaty, but with unconcealed regret and many misgivings, the President has decided to accept the plebiscite. He admits quite frankly that he is constrained to make a most unwelcome sacrifice, but he says: "At least, House, we are saving the Covenant, and that instrument will work wonders, bring the blessing of peace, and then when the war psychosis has abated, it will not be difficult to settle all the disputes that baffle us now."

House deeply regrets this decision. He considers it the most sinister of all the concessions that have been forced upon the President —to save the Treaty and above all the Covenant. He agrees with the

French that in Silesia the Germans will find all the ores that would be needed to rearm and wage another aggressive war.

April 20, 1919

Late last evening I was sent to the rue Franklin by my Colonel to show some papers to M. Clemenceau. They did not detain us long, and then as the bullet near his lung was preventing him from sleeping he asked me to stay and talk. How he loves to talk, and how natural that he should. He talks superbly. Tonight, however, the Tiger's thoughts were not on the present. He was in a reminiscent, or perhaps I should say in a reflective, mood. At first he talked about the Poles; then the small farmers in the Vendée, and above all about the peasants of Picardy—all very near and dear to him. What he wanted to say ran on about in this way:

"Klotz, that merciless collector of taxes [he is minister of finance in the Clemenceau cabinet] says I am too lenient with the peasants; that I will never approve of his budgets unless it is soft to them. *Ma foi*, for once Klotz is right. Our peasants have paid the heaviest taxes, by pouring without measure their precious blood on all the fronts, and I'll not let that terrible Klotz extract the last piece of money from their nearly empty woolen socks as he is always trying to do. As long as I live I'll not let him do it. 'Cook some more fat out of your greasy bourgeois,' I tell him. But he hates to do that. You see, birds of a feather flock together.

"And there's Jules Cambon. He says I take a much too romantic view of the Poles. He likes them all right, but he says that they are out for a sharp bargain in Silesia and everywhere else. How natural that is when you recall what they have suffered, what has been done to them in the past. Perhaps he is right. Perhaps not all the Polish claims can be justified by Holy Writ, but I answer shortly, whose can?

"Perhaps I am lenient to the Poles because they opened up to me the world of romance—the only real thing in life. The Poles also introduced me to the pursuit of politics. It has often proved disappointing, but if I had my life to live over again (God forbid!), I would not swerve from my predestined path.

"When I was a boy in Nantes the old seaport was filled with

Polish refugees, men who had escaped the ruthless suppression of some uprising at the hands of the Great "Red" Tsar (for believe me there never was a Great "White" Tsar except in poetry). They had lost everything but their hopes and their high spirits, and of course I played hookey from school and sat with them in the taverns. They had little to eat and nothing to drink, and most of them were trying to smuggle themselves on board ships and go to your land, the land of promise where at least they could survive—until the next revolution. Wonderful fellows they were, sustained solely by inner fires and unquenchable hopes. I sat at their feet reverently, and they told me all about the Polish Parliament in the happy days before the Partition and before the invaders came: What a splendid sight it must have been—at least as they described it to me. Each member came to the sessions on horseback. They remained in their saddles and only mounted men were permitted to enter the debates. From that very day I decided to be a parliamentarian and come to some future Diet mounted. I do not have to tell you what a sad moment it was, when at last, by the will of our people, I came to the Palais Bourbon—I sat in a horse-drawn cab. That was the first but by no means the least bitter of my experiences in politics.

"Yes, I have a long memory. It certainly goes back farther than most men here but not as far back as at times Mr. Wilson thinks. Several weeks ago he asked me for information about the battles that were fought long ago on the 'ringing plains of windy Troy,' but I brought him back to Poland. What a lot he does not know about that proud tenacious people. In this matter it seems to me he is ensnared by the flood of words which flows from Lloyd George, that tireless spinner of words—the kind that leave no trace, not even upon the memory of the speaker.

"I tell Wilson that mines of gold or of coal are of little importance; that legions of soldiers come and go, but that the unflagging sentiment for freedom and independence is what should be regarded, and that the Poles have it in a superlative degree. He comes to our talks with kilos of statistics under which our council table groans audibly, but I tell him it is the spirit that counts, not business ledgers—and I know I am right. This struggle with the Germans has been going on for nine hundred years, and unless we give the Poles defensible boundaries it will go on for centuries, indeed until the end of time."

[1941. Well, Poland was not given defensible boundaries. Lloyd

George won out, and the seeds of World War II were sown. Mr.
Wilson made another sacrifice to secure his League. Danzig was not
given to Poland and the unworkable corridor was invented. The
intricate solution of Danzig as a Free City with special port rights to
Poland only led to friction until at last racial hatred burst out into
the flame of a new world war, as Clemenceau the realist had said it
would.]

After a short pause M. Clemenceau continued. "I do not have to
tell you who have sojourned so long in what we call euphemistically
the 'troubled zones,' but I tell Wilson every day and I shall keep on
telling him the stark disagreeable truth in the hope that it will at
last sink in."

Now suddenly he switched to American (he had been talking
French), and very American his words were. "I say, 'Mr. President
you must not forget, not for a moment, that we Europeans are a
tough bunch.' Then I explain, 'Please do not misunderstand me.
We too came into the world with the noble instincts and the lofty
aspirations which you express so often and so eloquently. We have
become what we are because we have been shaped by the rough
hand of the world in which we have had to live and we have survived
only because we are a tough bunch. Please do not misunderstand
me, Mr. President; had our life lines been cast in the pleasant places
across the Atlantic, we too, I believe, would have developed and
clung to the noble qualities which you, Mr. President, assume is
the universal heritage of man. I do not think we are very different,
except in our experiences. After all, you are Europeans too, but you
have been translated to pleasant pastures and above all you have had
elbow room in a land of plenty. Yours has been the best of all possible worlds, but there are signs and portents, and it should be clear
that your happy, your privileged position, will not endure forever.'"

Then, after another short pause, M. Clemenceau went on. "When
I talk this way you must not think for a moment I do not appreciate
what you have done for us and the losses in men and money that
you have sustained. Your intervention has cost you dear, and that I
do appreciate. It is one of the reasons why I do not want it all to
have been expended in vain. I am grateful because your intervention
saved France from disaster and my gray hairs from defeat, and yet,
and yet I cannot close my eyes to the fact that before the Treaty is
signed and the overthrow of Germany as a military power is accom-

plished you are going home. Pershing is proud of the thousands of brave boys he is sending back every week, and Lloyd George, though he has joined me in my protest to Wilson against this precipitate step, is doing the same thing—but of course he is doing it on the sly. In view of the speed with which our armies are vanishing, the sluggishness and the bad faith the Germans are displaying in the process of disarmament to which they are pledged, for once I find myself in agreement with Foch when he says that if this disintegrating process is allowed to continue for a few weeks more, the German barbarians will once again be supreme in Europe—just as they were before you came in."

Here I interrupted with, "But even before we entered the war and came millions strong across the seas you were confident of success, you at least never despaired of victory. When the darkest hour came for France and the responsibility was turned over to you by the men who had failed, you said even if you had to stand alone you had no fear of the outcome."

"Of course I said that, my dear friend. But that was policy, politics, what will you. I said in that dark moment—I recall my very words— 'We shall fight before Paris. We shall fight in Paris. And then if we are pushed south, we shall fight with our backs to the wall of the Pyrenees.' And I meant that, and the best of my countrymen were with me heart and soul. But I had no hope of success until you came. A cunning, crafty enemy had caught us napping. I merely meant by my words, and how sincerely I meant them, that while our defeat was inevitable it would be a glorious defeat; we would go down fighting to the last; our children would not be ashamed of their fathers.

"I have differed from Mr. Wilson. Our viewpoints are so wide apart and at times our interests seem to clash, but these differences are not irreconcilable. They can be adjusted, 'ironed out,' as your wise Colonel so wisely says. Mr. Wilson dreams of a world which can only be indulged in if you are many thousand miles away from the Rhine, and perhaps even then you cannot indulge yourself in it with impunity.

"Tonight I am depressed. I fear we shall never attain the world situation that Mr. Wilson seeks unless I can bring him to see the world *as it is today*. It is upon that we must build and not upon the stuff that beautiful dreams are made of. Wilson is blind to the actual situation, and our negotiations will fail unless he can be brought to realize that we Europeans are a tough bunch and that our problems will have to be handled with gauntlets of iron. Soft kid gloves will get us nowhere."

I repeated to my Colonel what Clemenceau had said, as he had asked me to, on the following day, and he was deeply impressed. He saw great danger in the Rhine agreement which was then being trotted out as a consolation prize for the French, a concession which would help Clemenceau to get the unsatisfactory treaty through the Chamber of Deputies. But as to our Senate, the Colonel was quite confident it would not accept this long-termed obligation. He said, "Today I am haunted by an opinion which John Morley, at once a realist and an idealist, expressed to me some years ago. He said, 'I often think that the world turmoil in which we are all involved is not due to the realists but to the tireless and often thoughtless activities of those unyielding people I call *perfectibilitarians.*'

"Well, our job here is to achieve a working agreement between the idealists and the realists. A hard job in any event, even if, as the Tiger says—and he knows—these Europeans were not such a tough bunch."

CHAPTER VIII

Naboth's Vineyard: The Rich, Unhappy Ukrainians

January 10, 1919

If bitter experience had not taught me the danger of sweeping statements I would say that the Ukrainian problem is the most complicated of the many with which the Conference is confronted. Happily for them, at least, few of the delegates know it. There are probably forty-five million of these vigorous and interesting people, all hitherto held in leash (indeed often under the lash) by half a dozen alien rulers, and today unhappily they are divided in their allegiance to about the same number of ideologies. The Great Russians, who also claim to be *Herrenvolk*, are inclined to despise them as an inferior category of the Slav family and also maintain that the Ukrainian language, they call it a patois, is simply a degenerate Russian gone to seed.

Nothing so infuriates the Ukrainians as this slur upon their speech; they answer it by bursting into song, generally the ballads of Schevenko, with which my office has often resounded during the past weeks. "We are the free men of the border," they sing. "Our home is on the rolling steppes. We preferred liberty and struggle to tyranny in relative comfort. We are the men who stem from those who fled the slave-driving practices of the Polish and the Lithuanian landowners. Bringing with us only our democratic ideals we founded the state of the Free Cossacks, and soon our rich lands extended from the Vistula to the Black Sea. We are here to demand their return and our right to live as free men."

As to the authenticity of their language I maintain an attitude of strict neutrality, but there can be no question as to the richness of the lands they have acquired. In these starving, freezing days in southeastern Europe, indeed in all Europe, their grain fields, their oil wells, and perhaps above all their coal mines in the Donetz Basin have become very important factors in a desperate situation. In 1917, when the blockade was bringing the Germans to their knees, the fertility of the Ukraine "and the fatness thereof" seemed a plank of salvation to Berlin. Today, when all Europe is cold and hungry, unfortunately for the Ukrainians their possessions have assumed even greater importance.

Whether they are Ukrainians or Ruthenians or Carpatho-Russians, they all have broad flat faces, high cheekbones, and snub noses which probably reveal their Mongolian origin. Physically alike they are widely separated by their political experiences. Yet all of them dream of a greater Ukrainia with the fragments and the segments of their race joined together in one happy family—those who have been held down by Austria, or oppressed by the Magyars, by Russia, and even by little Rumania, brought happily together in one independent glorious state. But, and what a *but* it is, as to how this noble ideal is to be achieved and under what auspices, the good Ukrainians are as wide apart as the poles. The members of the American-Ukrainian committee who through political experiences in our country have learnt the wisdom of compromise often intervene with words of conciliation, but it is far from certain that these common-sense views will prevail. I confess I shall be surprised if they do. The Free Cossacks of the steppes place a higher value on the money contributions of the Ukrainians from Pennsylvania than they do upon their advice.

Here is the baffling situation, as it appears to me: All the neighbors covet the Ukrainian lands, and I fear that is not surprising. What is surprising is the fact that even after the terrible experiences which all the Ukrainians have experienced nothing even approaching unity of purpose has evolved. When you talk to them about self-determination and the right of all peoples to govern themselves, they are in perfect agreement. But when you suggest putting into practice these wise precepts, they rear and break away in a dozen different directions like Mazeppa's wild horses of the plains.

This want of harmony opens the way for the specious promises of covetous neighbors. The Russians say blood is thicker than water; the Poles say, "Come with us and we will confer upon you our world culture." Even the Germans have the audacity to say, "Without us you will not have law and order, there will be no peace, and no man or woman either can hope to live in peace and tranquillity."

Of course there are also conflicts of ideologies and of contrasting experiences at the hands of more powerful neighbors. At moments my visitors admit, "Russia must have our Black Sea ports of Odessa and Kherson, or cease to be a great power. Germany will have to have the oil fields, and all Mittel-Europa will starve without our grain." Sometimes I conclude that these people would be happier, much happier, if the land of their hard-riding forefathers was what my Virginia soldier in Vienna called Austria—"A porefolksy land."

February 16, 1919

Yesterday the Colonel demanded a résumé of the present situation, and I have submitted it today with, however, the express reservation that I am not prepared to vouch for any of the alleged facts.

When the fall of Russia became apparent in April, 1917, delegates representing nearly two million Ukrainian front-line soldiers got together and formed an association to cope with the situation and shape their future. At about the same time a sort of parliament, or Rada, was formed in Kiev, and while there was little harmony in their deliberations, a provisional government was constituted. A few days later a certain Petliura demanded of the then shaky government in St. Petersburg the right to constitute a national army and began to enroll Ukrainian regiments. On the eighteenth of June following, the Rada, or parliament, issued its first *Universal*, or manifesto, formulating the demands of the Ukrainian people in Russia and elsewhere. The principal demand was for the right of the people, without separation from Russia, to organize an autonomous government on its own territory and coupled with it was the announcement that the future form of government would be shaped by a national assembly shortly to be convened.

St. Petersburg, under the provisional government, rejected these demands, and the Ukrainians then announced that as Russia could not give them a stable government they would do what they could unaided. This brought Kerensky and Tseretelli post-haste to Kiev and after long debates they recognized the right of the Ukrainian groups to self-determination and self-government. As it soon developed, the groups that sat in this body were unfortunately far from harmonious. Some were Social Democrats and some were advocates of national independence, but at least they were united in their detestation of both their enemies, the Bolsheviki and the Tsarists.

Late in October (1917) the Rada called upon the Allies to aid the Ukraine. Russia was crumbling; Kerensky was on his way out; the Bolsheviki were getting the upper hand. Its members asked for an Allied force to aid the national army, to carry on the war against Germany, and to stem the Bolsheviki tide which was threatening to overwhelm all of southern Russia. On November 20 the Rada published its third *Universal:* it proclaimed the autonomy of the Peoples' Republic of the Ukraine and gave the war ministry into the hands of Petliura while Vinnichenko remained in charge of foreign affairs. Many Allied officers now appeared in Kiev, but apparently they brought only advice and no munitions. The Allied officers demanded that the war against the Germans be pressed but offered no substantial assistance. Among the Ukrainian soldiers, Bolsheviki tendencies now became apparent. Many withdrew from the front and some spent their time in pillaging. In his desperate plight Vinnichenko asked the Allies, as military aid from them was not forthcoming, to arrange an armistice along the Ukraine front with the Germans to stop the invasion and so to give him a chance to organize his forces to cope with the Bolsheviki, and he demanded the recognition of his regime as the *de facto* government.

The only result of these negotiations was an unhappy split. Petliura and his group of young soldiers declared that they were ready to fight the Germans to the last. As the old army seemed unreliable, he began to recruit groups of Free Cossacks and peasants who were anxious to defend their little farms against both the Bolsheviki and the Germans. This action weakened the Vinnichenko *de facto* government, and the civil war between the factions got under way, which has unfortunately continued to the present day.

February 11, 1919

Two more Ukrainian delegations appeared yesterday and frankly deposited their problems on our doorstep. They are a pleasant-looking group garnished with gay Parisian clothes, striped trousers and all that, but Cossack boots are not wholly concealed. Their leader, M. Sydorenko, speaks excellent French and has his indignation under diplomatic control. "How can we sit at a Peace Conference with the Bolsheviki, murderers and bandits who have invaded our country and are still burning our villages and committing crimes at which even the Germans would blush?"

Sydorenko gave me a very dramatic account of the vicissitudes to which his people had been exposed during the eighteen months of their recent existence as an independent republic. The clash with the Bolsheviki came in December, 1917. Apparently the young Republicans held their ground and the local Soviet Socialistic state was but a flash in the pan. Their more serious trouble came in April, 1918, when the Germans put in an appearance, ostensibly to protect the young republic but in reality to loot the only remaining full "bread basket" in Europe and to secure the wheat and above all the oil at the time so desperately needed in Germany.

"In this emergency our National Union selected General Petliura to command our forces, and we faced the struggle for independence on three fronts," said Sydorenko. "On one were the so-called 'White Russians,' mostly former Tsarist officers who were seeking to carve out for themselves estates in the lands which our peasants had long tilled and of which they were now in rightful possession. On another front were the Soviet forces whose purpose was as unsocial and as imperialistic as ever had been the emissaries of the Tsar. We were holding our own when the Germans threw off the mask of friendship and entered the field with large armies. We met at first with defeats, but in the end we conquered, and on December 15 we recaptured our Holy City of Kiev and about twenty thousand Germans who garrisoned it. Unfortunately their leader, Skorapadski, escaped to Berlin where he is still plotting against us."

"Our future is by no means promising," continued Sydorenko, "but now that we are united and all the Ukrainian peoples are as one in our struggle for liberty, we have no fear of the ultimate outcome. The Ukrainian brothers, from what was the Bukovina, the Hungarian Carpathians, and Austrian Galicia, have asked and received permission to join our patriotic union. The federal state which we are forming is larger than Germany and much richer in resources. We have come to the Peace Conference to demand that our undoubted right to self-determination be recognized. It is unthinkable that we should be returned to Russia now that from our devastating experiences it is quite clear that the Bolsheviki are as tyrannical as ever was the autocrat. You are restoring to the peoples today the rights that were taken away from them by the Russian Empire and by the monarchy of Austria-Hungary, and so we have come with our plea for the recognition of our just rights. Unless this is done a stable peace cannot be established."

I asked Sydorenko to put his plea in writing and promised to see that it would reach the President, M. Clemenceau, and the members of the American delegation. The memorandum came this morning and I have fulfilled my promise. But I have my fears; under various disguises, Europe is still in a predatory mood, and this land of the long-submerged Ukrainians presents to the underfed and overcrowded peoples of war-ruined states a very tempting picture of Naboth's vineyard.

April (undated), 1919

It is certainly no secret that some of the Ukrainians have no more love for the Poles than they have for the Russians. Today a committee, representing as they said the "former Crown land of Galicia in Austria," "an artificially created administrative unit which conflicts with historic and national rights," filed with us the following protest. It reads:

The representatives of the Ukrainian people protest against even the smallest portion of the Ukrainian territories of Cholm, Podlachia, and Wolhynia ever being added to the Kingdom of Poland which is in process of formation and regard any attempt in this direction as an outrage upon the living body of the Ukrainian people, as a violation of its historic rights and a mockery of the principle of self-determination of peoples. We declare we shall not abandon the struggle until the great Ukrainian nation has acquired the fullest rights upon the whole of its national territory.

I take it this means the death knell of many panaceas and compromise proposals which would be so satisfactory—if only they were practicable.

May 3, 1919

Today there is undeniably a crisis in our archives. There simply isn't any more room in our safe for the countless memoranda that I have drawn up and the innumerable statements that I have taken down from the authorized Ukrainian delegates and from the free-lance volunteers who also abound. I will not assert that what they have had to say has gone entirely unheeded by the commissioners, but it has not been as carefully weighed as in my opinion it should have been. In my judgment, if we are to bring the blessings of peace to Eastern Europe, forty million of its inhabitants should not be ignored. But what was I to do with this mass of neglected and also I must admit often quite contradictory information? This dossier weighs about ten pounds, and now that the safe is jammed full, where can I stow it away?

Fortunately an hour ago a "directive" came from Captain Patterson, the "executive officer" of our ship, the *Crillon*. He urges us not to throw into the wastepaper baskets memos and papers "that have outlived their usefulness" (what a charming way of putting it). He warns us that even in the precincts of our closely guarded domain the presence of spies is suspected. "Take your papers down to the cellar, personally," he urges, "and stand by the furnace until they are incinerated."

Well, I obeyed Captain "Dick's" injunction. I took the papers down to the cellar and placed them with my own hands in the furnace that was red hot; and then a surprising thing happened. The Ukrainian dossier did not go up in flames—it simply curled up and smoked and smouldered. When I reported this to the Colonel, he said, "I hope that is not prophetic." And so do I, but I have my doubts. The pleas and the supplications of forty million people have been, to put it mildly, disregarded; they will smoulder on and some day, perhaps at a moment even more inopportune than the present, they may break out into flames that will spread. I hope the League will do better by the problem and the opportunity than we have done.

May 4, 1919

I had a general roundup today of all the Ukrainian delegates that are available and listened once again to what they had to say. I urged them, as instructed, to compose their differences, to combine to secure what they all—or nearly all—want to see, a greater and an independent Ukraine on both banks of the Dnieper. Again they spoke at length of their past glories, of the Cossack republic, of their hard-riding ancestors who formed a living bulwark against the Tartar horde, of the Rus-Kiev state, so long the valiant outpost of Christian civilization. They denounced with equal bitterness the Russians and the Germans and the Poles.

"The Russians seek to destroy our belief in God, and the Germans try to rob us of our language, which is the voice of our souls, and take away our farms. We can trust no one, and yet, can we stand alone? Ukrainia must be re-established—but how? Our democratic friends are far away, and the predatory people who want our grain and oil are very near. The Allies, thanks to America, have won the war; but will they win the peace?"

One of the delegates from Pennsylvania says he has bad news from home. He is advised that people beyond the Atlantic are saying:

"Bring our boys home and let us leave Europe to its own devices."

Then a delegate from Galicia reveals that the Lenin program, "peace, bread, and land," has a strong appeal to his people who have suffered an imposed serfdom for generations.

"But can we trust the new Russian?" he asks. "Is he very different from the old Russian? Has the leopard changed his spots?" And who can answer that?

Then the Germans are discussed. They, at least, have not concealed their purpose. They covet the Ukraine as a war granary which would help them to regain the position they have just lost. All agree that the selfish purpose of the Germans is plain.

Again another delegate voices the familiar lament:

"America is so far away and we cannot stand alone." Then he makes a very intelligent analysis of the changes that have come over and so completely transformed the military scene:

"In America, the embattled farmers achieved freedom; they fought behind hedges and trees. At Yorktown and at New Orleans they met and defeated guard regiments, the trained soldiers of Europe; but today that is impossible. The farmer with such weapons as he now possesses cannot with any hope of success stand up against the trained soldier with modern equipment. We tried it against the Germans and we tried it against the Russians. The result has been the slaughter of our sons. And so we are forced to ask: 'Will the world stand by and see forty million liberty-loving people trodden under foot by despots whose purpose is to enslave the democracies—all of them?'"

After everyone has spoken, I have my say, as per instructions:

"You must place your trust in the League of Nations, which is being fashioned now by the forward-looking peoples. Its purpose is collective security and freedom for all. It will be vigilant and always ready to smash the land-grabbers. It will be watchful and ready to curb any movement that threatens the peace of the world. It has been created for that very purpose."

"I suppose it is our best bet," said the Ukrainian delegate from Pittsburgh—none too enthusiastically.

All the delegates nodded and silently filed out. I am sorry for the Ukrainians. After all, the Covenant is an untested experiment and the sealed book of the future may have surprises for all of us. America is far away and there are many among us who would like to withdraw still farther into our transatlantic shell. Today as so often before it is only too apparent that the President's "clearly distinguishable frontiers of nationality" is a pipe-dream. And, as my chief well says, "When you change a boundary line, look out for squalls!"

May 8, 1919

One of his henchmen came in this afternoon and whispered that Petliura, the great partisan who had perplexed us all by fighting under so many flags and on so many opposing fronts, had, after escaping many dangers by land and sea, reached Paris and naturally was most anxious to get in touch with the Colonel. "But there is difficulty," he explained. "There are many assassins wandering along the boulevards of Paris and many of these misguided men would not hesitate to shoot our noble leader on sight. In these circumstances, wisely I think, we have decided that he must not leave his hideout. Could you not visit him there and pave the way to a meeting with your chief, waiving the protocol and all those obstacles to fruitful intercourse?"

There was nothing I would have liked better, and perhaps personal contact would have cleared up many obscure points in the Ukrainian situation; but as in duty bound I consulted my chief, and he vetoed the adventure, although he admitted that to him also it had many attractions. "Perhaps he will give us the key word to the enigma that has for so long evaded our researches," I suggested. But the Colonel was adamant; he argued that these Cossack assassins are not sharpshooters; you might get in the line of fire. No! This invitation you must pass up—and I did so, regretfully I admit. . . .

[*1921.* For months Petliura remained in his hideout, and the assassins must have been discouraged; but they hung on, and two years later a young Ukrainian Jew came up behind him on the Boule' Mich and shot him in the back. He had the very German name of Schwartz-brod.

For many months after our failure to tackle the Ukrainian problem at Versailles, anarchy reigned throughout the Cossack lands. The murders and the other atrocities that persisted throughout 1919 and the first months of 1920 are said to have been without a parallel even in this unfortunate country until you reach back to the Cossack uprisings of the seventeenth century. By all accounts this rich and lovely land was again drenched with the blood of its children and of its invaders. Everyone was engaged in putting to death anyone they could lay their hands on. The so-called Whites went in for rather formal hangings, the Bolsheviki showed a decided preference for firing squads, and the peasants used their short, sharp knives very effectively on all invaders. The so-called Peace of Riga, celebrated in October, 1920, put an end to the anarchic conditions which had so long prevailed. For the most part the peasants were rescued from their Polish landlords, and outside of Galicia, at least, they settled down as a Soviet state closely affiliated with Moscow. It is clearly a temporary solution; but it is better, much better, than the anarchy that has so long prevailed.]

CHAPTER IX

Czechs, Slovaks, and Father Hlinka

December 13, 1918

World affairs, and these are what should be engrossing our attention, have taken a distinct turn in a new direction in the last week. In fact it might even be said they have gone into reverse. For days we have stood at the bier of fallen empires or investigated the murder of mighty Tsars; we have witnessed the dethronement of kings and the flight of princesses; but today a new ship of state is launched and has put to sea in the stormy waters of Central Europe. Czechoslovakia emerges from the maelstrom of war and her chief magistrate is in Paris to receive the fraternal accolade of the leaders of world democracy.

When the Bohemian peasant cohorts were smashed by the feudal lords in the seventeenth century at the White Mountain, those who survived swore a mighty oath: "We shall live again! We shall come back!" and here they are, and I should say they are very much alive. Of course in our midst there are many soothsayers and, as is the manner of their craft, many and varied are the prophecies they pronounce. Some say the new republic that swims into our ken out of the smoke of battle will prove a bulwark against the prolific German horde and its *drang nach Osten;* others find it no more valuable than a pop gun against siege artillery; and many, very many, say that soon, very soon, it will become a satellite to the great Slav Power, in its new incarnation—that it is destined to disappear in the whale's jaw as does the unwary minnow.

But Paris, wisely I think, lives in the day, and the Parisians are incorrigibly romantic. The Odyssey of the Czech legionaries, the march across Siberia, has captured their sympathy and won their admiration. Thus when on the morning of December 7 Thomas Masaryk, the recently elected president of the war-born republic of the West Slavs, reached the city on the Seine from the United States, he received a reception which compared not unfavorably with gala ceremonies of the days of pageantry before the war.

[On the outbreak of the Bolshevik revolution, the Czechoslovak troops serving with the Russian armies on the Eastern Front declared their intention to remain neutral toward the Reds and, under the leadership of the Slovak scientist, Stefanik, were supposed to be transported peaceably to France via Vladivostok. The dramatic complications and the heroic march that ensued, as related further on, caused a sensation in the Allied world and boosted the case for a Czechoslovak state. The National Czech Council (Masaryk, president; Durich, vice-president; Beneš, general secretary—with the Slovaks represented by Stefanik) was recognized as the future Czechoslovak government by Britain and America in September, 1918.]

December 14, 1918

In the interview that followed between the new president and Colonel House, it was increasingly apparent to both of us that Masaryk had aged greatly in the months that had elapsed since we saw him in America, and it was evident that the news he had received and was almost hourly receiving from Prague brought with it little refreshment. The birth of a nation is evidently a searching trial to the founding fathers, as is the delivery of a child to the mother. He told the Colonel that problems were awaiting him in Prague and he would shorten his stay in Paris because he felt he should get to grips with them immediately. He would leave the task in Paris to Beneš and to Kramar, the recently chosen president of the Council of Ministers.

"As for myself I find it would be unwise for me to await here the coming of President Wilson, much as I would like to. I feel that Czech problems, and there are many, have to be viewed and met on Czech soil, and I have been away from home so long, so long!"

Turning to me he said, "You, who have been with our people so much both at home and abroad, must know the old Bohemian ballad, the ballad that our wandering people sang throughout the world for three hundred years, 'Where Is My Home?' Now we know where it is and we must hasten to it. We shall never forget America or Wilson. America we shall always cherish because for decades, and indeed for generations, she welcomed and succored our wanderers. And Wilson! He is our Salvator. He held aloft the beacon of democracy and his brave soldiers saw to it that its light penetrated into the darkest places. When the Old World seemed lost he came and redressed the balance which could have been restored in no other way, and by no other man."

"The future?" inquired the Colonel.

"There are rough places in the road ahead of us that cannot, should not be denied," admitted Masaryk, "but all will be well if we keep to the covenant of fair-dealing which, as you know, the President is bringing with him. It would also be well if in a sense we could forget the wrongs and sufferings of the past; not entirely, perhaps, for they must serve as reminders of the dangers that yet await us. But we must not let these ancient wrongs rankle in our memory or shape our course."

Masaryk questioned me very closely as to what I had seen in Prague during my visit there in March, 1915. It was truly a mourning city then, and the Magyar soldiers were ruling town and countryside with the ruthlessness of the Huns in the days of old; but I did not stress the picture. What he did not know he would soon learn.

While the Colonel showed great reluctance to discuss the subject, Masaryk was not to be denied, and he went into the question of the President's proposed visit to Paris and the length of his stay there at great length. He had with characteristic frankness evidently imparted his views to the President while still in Washington. Now that the President had reached a decision and was coming to Paris, indeed would be on the water in a very few hours, Masaryk concentrated his objections against a lengthy stay. "I trust the President will not enter the arena or take any direct part in the battles that are unavoidable. I think it would be a very great tactical mistake if he should present himself as a delegate or stay for any length of time in Paris. He must remain aloof, otherwise his prestige will suffer, and that will be greatly needed to pull the Conference out of the mire."

House assured Masaryk that he appreciated these views and indeed that he shared them as did many others. He did think, however, that the presence of the President at the opening session was absolutely necessary. "Otherwise," added House, "the opening days may resemble Donnybrook Fair. I have said all I can say to the President on the subject with propriety, but I see no reason why you should not reinforce the arguments you advanced in Washington with the knowledge that you have acquired of the prevailing atmosphere since your arrival in Europe."

"I shall indeed write him," said Masaryk. "It will be some slight recognition of my obligation to him which I can never fully repay. I shall beg the President not to attend in person any of the meetings of the delegates. He must not become a participant in the struggles that are inevitable. He must remain the mediator. He is the only possible mediator."

Being shorthanded (his charming daughter Alice was working like mad on a mountain of correspondence in the adjoining room), Masaryk asked that I be directed to draw up a brief summary of the thoughts that had been exchanged to be placed in his confidential files which were only open to Beneš.

The following is a brief summary of what took place in the interview as drawn up by me and initialed by House and Masaryk. It was placed in the confidential files but a copy was also furnished Beneš who had now presented his credentials to the President of France and is everywhere recognized as the minister plenipotentiary of the new republic in Paris:

President Masaryk stated, first, that owing to his long absence from the land in which he was about to assume the duties of chief magistrate, he did not think it proper to formulate his ideas as to the proper political course to pursue until he had had the advantage of conversation with Dr. Kramar, the Prime Minister, and his colleagues of the Cabinet. He felt quite confident, however, that the troubles which his people had always had with the Germans would continue; that there was very little difference between the Pan-German Prussians, who sought empire, like the Emperor William, and the Pan-German seeker for new and exclusive markets, like Scheidemann. He said he feared that the Germans were planning serious opposition to the Bohemian form of government in those districts of so-called German-Bohemia, which are in large part inhabited by Germans. He said he was not inclined to let these people go to Germany as they were efficient workmen and necessary to the revival and the further development of industries in which they were employed.

President Masaryk spoke at some length as to his last interview with President Wilson, in which the President of the United States asked him his opinion as to the advisability of his (President Wilson) appearing at the Peace Congress. President Masaryk states that he answered the President in this manner: "I think it would be of great value for you to appear at the Congress to defend the principles which you have promulgated, but I do not think it would be expedient for you to enter into the discussions that will undoubtedly be provoked by the application of these principles to special cases that it may be thought come under their purview."

S. B.

December 16, 1918

At his request I had another talk today with President Masaryk an hour before he entrained for Prague to assume his post of president. He has been tireless during the short week of his stay here in trying to bring together the discordant elements from Central and Southeastern Europe who here abound. He told me of a long conference he has had with Take Ionescu, of the Rumanians, and also with Venezelos, the Greek Premier, for whom he expressed unbounded admiration. In his endeavor to bring about an understanding between the South Slavs and the Poles, the roaming Rumanians (the Wallachs) and the Greeks, he got a clear insight into the disturbing territorial disputes that separate them all and particularly the Serbs and the Rumanians. He admitted that he had not been entirely successful but thought that I was unduly pessimistic. Admitting that there were obstacles, very serious obstacles, in the path to concord, he protested that he still cherished high hopes.

"Solutions are still beyond our immediate reach," he admitted, "but I am confident we have cleared the ground for co-operation at the Peace Conference. These bickerings are undeniable, but we laid the cornerstone of the peace edifice at the Rome and the Paris Congresses of the Oppressed Nationalities and we started to raise the superstructure by our organization in America of the Mid-European Democratic Union." Cheerfully he added, "Don't let Colonel House get discouraged. Many of these noisy people are talking for what they call in that part of America that I know best 'home consumption.' Remember Rome was not built in a day, and it is natural that the New Europe, with its constellation of little states, will require patient and intelligent readjustment.

"I assured President Wilson when I first reached Washington from Siberia," President Masaryk went on, "that the prophecy of the great Komenski that the government of the Czech nation would come again, and soon, into the hands of the Czechs has been fulfilled, and indeed a little sooner than we had dared to expect. German-Bohemia, so called? These districts where the Germans are intermixed with our people is our territory, and ours it shall remain. We have recreated our state with assistance from the democratic world and most of all from my second country, America. We hope that these Germans may collaborate with us, but I for one understand the difficult position in which they find themselves. They were so ready to support the Pan-German attacks on the Czechs! They were intoxicated by the ephemeral military victories and failed to realize what was the true balance in the world situation. But because we understand these people who have remained strangers in our midst for so many generations is the strongest reason why we are not disposed to sacrifice our important and very precious Czech population who are their neighbors in what some propagandists call, mistakenly, German-Bohemia. [Sudetenland.] It remains where it belongs, our bulwark against invasion where the danger is greatest."

As I was leaving, President Masaryk brought up once again the problem which the presence of the large German minority in Bohemia undoubtedly presents. He expects that they will soon invoke the Wilsonian doctrine of self-determination. "Our first answer will be that these ideas were never expressed before the war. Not a voice was raised in favor of union with Germany in the days of Austrian rule. The present agitation is simply the work of Pan-German propaganda." Beneš, who had joined us, mentioned that some were advocating a division of the disputed territory. This he argued was far from practicable.

"The Sudeten hills," said Masaryk, "afford to us Czechs the only defensible frontier against our formidable and aggressive neighbor. A division of the territory in dispute is also far from practical. The three million Germans do not present a solid bloc which could be more easily dealt with. They are widely scattered, and in many of the districts which they have hitherto dominated are to be found almost an equal number of Czechs."

Masaryk then pointed out: "These troublemakers in Reichenberg say that they fear that Prague will attempt what they call the *Czechization* of their fellow Germans. It seems to me that this only would be possible if, as is proposed by some, two millions were ceded to the Reich. One, the remaining million, might be *Czechified*, if anyone were so foolish as to attempt it, but surely not three million! These Germans are as stiff-necked as the Poles, and we know how many hundred million gold marks the Berlin attempt to Germanize the Poles of Silesia cost and what a complete failure it has been."

A new and I think an important aspect of the situation was brought to light by the following words of Masaryk. "The present agitation is due almost entirely to the fact that under the Vienna government the Germans of Bohemia were favored, perhaps pampered is the more correct word, for obvious political reasons, and rightly they do not expect that this favoritism will be continued by the new government in Prague."

Beneš expressed the hope that the German minority after a little calm reflection would be willing to remain outside the Reich, just as the three million Germans in Switzerland are enthusiastic about remaining with the Bund. "From us," he added, "they will have no cause of complaint, once they have divested themselves of their pretenses to race superiority and their claims for special privileges. The only hardship that awaits them is that they will have to learn to live under a democratic government which guarantees equal rights to all, irrespective of race, religion, or language."

Both Beneš and Masaryk lived up to this promise. Only when Henlein and other agents of Hitler came with money and promises did irreconcilable differences develop and the Sudeten Germans lift their voices in complaint.

January 11, 1919

While, as he admitted frankly, differing from him on a number of important questions, and far from approving many of his plans for the future, Beneš sent General Stefanik to see me this morning and I took him out to a quiet place for lunch. He is just back from Siberia and has been preceded by a number of romantic stories as to his exploits, some of which are true. Apparently at no time was he a prisoner of war, as were most of the legionaries, but he did command them at a difficult moment when he, with his Czechoslovaks, had to face the Germans on one flank and the Bolsheviks on the other. He is a slight man of about forty, and his pale complexion and sunken burning eyes would seem to indicate that he is not long for this world in which he has played such a notable rôle.

Beneš had told me that in civil life Stefanik was an astronomer, and Stefanik explained to me how he had risen from a shepherd boy in Slovakia to become a famous stargazer in Paris, a story which I fear interested me more than some of his more recent and rather complicated adventures.

"A barefooted boy of twelve, thirty years ago, I left my village and walked to Paris. I wanted to learn all about the stars and the constellations that I watched at night as I guarded my uncle's sheep. I had heard there was a great observatory there, and there I would learn the secrets of the heavens. When I reached the observatory I put on my shoes (I had carried them on my back during the journey), it was my court dress as it were, and I waited on the steps all night though several people tried to shoo me away. In the morning the great M. Flammarion arrived, and through an interpreter I told him that I had determined to follow in his footsteps. He was amused, but seeing that I was half starved he gave me a little money and put me to work sweeping out his office. A few weeks later I had picked up some French, and the first sentence I framed was fired at my benefactor. "M. Flammarion," I said, "in fifteen years I shall be your assistant." He laughed heartily but he helped me a lot. I was a little better than my promise. I worked hard because I loved the work, and in twelve years I was his first assistant, his fellow traveler through the celestial regions.

"But when the war came I too came down to earth, and I have worked for Slovakia and for the peace of the world ever since." And now this remarkable man became diffuse. He was hard to follow and seemed to suffer from a Niagara of ideas and a lack of planning. I suppose the explanation is that he is a man of genius and that I am merely an ordinary fellow with a weakness for practical solutions. Suddenly he asked me if he could speak frankly with me, and I assured him that this was my wish. That in no other way could he help us or his own people.

January 15, 1919

How I wish I could record fully the details of the journey of the Czechoslovak army across Russia and Siberia which General Stefanik gave me this evening. They were interesting and, unlike so many of my memos, would have permanent value. Today I have only the time to jot down a few details of their wonderful adventure. From their own ranks I trust some day a modern Xenophon will appear. Throughout the four terrible years of the war the Czechs have exhibited all the qualities of a great people, but the story of their katabasis during the last eighteen months of the struggle would seem incredible were the facts not so fully authenticated. I have no doubt that Professor Masaryk will have success as the chief magistrate of this remarkable people, but nothing can surpass his achievement in forming this gallant little army and in placing it where it was needed.

The story begins with the signing of the infamous Brest-Litovsk treaty when the Czechoslovaks, about fifty thousand strong, were in Ukrainia near Kiev. To escape the Bolsheviki, the bewildered Ukrainians threw themselves into the arms of the Germans. This the Czechs, although equally bewildered, the world they sought to reshape having apparently been smashed to atoms, could not bring themselves to do. And it was at this crucial moment that with unusual cunning the Emperor Karl tempted them. Riding as he thought on the crest of the wave, he offered them "amnesty for past offenses and autonomy for the future." "They knew the Hapsburgs," commented Stefanik, "and spurned his offer."

"The roads to the west and to their homeland were held by the enemy in overpowering numbers," continued Stefanik, "so the little isolated force turned toward the east. Having failed to seduce them with promises they had not the most remote intention to keep, the Austro-Germans sought to destroy them. When the little army had reached Bachmac, about one hundred miles from their original position, they were set upon by a large German force. Our people drove them off, however, and now the Germans abandoned open warfare for methods of insidious intrigue and the situation became greatly involved. Our boys had no desire to take part in the Russian civil war. They wanted to get home and to take up their proper position on the Western Front. In Russia all was confusion; there in the west the war objective was clear. There they would be fighting for home and country, not for ideologies which many did not understand. A compromise was hit upon. Our boys agreed to disarm, partially, so that they would no longer be the least danger to Bolshevik supremacy, and in return these people agreed to smooth out the transport difficulties to aid our people to reach Vladivostok. Fortunately our boys did not disarm completely. The trains that were furnished proceeded at a snail's pace and the little convoys were often attacked by German agents and by Magyar prisoners who apparently were released and given arms for this very purpose. Our men were exhorted to join in the 'battle against world imperialism,' and when they turned a deaf ear, they were set upon. They fought their way through, but many weeks elapsed, and many died, before at last they were able to join up with the Allied forces in western Siberia."

No wonder that little Stefanik and the two lieutenants who are with him look like shadows, but they are the shadows of something glorious.

January 12, 1919

General Stefanik, the strange little stargazer with the pale face, the emaciated frame, and the burning eyes, lunched with me again today and he gave me vivid details of the march of the Czechoslovak legions from the plains of the Ukraine to the shores of the Pacific in which he played a notable part. The Czechs, generally spoken of as liberated prisoners of war although actually many of them were patriotic deserters from the Austrian regiments, were being armed to serve against the Germans when the Russian Empire fell and the succeeding government changed its policy of assistance to the Allies to one of peace at any price. This placed the Czechs in a difficult position, and soon the inevitable incident occurred which led to hostilities.

They were quartered in a prison camp near Tchelyabinsk, and near by were many German prisoners. In an affray a Czech soldier was wounded, and his comrades killed the aggressor. The German and Magyar prisoners joined in the resulting riot and many were killed on both sides. The local Bolsheviki sided with the Germans, but the Czechs were successful in securing arms and soon they had wrested possession of the town from the Soviet. There was no possible help to be expected from the outside, but unaided the legion advanced to Penza and captured that important town. Meeting with but little real opposition, they proceeded down the Volga and, after capturing Samara and Kazan, they crossed the Urals.

From now on the attitude of the Soviets is difficult to define, much less to describe; after some desultory fighting an order came from the Moscow Soviet, signed by a certain Stalin,* ordering the local au-

---

* This is the first official reference to this remarkable figure that I have come across. S. B.

thorities to give the Legion free passage to Vladivostok; but several days later came a telegram (which the Czechs intercepted) from the same untrustworthy source, ordering that the refugees should be stopped, disarmed, and transported to a concentration camp near Archangel.

There followed now inconclusive skirmishes and desultory negotiations which are equally difficult to follow. At one point Stefanik admits a brigade of Czechs agreed to give up their arms on the ground that these weapons were Russian property distributed at a time when Russia was still an ally of the Western Powers. At this critical moment America and Japan came to an agreement (August 3, 1918) "to render the Czechoslovaks (in Siberia) such assistance and help as might be possible to combat the former Austrian-German war prisoners who were attacking them."

"That was the original purpose of the American Siberian expedition about which so much misinformation is in circulation," Stefanik insisted. "As a counterstroke the Soviets asked the German high command to send arms to their former soldiers, now prisoners; but doubtless, with the best will in the world, this they were unable to do, and so the great mass of our legionaries continued their long trek across Siberia."

Stefanik frankly admits that some, although not many, of the Czechs fell away from the flag. "It was a most difficult and a very complicated situation," he explained. "Here they were starving and hopeless, thousands of miles away from home and succor. They had always hated imperialism, and here the men who had overcome the Tsars were tempting them with their attractive ideologies. Some but not many succumbed and were swallowed up by the Soviets. But the main body resisted the temptations and now they are on the Pacific coast awaiting the coming of the transports which will bring them home to where they are as greatly needed as they were on the Western Front in 1918. [Following the Armistice there was a letdown and the transports were slow in assembling. The first contingent of the Czechs did not sail until December, 1919, and their repatriation was not concluded until well on into 1920.] And they are not idle; in that benighted land of eastern Siberia they are bringing in the light of a new day. They are organizing workingmen's clubs, peasant's banks, and a postal system. They are doing much good; those poor Russian serfs are profiting by their presence."

One of the charges against the Czech legionaries which is listened to in our present atmosphere, so receptive to muckraking, makes Stefanik very angry. It is the charge that indirectly they were responsible for the murder of the Tsar and his luckless family in Ekaterinburg on July 16, 1918. "As a matter of fact, our people did not reach that place until nine days after the murders were committed," said Stefanik. "And they had not the slightest intention of liberating the Tsar or in any way taking part in Russian politics. They were simply straining every energy to reach their distant homes." I have no doubt that Stefanik is quite correct in this statement. His people wished to remain aloof from the internal struggle, but I am afraid the local Soviet which, with or without orders from Moscow, committed the foul deed were not convinced of this.

*   *   *   *

September 19, 1919

The day after our return to Paris from London and the Conference on mandates, Jean, the bright-eyed veteran who ran one of the elevators in the Crillon, famous for his nimble wooden leg and his breast covered with the decorations he had won in the gallant defense of Verdun, told me that several Slovaks had arrived in Paris and were anxious to see the Colonel. I advised him of the coming of this belated delegation, but House decided that at this late day he should not intervene in the matter.

"I will, however, ask Frank Polk, who now presides over the delegation, to see them. As you know, I have many misgivings as to the justice of the settlement that has been reached in this thorny Czechoslovak problem. However, there is comfort in the thought that at least we have, under the provisions of the Covenant, called into being international machinery which in the end should effect a just settlement. You can tell them if you see the Slovaks that this is my hope."

On the evening following their first call, Jean appeared at my room, acting in an unusually secretive manner.

"The Slovaks are here again," he whispered. "I have them on the back stairs. Shall I bring them up?"

"No, put them in touch with Mr. Polk's office."

"But they have a letter to you personally from General Stefanik. I knew the General was your friend; otherwise I would not have admitted them."

This was indeed mystifying. I knew—all the world knew—that Stefanik had met with a tragic death on a flying field near Bratislava three months before. My curiosity was now fully aroused and I asked Jean to show them in. One was a Catholic priest evidently, although he had discarded his clerical garb. The other was a small farmer with a very engaging face. They produced the letter, I recognized that it was authentic and I saw that it had been written only a few days before the Slovak soldier-leader embarked on his last flight. It read:

"Do what you can for my friends. I hope to join them in Paris soon. If possible, secure for them a hearing by the President or by Colonel House. I can vouch for the absolute truth of the statements they are authorized to make."

Both of the Slovaks spoke a strange Magyar-German to which every now and then the priest would attach a Latin tag, but they made their purpose perfectly plain.

"Many obstacles have been placed in our way," they explained. "All permits to travel were denied us. It has taken us three months to reach Paris with our protest, and as our presence here is illegal, we have taken refuge in a monastery where the good fathers do not have to make reports to the police or announce the arrival of guests. Our General has been foully dealt with [at the time I did not understand the full significance of these words], but with us we have brought our leader, Father Hlinka. He is ill, worn out by the hardships and the uncertainties of our clandestine journey, but he hopes you can come to him. He would like to explain the hopes and the fears of our people."

"Come at this hour tomorrow night," I replied, "and then I will go with you or tell you why I cannot do so."

In the morning I explained to the Colonel what had happened and he gave his permission for me to go. "If," he said, "you have no doubt about the Stefanik letter."

I had none and was eager for an adventure which smacked of E. Phillips Oppenheim. Late on the following evening we left the hotel by the baggage entrance, coming out on the rue Boissy d'Anglais. We walked along in the pelting rain for several minutes before my mysterious escort would allow me to hail a cab. Then, to my amazement, they said, "Drive to the Luxembourg." For a split second I hesitated, but after all the letter they had brought was authentic and I was clearly in the hands of Stefanik's friends. Once at the Gardens, which were closed for the night, they dismissed the cab and we wandered about for ten minutes or so in narrow, unfamiliar streets. Twice we turned sharply and reversed our course. Only when convinced that we were not being followed did my escort lead me into what seemed to be a blind alley at the end of which we came to a halt before an iron-bound gate which, after three carefully measured knocks, was opened to us. The guardian seemed to be a priest, but as he remained in the shadows, only throwing the feeble light of his flickering lamp upon us, I could not be certain. We went on now through a gloomy garden to another gate which was open and unguarded and along a narrow corridor for about twenty yards. At the end was an alcove cell, damp and dark, where by the light of a tallow dip I saw a man fully clothed lying on a narrow iron bed reading, in low tones, his breviary. The disguised priest, my escort, said:

"This is Father Hlinka, the leader of the Slovak Peasant Party," and with that he and his companions withdrew into the darkness of the corridor.

I assured Father Hlinka that I would listen to what he had to say and report it carefully to Colonel House; but, I said: "You have come late, and for the moment I fear nothing can be done. You see, on the tenth the Treaty of St. Germain was signed. There can be no further change in the structure of the Succession States of the former Austro-Hungarian Empire until the meeting of the Council of the League—some months hence."

"I feared as much," said the Father, with a sigh. "And that accounts for the extraordinary steps which the Czechs have taken to delay our arrival here. Ten years ago Slovakia was but a two-days journey from Paris. Today in the New Europe, which the Czechs control, it has taken us three months to reach the City of Light, and only to find then that the light has been extinguished. I have come to protest against the falsehoods of Beneš and Kramář, and they have, not without reason, hampered me on my journey in every way. Even so, they would not have triumphed had they not silenced the voice of General Stefanik. To him, our great leader, all the assembled envoys would have listened because he worked not only for his own people, but for the Allies in the Siberian campaign and on the Italian front. Well, they silenced him—in a most dastardly manner."

"What do you mean by this?" I inquired.

"You have been told—the whole world has been told—that General Stefanik came to his tragic end in an airplane accident. There is not a word of truth in that story. The plane that brought him from Italy made a successful landing, but as he stepped out he was shot down by Czech soldiers placed there for this diabolical purpose by Beneš. Many know the details of this crime and by whom it was plotted, but in the present state of affairs, what can they do? The truth is also known to the general's brother; but he is a prisoner in his village, and should he dare to say a word he would be brought before a firing squad."

[I did not believe this story at the time, or for that matter later, when several of Stefanik's adherents, having escaped over the mountains into Russia, told it to the world; but Hlinka believed it, as did many of his partisans, and it was this belief that made all the efforts toward a reconciliation with the Czechs hopeless.

January, 1933. I have recorded in my diary the terrible charge which Father Hlinka brought against Beneš as to the manner in which General Stefanik met his death. I had neither the opportunity nor the authority to investigate his indictment, but I would not feel justified in suppressing it. The fact that he believed in it explains much that followed. I greatly admired Beneš's behavior at the Conference, and it was certainly extremely fortunate for the Czech people to have such a resourceful leader.]

"One of the difficulties that will confront you when the time comes to reopen the question will be the documents you have filed with the Conference," I suggested as delicately as I could. "Voicing the wishes of your national committee, both you and Stefanik are on record as asking for union with Prague for many and cogent reasons—the ever-increasing disorders, the encroachments of the Bolsheviki . . ."

Poor Hlinka groaned. "I know, I know. We did that very thing. May God forgive us. The Czechs spoke us fair. They said that in union there was strength, that many, very many Slovaks had fought with them on many fronts. We had been brothers in war, and now that peace was at hand, a troubled peace to be sure, why not stand together? 'It is only a temporary measure at best—or at worst,' they explained. 'It should be regarded as a trial marriage, and then should the union prove irksome, we could each go our several ways without let or hindrance.' But in three months, indeed, after only three weeks, the veil was lifted.   In this short time we have suffered more from the high-handed Czechs than we did from the Magyars in a thousand years.   Now we know *extra Hungariam non est vita* (outside of Hungary there is no life for us).   Remember these words, time will prove their truth.   Beneš is an ambitious knave.   He even wants to absorb Polish Teschen."   [And as a matter of fact, rightly or wrongly, he did.]

"But your union with the Magyars—that sins against the principle of ethnic solidarity which is in such high favor now," I suggested.

"I know, I know," interrupted Hlinka.   "It runs counter to the popular current.   We cannot mix with the Magyars and we do not want to, but economically, and above all religiously, we can get along with them better, much better, than we can with the irreligious free-thinking Czechs who, as we now know, have no respect for God or man.   We have lived alongside the Magyars for a thousand years and the traditional tie is strengthened by the lay of our respective lands. All the Slovak rivers flow toward the Hungarian plain, and all our roads lead toward Budapest, their great city, while from Prague we are separated by the barrier of the Carpathians.   But the physical obstacles are not as insurmountable as are the religious barriers, which shall, I trust, always keep us Catholics apart from those who were Hussites and now are infidels."

Although I tried to turn his thoughts away from the unfortunate move he and some of his adherents had made in the hour of victory, I was not successful, and he returned to it time and again.

"Yes, I did sign the declaration which went to the Powers a few days after the Armistice.   I did say, may God and my unhappy people forgive me, that we Slovaks were a part of the Czechoslovak race and that we wished to live with them with equal rights in an independent state.   Why did I do it?   I cannot explain—not even to myself—but I will tell you some of the reasons that swayed me then unfortunately. In the Pittsburgh declaration of our independence which the American Slovaks sent on to us, I read that Masaryk had guaranteed the independence of Slovakia and had further agreed that we should be represented at the Peace Conference by our own delegation.   Even then I had my doubts as to the wisdom of the step I was taking, but what else was I to do?   When the people in Prague saw that I was hesitating and the reason why, they reassured me by saying, 'This is merely an emergency move, and you can make it with mental reservations. When Europe settles down you can make your own final decision.'

"And of course I saw the plight of Hungary. Having accepted the role of cat's-paw for the Germans, she was powerless, while the Czechs were in a strong position. Some said to me: 'We must spread our sails to the prevailing winds,' and I agreed. God has punished me, but I shall continue to plead before God and man for my people who are innocent and without stain. For long and fateful years we fought for our religion and our freedom shoulder to shoulder against the Magyars. Our relations with them were not what they should have been, but during all those years we did not suffer one tenth of the wrongs that we have had to bear at the hands of the Czech soldiers and the Prague politicians in the last few months.

"The Czechs regard Slovakia as a colony, and they treat us as though we were African savages. Abroad they shout that we belong to the same race, and yet at every opportunity they treat us as helots. Within the borders of what they are pleased to call Czechoslovakia, they only treat us as hewers of wood and drawers of water for their High Mightiness of Prague."

(The fact that the people of Prague speak of the newborn state as *Czechoslovakia* and not as *Czecho-Slovakia*, is a grievance which also rankles.)

Three days later, still under escort, I was back at the mysterious monastery bringing to Father Hlinka a copy of the Covenant in Slovak, with the article indicated through which, upon the assembling of the League, he would be entitled to ask for a review of the decision and, indeed, of the treaty. The Father was now sitting up and, to explain his physical condition and his delay in reaching Paris, he told me many details of the hardships he had experienced on his three-months' journey. It was a checkered land-Odyssey, but unlike the second Korean Mission headed by my old friend of Seoul days, General Pak, which never got beyond Lake Baikal, the Slovaks, though battered, and limping, and above all, late, had now arrived.

"We had the best of reasons for knowing," explained the Father, "that the new people in Prague would not assist us with passports; in fact, we were confident they would throw every possible obstacle in our way; so we sneaked out of our villages by night, and wandering across country, often on foot, through Teschen, we came to Warsaw. Here we were well received by Marshal Pilsudski. He had many troubles of his own. His people were, as you know, in a desperate plight, and so he was only able to give us words of encouragement. Even the French traveling passports which he asked of the French Embassy were refused. His parting words, however, sustained us in many a trying hour of our journey. 'You are entitled to your independence as much as we are,' he said. 'I shall instruct our delegation in Paris to assist you all they can.'

"We also received kind words from another great man, Achille Ratti, the Papal Nuncio in Poland.* He gave us his Apostolic blessing. He, too, deplored that Christendom had placed the devout Slovak congregations under the tyrannical rule of the enemies of the true Church. But he begged us to give up our journey, at least for the moment. He asserted that conditions were too unfavorable; that for the present they could not be overcome. He urged us to stay with him, to watch and pray, to pray for the peace of Jerusalem. This we regarded as a counsel of despair, and so we pushed on, without credentials and with little or no money. Often our poverty-stricken countrymen, exiles in strange lands, saved us from starvation and by their contributions enabled us to travel many stages of the journey at least in fourth-class cars; but progress was slow and often, very often, we had to stop and retrace our steps because of the political conditions by which we were confronted. Germany we knew was unsettled. We were warned there was not one chance in a hundred of getting through there. The longest way around gave better promise, and so we wandered on through Yugoslavia to Italy and at last to Switzerland. Once there we did not have to sleep out under the stars or go supperless to bed, as had become our habit. A committee of good people from our unfortunate country took us in charge, arranged for our stay with our brothers in Christ, and brought us to Paris in that relative comfort—which we had not enjoyed for so long . . ."

Five days later I called again on Father Hlinka, for no reason in the world but that I wanted to have one more, and what I feared would be a last, look at what they would call in Maryland his "honest affidavit face." And now I needed no guide and could reach the monastery unescorted. It was the Paris home of the Pères du Saint-Esprit, with whom evidently the Catholic Slovaks had close affiliations. The

* Later Pope Pius XI.

gatekeeper wanted to send me away in short order. "The Slovaks are gone," he said. But I insisted on seeing the Abbot, and from him, between his lamentations and self-reproaches, I learned what had happened.

"A week after our dear brothers arrived," he explained, "we had to make room under our roof for those who came to take part in the annual assembly of our Order. We secured rooms for our Slovak visitors in a little hotel a few steps down the street. There we hoped they would remain as our valued guests until once again there would be available space for them under our roof. They were loath to leave, and now too late we recognize how right they were. Apparently their presence was immediately announced to the police by the keeper of the hotel and they were called upon to show their papers at the prefecture. These were not in order; in fact they had none, and so, twenty-four hours later, in spite of our protest, they were escorted to the station and placed on an eastbound train.

"It was a great triumph for Beneš and his infidels," lamented the Abbot, "and we shall never forgive ourselves for unwittingly assisting them. Father Hlinka was sure that Beneš brought about his expulsion and so am I. But how could a country, how could France, that at least until recently was the eldest daughter of the true Church, lend itself to such a dastardly act?"

I chose to think that neither the government, except in a perfunctory, routine way, or for that matter Beneš, had anything to do with the expulsion. Perhaps Hlinka and his friends were simply victims of the newspaper crusade against unregistered aliens and others that the Paris press had preached, with the warm approval of the delegates to the Peace Conference, as a result of the murderous attacks upon Clemenceau, Venizelos, and other delegates. Reproached for their criminal laxity, the police with many indiscriminate *rafles* now made a clean sweep of the lodginghouses of Paris. I trust this is the explanation of the unhappy and most untimely expulsion of the Slovak Mission, but I must admit that the good Abbot would not accept it and as long as I stayed with him kept repeating, "Beneš and Tardieu, Tardieu and Beneš, they are the villains."

Tardieu, at least, I think was guiltless and had not the remotest idea that the Mission had been in Paris, for when some days later House broached the subject of their dissatisfaction with the St. Germain settlement, he thought it was based entirely on protests that had reached us from the American Slovaks, residents for the most part of western Pennsylvania.

Colonel House was impressed by Father Hlinka's story and deeply touched by some of the details of his hazardous and necessitous journey which I gave him. "I had thought," he said, "that all roads led to Paris and that the Conference was easy, perhaps too easy, of access—but at least in this instance I'm mistaken."

When the Colonel recovered his health, the Slovaks had been expelled, but he brought the memorandum which I drew up for them to the notice of our delegation and also called the matter to the attention of Tardieu when he came to the Crillon on one of his frequent calls. Tardieu admitted that he had heard of the schism between the Czechs and the Slovaks, which was increasingly apparent, but had consoled himself with the thought it was due merely to a misunderstanding which could and should be cleared up.

"At times," suggested the Colonel, "I fear you are not going about the foundation of a strong Czechoslovak state in the best way," and Tardieu promised to study the matter very carefully, indeed "prayerfully." He admitted that he had been startled and impressed by the plea of the Slovaks.

"Of course we knew," he went on, "that a plebiscite would disclose a number of minorities in the new state. There are the Germans and Hungarians, and those strange Carpatho-Russians, all very difficult to understand, much less to assimilate. But what could we do other than what we have done? It would be absurd to turn this section of Europe into a hodge-podge of governments, a crazy quilt of little nations. On the other hand, the government in Prague is a liberal one. It was and is our staunch ally and we have every reason to believe that in an autocratic world it will prove a bulwark of democracy. It seems to me that we have the right, even the duty, to make that government as strong as we can."

[1938. On their arrival in Vienna, the expelled delegates separated, Hlinka going to his native village of Ruzomberck to work with his people, while one member of the delegation was sent to Budapest to keep in touch with the Magyars. Hlinka decided to enter parliament and there, in what he was told would be an open forum, fight for the liberties of his people. Some weeks before the election, however,

Czech soldiers broke into his house at midnight and, before his ador-
ing peasants had any idea of what was happening, carried him off to a
distant prison. This high-handed act provoked an insurrection that
was only suppressed after much bloodshed. Hlinka remained in
prison for many months and was treated with such cruelty that he
never recovered his health.

He fought on, however, and in 1938 came his hour of triumph.
Some American Slovaks brought to Europe the long-concealed original draft of the Pittsburgh Pact between the Slovaks and the Czechs,
reached in 1918. It demonstrated the fact that, although he had taken
some part in drawing it up, Masaryk was honestly mistaken as to its
terms and that Hlinka was fully justified in maintaining that complete
autonomy had been promised his people and further that they were
assured that on a basis of equality they would sit with the Czechs at
the Peace Conference. Andred Hlinka died a few days later. With
his last words he again demanded the plebiscite too long denied.
Even had it been granted it would now have proved too late. The
discord between these two branches of the Western Slav family,
which would have taken years of fair and friendly dealings to remove, made the conquest of their common country by the Germans
in 1939 a matter of but a few days.

I retain pleasant memories of my intercourse with the Slovak
priest. At times I think of him as the most sympathetic of the many
agents of the scattered and disinherited ethnic fragments with whom
I was brought in touch. He had dark luminous eyes of rare beauty;
they were indeed the windows of a soul that was transparently sincere. His speech was straightforward and convincing, but here was
the rub. It was not words alone that could set his people free, and
apparently his bitter memories made it impossible for him to listen
to, much less accept, the compromises and the adjustments the situation demanded and which might have saved it to the ultimate advantage of all.

July, 1943. Thanks to the way in which Hlinka's teachings
swayed them, although he, their apostle, was now dead, the Slovaks
escaped the inhuman, barbarous treatment by which the Austrians,
the Czechs, and, above all others, the unbending Poles, have been
crucified. But they cannot be congratulated on their "escape."
Some, blinded by their unbrotherly strife with Prague over Teschen,

believed that Hitler would live up to his promises and that their dear country would be comfortable, well fed, and happy—even as a satellite state.

But today the Slovaks know the truth; even the puppet president, Tiso, admits that their situation is hopeless, that they have lost faith in themselves and their leaders. All their food and movable property have been looted, and those who survive are treated as serfs. The divisions they were forced to send to the Eastern Front have been annihilated except for a few fortunate units which, honoring their ancient Pan-Slavic creed, deserted to the Russians whenever the opportunity presented itself.

Today it can be said that 90 per cent of these unfortunate people are praying, and as far as it is in their power, are working, to re-establish their country as a free part of an independent Czechoslovak state. Poor Father Hlinka has really deserved a better fate than the crown of thorns that is his today. He and his teachings have helped destroy the people he loved so well and so tragically misled.]

CHAPTER X

Beetle-Browed Bratianu and the Rumanians

January 10, 1919

Duly announced with a flourish of trumpets over the telephone from Rumanian headquarters, M. Goga came to see me this morning. Fortunately I had heard that a man of this name, the "bard of Transylvania," was expected to join Bratianu [prime minister] and bear testimony to the pure Rumanianism of the people who dwell in that beautiful mountain country where the Telekis and the other Hungarian magnates have lorded it for centuries and carved out for themselves quite sizeable estates which, not unnaturally, they are extremely reluctant to give up.

Goga said what he had to say and he said it beautifully. Transylvania was the cradle of his race. Here on these mountain slopes and in these sunlit valleys the scattered remnants of the Roman legions had taken refuge from the Dacian hordes. He mentioned Varus and Trajan, the Latin leaders, as glibly as we talk about Joffre and Foch. Here these refugees had found safe harbor and prospered while Mother Rome sank into insignificance and decay. Then, alas, into this paradise where the Christian faith and brotherly love held sway there came another horde of invaders, the Moslems under their green banners; and the war for land and religion was waged with varying fortunes for generations.

"At times we fought alone," explained Goga, "at others the Christians of the West aided us—but not unselfishly. In the last campaign, Magyar lords fought at our side, but when the war was won they parceled out our lands and our peasants to suit themselves.

This is the history, the sad history of my people," insisted Goga, "and our day of redemption only dawned when Wilson sent his soldiers across the seas and liberated Europe." That was his story, and it was perhaps a fair one of the land of his birth; but of course I fail to do justice to the poetic prose in which it was unfolded.

I told Goga that America had no special Transylvania policy, but that I had no doubt that his aspirations were fully covered by the Wilsonian doctrine of the self-determination of peoples. "We can now take care of ourselves," he went on. "We have rifles and we know how to use them. We do want medicines and perhaps a little food. The Germans swept out our storehouses and devastated our farms, and the Russians who came to our aid brought us the plague of typhus. Our need for medicines is great, but Bratianu has already spoken to Mr. Hoover about this and he has promised to do what is possible." With this I thought the interview was at an end, but suddenly the poet darted off on another tangent.

"I came to Paris in a roundabout way," he said, "and with good reason; throughout the war my voice had been raised against them, so when I was selected to represent my province of Greater Rumania at the Conference I had to avoid the lands of the Germans and the Magyars. So, I floated down the Danube and across the Black Sea to Constantinople. There I shipped for France, but not for Marseilles as I had hoped. My ship was bound for Bordeaux and the captain would not deviate from his course. This meant a delay of a week, but what a fortunate delay it was! I now sailed through the Pillars of Hercules, and as I looked out across the boundless Western Ocean a song straight from my heart fell from my lips. It was my salute to America from where our salvation had come. It was an ode of Thanksgiving to the American people, and when it is perfected I shall send it to you."

[The poem never came. Perhaps it was never "perfected." The atmosphere that now prevailed in Paris was not helpful to expressions of gratitude. In fact they all went out the window. Years later Goga, the poet-politician, became Prime Minister of Greater Rumania (1937). He made a mess of his difficult job, and his ministry that was distinguished for anti-Semitism soon fell. So Goga, my charming visitor, died, it is said, of a broken heart and was carried back to his beloved hills by a cortege which included all the poets of his land.]

All this was interesting, but I was a hard-driven man and my desk was piled mountain high with prosaic communications that had to be attended to, so perhaps the gesture of impatience which I now permitted myself was pardonable.

March (undated), 1919

One of President Wilson's marked dislikes is his aversion for Bratianu, the beetle-browed prime minister of Rumania with the notorious Byzantine background. Up to the present he has avoided the *tête à tête* with him which the Bucharest leader so ardently desires. He puts him off with messages through House. "Tell him," says the President, "that the frontiers we are tracing are temporary, certainly not final, and that later on, in a calmer moment and informed by longer study, the League of Nations will intervene to adjust provisional settlements which may be found to be imperfect."

Last week, however, the Colonel said to me: "Bratianu insists upon an interview with me and I do not think it wise to put him off any longer. I have every reason to think it will be stormy and I want you to be present. Misu, the Rumanian Ambassador, is coming with him, but I prefer to have you interpret."

The interview was more stormy and the language of the Bucharest "Bull," as he is sometimes called, was even more outrageous than had been anticipated. Little Misu did what he could to soften the words of his chief, and in asides to me was often apologetic, but it is difficult for a mere ambassador to stand up against his chief, a prime minister.

Bratianu's blast began by a violent and yet by no means an untrue account of how after entering the war Rumania had been let down by the "promising" Allies. "Solemn pledges were given us that a great Russian army would come to our aid, and that, as the Germans would be held by intensive operations on the Western Front, the invading army of Mackensen would not be a force larger than we could cope with. Now what happened? The Grand Duke did not move, and on the Western Front the Allies went to sleep. An unholy calm settled down on that sector, and Mackensen drew from there all the divisions he needed to overwhelm our gallant resistance. But mark you, we have learned our lesson; it has cost us the complete devastation of our country; so for its restoration we are demanding naturally something more substantial than verbal pledges. We know now what these are worth."

After excoriating Briand and Lloyd George (as to Clemenceau he was reserved), suddenly the Rumanian scold went after Hoover. "He will not permit us to have loans, or food, except in return for oil-land concessions. Without these we can expect no help, he says. I have been advised that no assistance of any kind will be forthcoming unless special privileges are granted our Jewish minority. And the American Jews, bankers and big businessmen, seem to think that our country is to be turned over to them for exploitation. Their agents in the thin disguise of food organization officials are on hand and they are earmarking industries and concessions which they must have, they say, otherwise no assistance can be expected. Once for all I have come to say that these people may go to Palestine, or to Hell for all I care, but I shall not let them settle down upon my country, devouring locusts that they are!"

This went on for three quarters of an hour. It should in all fairness be admitted Bratianu was in a nervous condition, although not "concerned in liquor," for which he should not perhaps be held responsible. Several times Misu intervened with placating words, but without success. He, however, whispered to me: "His Excellency has had very bad news from Rumania in the last few days . . ." Then, shrinking from the fierce frowns of his chief, he stopped short, and so the details of the bad news were not forthcoming.

Suddenly the Colonel's patience was exhausted and he ended the interview with, "I think you will admit that I have listened to you very patiently. If you furnish me your charges in writing I can assure you that they will be carefully investigated and answered. And now, Mr. Prime Minister, I bid you good day."

Misu was most embarrassed; throughout the tirade of his chief he made deprecatory gestures and now and again he had murmured, "Yes, but . . ." Evidently he wished to pour oil on the stormy waters, but all his efforts only tended to infuriate "Bull" Bratianu. Shouting, "I shall file with you a memorandum dealing with the matter, officially," Bratianu bounced out of the room while little Misu slunk after him with an apologetic smile.

After a moment's reflection the Colonel said: "I must ask you to make a record of what has been said. It will furnish a basis of comparison with the Prime Minister's charges when they are put in writing. When, and if, this is done, in justice to Hoover we must make them a matter of official record. I think Bratianu, when he comes to himself, will hesitate and that the formal charges will never be filed. In the meantime I must ask you to type out what he has said and give it to me for the confidential file. It must be 'graveyard,' even to our stenographers."

The result was I made almost a night of it. Never expert in typing, I had not tapped on my old-fashioned Blick for months. It was near morning when I concluded the unusual task. My hatred of Bratianu was unbounded. At sight of me little Misu always slunk away. My transcript was placed in the confidential files and as we say in conference circles "the incident is closed."

The memorandum that Bratianu agreed to file never came. Perhaps on second thought he never wrote it. More likely, however, little Misu intercepted it. That is one of the things that a wise ambassador sometimes gets away with. On the following day House advised Hoover in general terms of what the Prime Minister had said. He received it with the most perfect equanimity. "Bratianu is a liar and a horse thief—that's all there is to it." Then as an afterthought, "I hope God will help the Rumanians—I cannot."

[Months later Bratianu indeed had a short day of popularity. When his armies invaded Hungary and flouted the veto of the Supreme War Council, many delegates of countries who would have liked to do the same, had they dared, cheered Bratianu—at least under their breath. And there was something in Bratianu's contention at this moment. "We are looting Hungary, it is true," he said. "But we are only taking back what the Hungarian regiments stole from us when as an important contingent of Mackensen's army they invaded our country."]

Bratianu is undoubtedly the most unpopular of the prime ministers who are assembled here. He is not, however, the only one of the statesmen present who during the war fell between two stools and flirted with the opposing forces, but it would seem that he fell more awkwardly than the others and that his flirtations were the most shameless. And it should be said that his shortcomings are emphasized and perhaps magnified by the diplomatic and social activities of his adroit rival, Take Ionescu, whose prophecies as to the outcome of the war have been justified. He is having a splendid time running around and saying, "I told you so! But Bratianu . . ."

Much of the correspondence in regard to the entrance of Rumania into the war is still closely guarded in the secret files, but on the facts that are known, Bratianu's policy, whether in power or out, was anything but adroit. It landed his unfortunate country in disasters which many think might have been avoided. At the outbreak his sympathies seem to have been with the Entente, but there was the Hohenzollern king who had to be "managed," and the burly Rumanian statesman had quite a soupçon of the Italian *sacro egoismo* in his composition. Ionescu traveled up and down the country shouting, "Our rôle is that of an unconditional ally of the democracies. We must not drive a bargain. We should and can rely on the appreciation of our allies when the victory is won."

Not so, decidedly not so, Bratianu. He wanted military guarantees and blueprints of territories to be annexed in advance of mobilization. He blew hot and he blew cold, and always at unhappy moments. His timing was always bad. He fascinated the Queen Marie who is now here bringing her undeniable charm to bear upon some of the more susceptible statesmen. As a granddaughter of Queen Victoria, she always thought as an English woman, and Bratianu assured her that she "would come out of the war as Empress of all the Rumanians wherever they were seated."

In the early years of the struggle, when the adherence of Rumania could have been of great assistance to whichever of the powers that secured it, the great talking point and the preferred prize of all the Rumanians was the possession of Transylvania—"The cradle of our race," says the Queen Marie (the daughter of Edward VII's brother and a Russian Grand Duchess). Czernin, who had served as minister in Bucharest and understood Rumanian aspirations fully when he took charge of the Austro-Hungarian foreign office, certainly toyed with the idea of ceding some districts of Transylvania to the Rumanians as a bribe—to keep them in line—but the Hungarian Premier Tisza was strongly opposed; the project came to nought, and all thought of it was abandoned when the Central Powers made their break through at Görlitz and captured Warsaw. The result of the shilly-shallying and at times bare-faced bargaining was that Rumania joined her forces with the Western Powers just as Russia began to disappear as an important factor on the Eastern Front. Three months later Field Marshal Mackensen was in Bucharest and in possession of the coveted oil fields.

When his armies were defeated and his country almost completely overrun, in the opinion of the military men of the Supreme War

Council, Bratianu's behavior was neither loyal nor intelligent. They assert he capitulated too soon and bargained too promptly with the Germans; they insist that the remnants of the Rumanian armies were in fine fighting trim and had they but stood up they could have held in Rumania many, very many, of the German divisions which were then needed so desperately on the Western Front. So, rightly or wrongly, Bratianu is charged with entering the war too late and of having surrendered too soon, a difficult position from which only a diplomat of great tact could have extricated himself. However, he plumes himself upon not signing the Treaty of Bucharest. Take Ionescu is on the worst of terms with the Bratianu group now in power, but he represents, as president of the National Council of United Rumania, the will of his people. At least that is his claim. He is a voluble talker and inclined to boast about his four pre-war prophecies all of which came true. "It is a too perfect score," I remind him and shut him off, a proceeding which he accepts with the most perfect good nature. He is strong for the League, however. He calls the Covenant the Fifth Gospel and American participation the hope, the only hope, of the European world.

Undated—probably March 6, 1919

The event of the week, with all its social, political, and economic repercussions, is the expected arrival any day now of the beautiful Queen Marie of Rumania. While like almost everyone else she comes a-borrowing, the ceremonial officer has decided that in homage to protocol some important member of our delegation should be at the station to greet her, to see that the red carpet is worthy of royal feet and properly spread. Frazier and I discussed the matter without any particular personal enthusiasm and we decided that a flip of a coin would decide who should perform this diplomatic chore. Gordon Auchincloss, son-in-law and secretary of our Colonel, overheard this conversation, at least in part, and, "getting us wrong," advised the Colonel that in his judgment the most beautiful woman in Europe should not be greeted on her arrival in "gay Paree" by men whose hair was gray or at least on the "graying side." And he offered to go to the station himself.

This remark started quite an uproar in the "family." It was promptly quelled by the Colonel deciding that as the Queen was coming to borrow money for her bankrupt country and food for her unfortunate subjects we might well await her appearance at the Crillon. He was confident she would not fail to put in appearance, and soon.

So the affair was settled by our chief with his usual wisdom, but the remark about the graying hair rankled. Then a copy of the *Temps* and an article which spread over several columns arrived which exalted us and gave sweet revenge. It was written by Mentchikof, the great scientist, biologist, and anthropologist, and the present head of the Pasteur Institute. He said that for some years now (in the midst of the greatest war in history) he had indulged himself in an intensive and extensive study of mammals. One of the discoveries he had made was that the superior animals of the fauna family, with the passing of the years and the coming of age, turned gray, while the inferior animals "moulted." We placed many copies of this informative article on Auchincloss' desk and others came to him by mail and special messengers.

And was he angry! The joke, at least from our viewpoint, is that while A. is quite young and, as some think, even juvenile, his head is as bare of hair as a billiard ball. He, like other members of the inferior tribes, must have "moulted" years ago. Jests such as these relieve the tension of world-shaking events.

CHAPTER XI

Greater Hellas and the Overseas Greeks

December 4, 1918

Even at this early stage of the diplomatic battle I have been drawn into the circle in which Venizelos, the Greek Premier, exercises his fascinating and, as many think, his dangerous influence. Last week he came to the Colonel, ostensibly to place before him some documents, very illuminating he thought, as to the actual conditions within the Reich. I was called in to test the translations and found that many of them were misleading. Sighing, the Greek leader said: "When you were studying at Heidelberg and Bonn, I was hiding from the Turkish *zaptieh* in the mountain caves of my native Crete. For months I never saw a book. What chance had I to study and to learn. What a handicap this is to my country."

I consoled the great man by insisting that his years of guerilla warfare in the mountains had resulted in the reunion of Crete with Old Greece and that now "he was on the eve of achieving Greater Hellas, the dream of his people for centuries."

[Eleutherios Venizelos, whose political fortunes rose and fell with sensational rapidity, bitterly opposed the pro-Bulgarian, pro-German sympathies of King Constantine. When that monarch was ousted in 1917, Venizelos formed a ministry and led Greece into the war on the Allied side. One of the most popular delegates to the Conference, he survived exile, death sentence, wars, and revolutions to die in 1936 still a controversial figure.]

When this was out of the way, the charming old buccaneer put his arm on my shoulder and said: "Alas, none of my staff knows German and I have come across an important volume in that language by a Herr Oppenheim. Some years ago he traveled in Asia Minor and he enumerates the purely Greek villages that he found there. His work is that of an impartial scientist and his researches were made to ascertain the truth, not for propaganda purposes. And now every night when my daily task is done with the aid of a French-German dictionary I dig out the facts which his travels have brought to light. Would you be so kind as to come to my apartment this evening and check up on the accuracy of the translations I am making under these difficult circumstances?"

I went to his hotel in the shadow of the Arc de Triomphe that night, and indeed the two following nights also found me busily engaged there. We extracted from the volume everything that was comforting to the Greek cause. We followed Oppenheim from the Mediterranean to the Persian Gulf, and along this path of empire his trail was dotted with the ruins of imperial cities which once were great and of vigorous Hellenic settlements that gave promise of a glorious renaissance. The Greek statesman was profuse in his thanks for my assistance but, as a matter of fact, the obligation, if any, was on my side. A few days later the resulting report, setting forth the extent and numbers of the Greek colonies in the disputed territory, was filed with the Supreme Council. In his compilation I thought that Venizelos stressed the Greek talking points and left out some information that was not helpful to his cause. But that was to be expected, and I have no doubt the members of the Council discounted it.

The charming Venizelos is greatly distressed at the present situation. He has most certainly the good will of all who know him, but is that really helpful? He enjoys the sympathy and the esteem of all the delegates and all the plenipotentiaries, but also they fear him because of his well-known and incontestable charm. Perhaps we shall all have to change our measure of success. Is charm as potent in securing results as nuisance values? This is the thought that is evidently uppermost in the mind of the great Greek as today he surveys the progress that has been made toward a Greater Rumania and the meager harvest that has been realized down to the present by himself and the advocates of a Greater Hellas. When the uncouth and beetle-browed Bratianu comes barging in, the plenipotentiaries seem to think that no price is too great to pay to get rid of the fellow.

But when Venizelos comes in they say, "I must be very careful. This fellow can conjure a bird out of a tree." And so they harden their hearts and turn a deaf ear to his pleas. In this instance at least nuisance value apparently does outweigh charm

January 22, 1919

Venizelos has had a series of long talks with the Colonel during the past week. He is evidently greatly perturbed over the outlook which seems to me, and evidently to him also, rather nebulous. He is convinced that Wilson will not accept for America a mandate for Constantinople and the control of the Straits that has been offered. Of course, he was never an outspoken advocate of this arrangement, although he did not openly oppose it. He was evidently convinced that, if accepted, in a short time Washington would tire of this responsibility and withdraw after things had settled down, and then Greater Greece would emerge. Now he thinks that the President has been won over to another plan, one far from favorable to Greek aspirations, and that this plan will shortly be submitted to the Supreme Council. He would like to have it reshaped ("reformed" he calls it) before it reaches this stage.

Last evening, at the suggestion of the Colonel, Frazier had Venizelos and myself to dine at his charming apartment on the Avenue du Bois. The nerves of the Greek Prime Minister are evidently worn to a frazzle, and we did not get away until long after midnight. While greatly condensed, I think these notes which I made on my return to the Crillon do justice to his plea, although they are not always given in his words.

"Flesh and blood, not even Greek flesh and blood, can stand further delay in the approach toward a settlement of our problems," he said. "For six months now we have had two hundred and fifty thousand men mobilized and in the field at the request, I might even say at the order, of the Allies. This has cost us millions upon millions of drachmas which we haven't got, which we have borrowed and shall have to repay. Mobilized, yes; but mobilized for what? We are not told. 'Wait and see,' whisper the members of the Supreme Council— but of course quite unofficially. Apparently we are not mobilized to take over Constantinople, although that has been our dream for centuries, or even for a large slice of Thrace. Lloyd George points significantly to Smyrna and the fat lands around it where there is such a large purely Greek population. 'There a great future awaits you,' he insists, but within the hour he is urging Italy to jump in there on our right flank, and you can't help concluding that he has earmarked Adalia and the rich near-by districts for the Italians.

" 'What are we mobilized for?' I inquire, and he answers jovially: 'Have a little patience. You will learn very soon. Be assured the Council is not neglecting your problems.' I can wait, but it is quite clear that the Greek treasury can't stand the strain, nor, as a matter of fact, can our soldiers. Last September the morale of our men was excellent. They were eager to fight and to go anywhere, but now they want to go home, to get away from the stinking camps."

Then his great grievance came out. We could not answer it because it deals with an alleged proposal of President Wilson about which House has not been informed and of which we know nothing. Venizelos has what he regards as reliable information to the effect that as a substitute to the American mandate he, Wilson, is proposing an international state or administration for Turkey in Europe.

"This plan, if carried out," he maintained, "would take away from us over 700,000 Greeks, that is, at least 28,000 in western Thrace, 306,000 in eastern Thrace and about 360,000 in the vilayet of Constantinople. It is probably true that in this territory there are about 700,000 Turks. This I admit is a problem, but the way to meet it is not by placing this great number of our people under non-Greek sovereignty right next door to Greece. The result would be constant agitation and I fear civil war.

"There are in Greece, in Thrace, and in Asia Minor about seven and a half million Greeks," he continued, "but if this plan, which they ascribe to Wilson, is approved by the Supreme Council, at least a million of our people, whom we thought to 'redeem,' would have to live outside of our boundaries and under an alien administration. This should not be done. How can it be done? In its original form the proposal of an international administration to cope with the problem of Constantinople had a simple and limited objective which was to guarantee the freedom of the Straits for all time and against all comers. As at first proposed, the Enos-Media line was to be the frontier with Europe, but in its expanded form it takes away from us nearly a million of our people and the resulting international state could never prosper. Indeed, it seems to me to be designed to keep alive the racial conflicts which we had hoped with the coming of peace would subside if not wholly disappear."

M. Politis, the Greek Minister to France and a delegate to the Conference, came to the Crillon this morning and he certainly crossed the *t*'s and dotted the *i*'s of the Venizelos talk. He read and left with House an informal memo to the following effect:

Unless the project now under discussion is rejected by the Supreme Council in a few days, the Greek government will file a formal protest. I beg to remind you that M. Venizelos brought our country into the war spontaneously without making any conditions. He simply rallied Greece to the side of justice. Since the Armistice he has listened to the counsels of the Allies and complied with all their demands—at times against his better judgment. Since Armistice Day he has mobilized three new divisions, making twelve divisions under arms. As requested, he has in this way held himself in readiness to carry out the instructions of the Conference, either in Smyrna or more recently, with due regard to the menace of Bulgaria, in Thrace. It must be clear that this proposal [the changed frontier with Turkey in Europe], ascribed unjustly we believe to President Wilson, if approved, would place Greece and the present government in a most unenviable position, although its deserts are certainly greater than those of any of the other countries of Southeastern Europe who have been so greatly favored, particularly Rumania. Unlike the situation in many of the districts granted to the Bucharest government, the lands which we should have, and are apparently in danger of losing, are occupied by Greek populations.

In conclusion Politis said: "What I am about to say is not authorized by M. Venizelos, but it is so important that I think you will pardon my indiscretion—if it is one. If this plan is approved, the first result would be the fall of the present government in Athens and the return to power of King Constantine and the pro-Germans. Even now these people are saying that we have failed to secure the benefits we fought for and were fully justified in demanding."

[*1922.* On the first of September following, the Supreme Council rejected the plan, described it as one contained in Mr. Wilson's letter for "reasons ethnographic, political, and moral," and requested Mr. Polk to draw the President's attention "to the desirability of seeking a solution to this question more in harmony with the general bases of the peace, one less unfavorable to Greece, and one more proper to avoid future incidents in the Balkans." This was one of the least happy of the President's interventions; fortunately the results were not as lasting as his abandonment of the Austrians in the South Tyrol.]

House had a long conference on the following day with the President and placed the information contained in these memoranda before him. He came back still rather uncertain that the plan which the Greeks opposed could be ascribed to Wilson. The President's memory on the subject was apparently not quite clear.

February 10, 1919

M. Coromilas, the No. 3 Greek delegate, came in today and "after compliments" made an open attack on my table of the languages spoken in that salad of wild tribes which is the Macedonia of today. He objected to my "mother tongue" definition as to the ethnic factors in this land of Babel and yet that is, as far as I can see, the only yardstick we have to rely on.

"The situation is not as simple as you present it," he objected. "For instance, you leave out the Bulgaro-phone Greeks (Bulgar-speaking Greeks)—and yet they are an important factor in the complicated situation. They are of straight Attic descent and the land is full of them; but to pacify their ferocious Slav neighbors, and so that they may be understood in their daily life and pursuits, they have gotten into the habit of speaking Bulgarian and many of them have lost all knowledge of their mother tongue. What are you going to do about that?"

I did not commit myself, but I did tell him of an incident that occurred years ago when I was engaged in my early linguistic studies on the Vardar. I was walking along the noisy river with Spiridon Gopsevich, the apostle of Pan-Serbism in these parts. We met a poor peasant staggering along the path under a load of wood for his cabin fire. Thinking to do a little spot of propaganda, Gopsevich said: "My good man, what is your nationality?" "*Ja sam Bougarin*" (I'm a Bulgarian), the thoughtless fellow answered. Gopsevich was nettled and blazed out: "My poor fellow! you are mistaken. By the very words that come from your mouth I can see that you are a Serb." I left them to argue it out and went on my bewildered way.

"That Gopsevich was just one of those common garden liars that were sent out by Belgrade to complicate the situation," commented Coromilas, who from long service in Chicago spoke good American.

"Perhaps, perhaps," I answered, "but he was not the only one."

If truth is to be found in Macedonia, it is at the bottom of a very, very deep well. Certainly I never plumbed it.

March 8, 1919

Three of the strangest looking men wandered into my office yesterday morning. Their dark mysterious faces and their stealthy tread excited the suspicions of our guardian sailors, but soon they produced a letter from Venizelos which authenticated their mission. The Greek Premier said they were the properly accredited representatives of the Overseas Greeks, as yet "unredeemed," of the Euxine Pontus (better known in the western world as the Black Sea). But on closer inspection of the letter from the Cretan mountaineer and guerilla fighter, who in the last ten years has developed into the smoothest of diplomats, it appeared that it was couched in more reserved terms than was usual in his writings.

"Down to the present," he said, "our Council of State has not decided to include the colonies or settlements which these gentlemen so worthily represent in the picture of Greater Hellas which we are about to present to the Conference. Yet these, our noble kinsmen, are in great need of supplies, indeed of even the bare necessities of life, and I am writing in the knowledge that their unfortunate plight will excite sympathy in America, from where alone help can come."

House told me to take them to the Food Administration; it was a walk of several parasangs, but I enjoyed every foot of it. We talked about the misnamed Anabasis and it was as fresh in their minds as the retreat from Mons in mine.

Hoover * received us with his most ferocious glare. They were all of a tremble, and my knees, too, were knocking together. In a quavering voice one of them told their story in a sort of bastard Italian, the *lingua franca* of the Mediterranean, and I passed it on to Hoover as best I could. He told how all navigation on the Black Sea had been arrested by the war conditions, and so no longer could their usual foodstuffs reach them from South Russia; and how outside Trebizond Anatolian bandits were lurking so that the peasants in the interior, the few who had any, did not dare to bring their produce

* Herbert Hoover was chairman of the American Relief Administration, the 1918 counterpart to World War II's United Nations Relief and Rehabilitation Administration.

to town. With what seemed a contemptuous smile, Hoover listened
and then, just as I thought he was going to have us all thrown out
through the open window by the side of his desk, he said: "Tell 'em
I'll feed 'em. They must be here tomorrow—sharp at nine—and we
will work out the details."

For five minutes the Pontus Greeks confounded themselves in
salaams and genuflections, but Hoover paid no further attention to
them. He had lit another cigar and with sheafs of telegrams in his
hand he was immersed in other tales of woe.

The delegation was so jubilantly excited that I did not dare to
leave them alone in the mazes of traffic outside. I walked them
another parasang or two to a boulevard café and ordered drinks
which I hoped would prove soothing. Several of their countrymen
who were lurking in the background joined us and all burst out in
paeans of victory. They agreed that Mr. Hoover was the greatest
man who had lived since Alexander and that I was evidently a favorite
son of Hermes. I wanted to hear something about the war as viewed
from their distant standpoint and also about their relations with
Mother Hellas, and they were not at all loath to enlighten me.

"We, too, helped not a little in winning the war," one asserted.
"Of course, our war chariots of the Homeric days were the fore-
runners of the tanks."

Soon they were telling me the story of the fate of their nation,
alas, for so many centuries submerged by the unspeakable Turks.

"We represent the oldest overseas Greek colony in the world,
several centuries older than Marseilles; of course, to us the French
port is a mere parvenu," they insisted. "Our noble city of Trebizond
[on the Black Sea], the Attic atmosphere of which none of the
barbarian hordes has been able to destroy, should really be called
Xenophonopolis. Now this is why: When Xenophon brought his
men back from the Persian campaign with Cyrus and once again
they were all cheered by the sight of the Pontus, 'Here,' he said, 'I
want to found a great city—a home for the overseas Greeks, a bulwark of Hellenism against the barbarians on the dark shores of the
Great Sea.' At first the plan was warmly applauded; with trained
oxen the confines of the city that was to be were being drawn when
—ah! that was terrible, I should not tell it—"

But I insisted, and at last the sad tale came out.

"There had slipped into that noble band of Greeks an unreliable soothsayer, a despicable sorcerer. We recall his name to cover it with infamy, and if you will allow me I will now expectorate. (All three delegates spat in unison.) His name was Silanus of Arcadia. He had cozened up to Cyrus and extracted much money from him and he did not care about founding a noble city, a bulwark of civilization; he wanted to return home and 'revel' with his money. So he told the hoplites that Xenophon was deceiving them, that he had no thought of building for them homes; no, he was planning to lead them back into the deserts of Asia from which they had so recently and so narrowly escaped. And that sorcerer was a cunning man. Every time he consulted them, the entrails told the same story. They said, 'Go home.' So the great plan was defeated, or rather postponed for several generations, and Xenophon returned to Sparta where, though broken-hearted over the failure of his project, he had a good time hunting and raising dogs and writing histories."

Stories of the founding of cities almost always start controversy, and this story of how Trebizond was or was not founded is no exception to the rule. One of the delegates would not admit that when the Ten Thousand reached the sea the shore where the noble city now stands was a lonely strand.

"It was not like that," he insisted. "Ours has been a noble city, a Greek colony since the dawn of history, long, long before Troy. It is recorded in our archives that when the Ten Thousand arrived they were escorted by the City Elders to the Shrine of Hercules and there they made appropriate sacrifices to the conductor who had led them, not unscathed, but still safely, through many dangers, to the dancing sea."

Quite an argument now arose, but I brought it to a conclusion by the statement that by going back to Xenophon their claims would have priority over all other colonial adventurers. It would most certainly suffice.

A few hours later Venizelos came back and thanked us warmly for bridging over the gap between Hoover and the Euxine Pontus.

"But I have told them that I cannot claim the south shore of the Black Sea, as my hands are quite full with Thrace and Anatolia. I told them to 'go home, make all the money you can, and send it back to the mother country. If you do that, we shall always cherish you' —and they went away well pleased." Then, as an afterthought, the Greek Premier said: "Often it seems to me wiser, and certainly more helpful, to have commercial marts rather than political colonies beyond the seas. But for the contributions that came from them in a steady stream we never could have faced the financial strain of this cruel and most costly war. It was our merchants in Cairo and Constantinople, in Liverpool and in Norfolk, Virginia, who kept us afloat."

March 12, 1919

As is now only too evident, it was unwise of me to communicate to my colleagues of Colonel House's "family" the flattering tributes that were showered upon me by the grateful delegates from the Euxine Pontus. They had hailed me as "Stephen, garland-crowned son of Hermes," and, of course, it was after all no mean feat to secure food from Mr. Hoover, or at least the promise of it, in twenty-four hours. I was also, I think, deserving of praise in squelching the plan of the delegates, which they developed as I regaled them with drinks at Weber's, to re-establish the long defunct empire of Mithradates. With liquor on the table and food in sight, they were hard to hold back. No, I told them, the atmosphere of the conference was unfavorable to the founding of empires, and at last they agreed. But I fear they will take up the matter at a more auspicious moment.

My envious colleagues have been looking up Hermes from whom, according to the Pontus Greeks, I stem, and while the classical dictionaries admit that he was a personage of great charm, and the tutelar saint of early diplomatists, the protector of travelers, of heralds and interpreters, they also reveal that in some respects he was a rather unscrupulous fellow. For instance, they relate that, while yet an infant, Hermes stole fifty head of cattle from his brother Apollo, hid them away in a cave, and then calmly returned to finish his nap in his cradle!

Hearing the uproar in his "family," the Colonel barged into the controversy. He, too, looked into the classical dictionary and eloquently took my part. "Great Zeus approved of this juvenile exploit," was his decision, "and while admittedly there was in some unfriendly quarters unfavorable gossip, still Hermes was the patron saint of those who were 'strong of voice and retentive of memory.' In our family, that means Bonsal." So my persecutors were silenced and slunk away. But I have learned my lesson. Should in the future compliments be bestowed, in my experience a rare occurrence, I may gloat over them—but only in private.

Not the most important, but certainly the most acute, of the Greek problems is how to settle the boundaries with Albania. Both are roving people, like most of the Balkan tribes. There are certainly many thousand Albanians in northwestern Greece, and there are many sons of the Eagle in Italy, and indeed nearer home in New England. And, worse luck, there are many thousand Greeks within the boundaries of Albania as established at the Conference of London. Another complication which adds fuel to the discussion: there are many important men in both Italy and Greece who boast of their Albanian ancestry. Undoubtedly the problem could be solved by an exchange of population and some slight frontier changes, but no one will accept either the one or the other. The Greeks will not yield a village or an inch of territory, and my friend, Essad Pasha, says the plan infringes on the Law of the Mountains and contravenes the Code of Lex, which he says has been honored by his people since the days of Moses, the Lawgiver.

If possible, even more acute is the clash of the Albanians with the Yugoslavs in the Kossovo district, where on the Field of the Blackbirds the Cross fell before the Green Banners and the Serbs became the serfs of the Ottoman Turks. Certainly the Albanians, with great arrogance, are encroaching on this territory, as I described their activities after my visit in 1892, and it is only in the last few years that the long down-trodden Serbs have had the courage to complain and at last to oppose the unwelcome intruders. This region was undeniably a part of the great Serbian Empire in the thirteenth century. Should it be restored to Belgrade now? Should California and New Mexico be restored to Spain or to Mexico? I don't know. I fancy a statute of limitations will have to be established. Of one thing I am certain: in both cases the restoration would require the employment of large military forces. All would be well if friendly relations could be established between the disputants, but unfortunately all the experts say this is impossible; on this point at least they are in full agreement

CHAPTER XII

Armenian Disaster

March 4, 1919

Even before the Conference assembled, the Armenian delegates, official and otherwise, were on hand. Perhaps today I should review their activities as far as they are known to me. They hail Mr. Wilson as their liberator after twenty-four centuries of slavery; and as one of them told me, the Fourteen Points, their charter of liberty, they regard as Holy Writ. "Your Wilson came from Washington," said Aharonian, chairman of the delegation, "but he was sent by God."

They have had their day before the Council of Ten (on February 26), and Lord Bryce is working for them day and night. My sympathy has been with them from the beginning, and I have been as helpful as I could be with propriety. (How silly that sounds, and yet it is the simple truth.) I do not have to read the atrocity stories which Lord Bryce has filed with us because with my own eyes during my days in Turkey I saw things that were even more bloodcurdling. I do not close my eyes to the crimes which the Armenians have since committed in the way of retaliation from time to time when the rare occasion presented against the diabolical Kurds and the Turkish irregulars—the Bashi-Bazouks. Indeed, I approve of them.

One, and I sometimes think not the least, of the handicaps of this unfortunate people is that in their church allegiance they are divided. Many of them are Gregorians, some are Roman Catholics, and not a few are Protestants. There is even a group of Nestorians. The result is, absurd as it seems, the Armenians do not benefit by the zealous and undivided support of any of the great churches. How strong are these sectarian animosities was brought home to me during my stay in Jerusalem. The political and social life of the "holy" city is poisoned by it. If there had been any other halfway decent place for me to lodge, I would have left the Greek Hospice and the stern control of Brother Stephanos, who kept such a watchful eye upon me. He deplored my relations with the Abyssinians, although he knew what very definite obligations their pilgrims had placed me under. Brother Stephanos admitted that the Armenians belonged to the Christian tribes, but yet as schismatics they were beyond the pale. In the Holy City, how these Christians do *not* love each other!

March 5, 1919

A long talk with Nubar Pasha (the ranking delegate of the Egyptian-Armenian contingent) today. He takes me back to the cradle of his unfortunate people. He says the Armenians are closely related to the Hittites, although he admits that some of the Arab clans in Syria claim, mistakenly of course, similar descent. I refuse to follow Nubar back to the dawn of history. There should be limits as to the research of national paternity, I insist, and finally he agrees. He maintains that the pure inhabitants of the Van plain do not know what you are driving at when you call them Armenians. They call themselves *Hai* and trace descent to a certain great chief, who may be mythical but who for all that is very real to them, called Haik. What we call Armenia is to them Haiistan, and the word Armenia, being of Persian origin, is most distasteful. However, Nubar is not dogmatic and is inclined to be lenient with our mistakes. He insists, however, that in the days of Herodotus western Asia was better known to the civilized world than it is today, even to our most expert geographers.

Skipping many epochs and ignoring many national vicissitudes, I bring Nubar down to date, or almost, and I am rewarded by facts that will have a bearing on the settlement of the question, if one is reached. He concedes that in many districts of Anatolia in Turkey before the war the Armenians had sizeable majorities—which were indeed before the massacres of 1896 overwhelming majorities—but that they are now minorities. "But," he argues, "should our people lose their homes and their lands because they have—that is, so many of them—lost their lives?"

I can see, too, that this, like the Silesia problem with its crusade of Germanization, is not one that can be fairly settled by the application of our American panacea of a "free and fair election." That would only be the case if the murdered and the exiled could come to the ballot boxes.

March 6, 1919

One of the reasons why we are making so little progress in carving up Turkey is undoubtedly the confusion in the plans and proposals of the Giaours, for which all good Moslems pray every day at the afternoon prayer—and, apparently, these prayers are heard. The President's original plan, or purpose, contemplated international control for Constantinople and the Straits. This is now interpreted by many as meaning that the Turks are to remain masters of Anatolia. When we look at Point Twelve for guidance, we read:

The Turkish portion of the present Ottoman Empire should be assured a secure sovereignty, but the other nationalities which are now under Turkish rule should be assured an undoubted security of life and an absolute, unmolested opportunity of autonomous development.

These words do not warm the hearts of my Armenian visitors. The same assurances were given them at the Congress of Berlin in 1878, and Great Britain, France, Russia, in fact all the Great Powers, sponsored the arrangement and accepted responsibility for its fulfillment. But nothing happened, and Turkish rule continued its ruthless sway. After all, the Armenians ask, what does autonomous development mean, what does it promise? Certainly not an independent sovereign state. Autonomy on the tongue of the Turk, the Armenians say, means nothing except the prelude to another series of massacres, and they cite many instances in the history of the last fifty years to support this interpretation.

And turning to the commentary on the Fourteen Points as drawn up by Frank Cobb and Walter Lippmann during the armistice proceedings (as we are officially urged to do in seeking light), and which when cabled to the President received his approval,* we find more confusion than clarification as regards Point Twelve:

Anatolia should be reserved for the Turks. . . . Armenia must be given a port on the Mediterranean and a protecting power established; France may claim it, but the Armenians would prefer Great Britain.

Of course it is impossible to carve a new Armenia out of Anatolia if that region is to be "reserved for the Turks." And the coastline on which the Commentary says the Armenians should have a port, their ardently desired "window on the western world," has been earmarked for the Italians, the French, and the Greeks, and they are all fighting briskly over their allotments provided for in the secret and conflicting treaties. It is plain that some of the slices of Turkey will have to be curtailed, and perhaps even worse is to come. At times, Lord Bryce fears that the whole idea of a free and independent Armenia, to which we are all pledged, will be dropped. I hate the whole wretched business, and from now on I shall decline to urge the Armenians to cherish hopes which I fear will never be realized.

Today (*March 8*) Boghos Nubar Pasha had his hour in court, and while his statement of the Armenia case was somewhat rambling, all agreed that he acquitted himself well. He first spoke in impeccable French for M. Clemenceau, and then in High Church English for the benefit of President Wilson and Mr. Balfour. Right at the beginning he pitched into the middle of things.

"It would be shameful," he announced, "to leave us under the domination of the Turks. We are as deserving of liberty and independence as are the Greeks, the Arabs, and the Zionists, although, I admit, not more so. Indeed, we have the same aspirations and pursue the same high ideals. Nothing can divide us from these noble peoples who have suffered similar hardships and vicissitudes—not even the question of Trebizond—although of course Armenia to survive must

---

* *1923*. As this statement has been challenged in some quarters it is perhaps proper for me to say that, as instructed, I drew up the dispatch in question and decoded the President's reply from Washington, dated October 29, 1918. In it he accepted the memorandum as "a satisfactory interpretation of the principles involved." In the circumstances, House was certainly justified in regarding the Commentary as a complete elucidation of the President's world program; and as a matter of fact in the course of the Armistice negotiations, when queried by the delegates for more precise information as to points which were regarded by some as obscure, he read aloud to them the explanations which the President had formerly sanctioned. S. B.

have an outlet on the Black Sea.   Between people of our culture this problem can and will be adjusted.   To negotiate with a noble man like M. Venizelos is a very different affair from negotiating with Abdul Hamid * and those who have come after him, who have only changed their names but who pursue the same diabolical objectives.

"I trust that no one here will seek to restore the Turkish Empire even on a reduced scale.   It has been kept alive for generations by the unhappy rivalries of the European Powers with the result that it has generated wars and revolutions, rebellions and massacres without end.   Turkey was given a chance to reform and to survive in 1914.   Had she not joined the Central Powers, had she remained at least neutral in the struggle, something might be said today in her behalf; but she joined up against civilization and by her action prolonged the war for at least two years.   Had she remained neutral, Bulgaria in all probability would not have entered the struggle or, in any event, could have been easily and quickly crushed.   How many millions of dead is she responsible for?   The flower of our generation is gone!

"There can be no mistake about it.   Civilization must not permit non-Ottoman peoples to remain under the yoke of Turkish oppression.   The extinction of Turkey is essential to world peace.   Otherwise it will prove an idle dream and indeed a cruel one for which thousands will have died in vain.

"We deserve independence on another score: We have fought for it.   We have poured out our blood for it without stint.   Our people have played a gallant part in the armies that have won the victory.

"I disagree with those who assume that in the hour of triumph the suffering and the blood shed by my people, our contribution to the common victory, is to be forgotten, and I shall be precise in telling you what we expect at your hands.   It is an independent Armenia embracing Cilicia and the six Armenian vilayets of Turkey; and to these must be joined the Armenian provinces of Russia whose inhabitants, numbering over two million and having the advantage of forming a compact body, have already been successful in forming an independent government of their own.   This reunited and inde-

* Abdul Hamid, Sultan of Turkey (1876–1909), was very pro-German and, as the instigator of the horrible Armenian massacres of 1894–1896, he was dubbed the Great Assassin, the Red Sultan.   He was dethroned eventually by the Young Turks.

pendent Armenia, we think, should be placed under the collective protection of the Christian nations, or under that of the League, which is to us the hope of the world. We also ask for the particular guidance of any one of these nations to stand by us in the transition period we are entering upon. It is clear that this aid and guidance will be indispensable to us as we begin the reconstruction of our devastated country, now reduced to ashes, blackened fields, and heaps of rubble by the Turks in retaliation for our unflagging devotion to the cause of the Allies."

Nubar's statement and his appeal were much more eloquent than would appear from the scrappy notes which I here recall. He was listened to with sympathetic attention by the great men who today hold the balance of power. But there was a faraway look in their eyes and no promises were made. That indeed is the trouble. Armenis *is* far away, and other problems nearer at hand and hence thought more urgent are coming home to roost.

March 3, 1919

Yesterday Sir William Wiseman of the British Intelligence Service dropped in and it was evident he had something on his mind. He often acts as a messenger for Lloyd George and not seldom he comes on missions that are evidently self-imposed. During the war, when he served in New York, Wiseman had many contacts with the Colonel, who thinks that they were to his advantage. On this point we of his staff are not in complete agreement. After beating about the bush for some minutes, Wiseman came to the point.

"I wonder if you could tell me, and through me, the P.M., confidentially of course, when the President is planning to bring the Armenian question before the Council for final adjustment."

I answered I could not, and then suggested that the President, perhaps, would not intervene in the matter at all. Wiseman registered surprise and then, "Why not?"

"Of course I do not know, but possibly he thinks he should not interfere with the British plans in this quarter."

Wiseman registered even more complete surprise and asked me to be more explicit. I then showed him a copy of the Prime Minister's speech made at the Guild Hall in 1916, which with malicious purpose I had held on my desk for some weeks. As he seemed to shy away, I read it aloud: " 'Britain is resolved to liberate the Armenians from the Turkish yoke and to restore them to the religious and political freedom they deserve and of which they have been so long deprived.'

"It seems to have been your job, and you accepted it at least a year before we entered the war. Why should the President barge in? *Après vous, messieurs les Anglais!*"

Wiseman scurried away with a bee in his bonnet, perhaps even a hornet, and doubtless reported my discourtesy in exalted quarters. If bad temper ever can be justified, I think mine was on this occasion. Among the things that the deplorable treatment of the Armenians reveals is the skill of the Powers with whom we are associated in "passing the buck." Both England and France before we entered the war officially announced that they would re-establish the Armenian people in their ancient rights and within their traditional boundaries, but as the extreme difficulty of their task becomes more and more apparent, they have earmarked the ugly job for Simple Simon, that is, for Uncle Sam.

As a matter of fact, the Armenian problem is a hard nut to crack and the anxiety expressed by their delegates here, and by Lord Bryce, their sponsor, is fully justified. The survivors of the massacres that have raged almost without interruption for four decades are hemmed in by enemies and the few localities that they still defend are difficult of access. Should a rescuing force be sent for their protection, the losses would be heavy, and it is quite apparent that none of the Powers who promised protection and rehabilitation for these unfortunate people have stomach for any further expense or casualties.

Indeed, we are hearing with increasing frequency of another and, what seems to me, a most faint-hearted solution of the problem. It is to transfer the remnant of this unfortunate nation to the once Turkish province of Cilicia. These regions border on the eastern Mediterranean and the naval powers that rule the midland sea could extend protection. The Armenians do not wish to move. They prefer the mountains and the caves of their ancient territory which, as their delegates explain, they have defended against all comers for twenty-four hundred years.

There is another and, I fear, a more potent reason why this plan will not prosper. It is increasingly apparent that both France and Italy have other plans for Cilicia. They do not harmonize with the new doctrine of self-determination and the rights of people to control their destiny. These plans clearly reveal a relapse into the practices of imperialism that brought about the present world disaster. And Cilicia? Well, we can find it on the map, but further than that even the most voluble of the ethnic experts maintain a discreet silence. I have a vague idea it is the country which Cicero, as pro-consul, looted so that he might have the means to build his villas and his fish ponds and where he received those charming gossipy letters with which his good friend Atticus enlivened his months of exile from Rome.

March 10, 1919

The Colonel is willing—indeed more than willing, he is *eager*—to accept our share of responsibility for the Armenian settlement, but he is not willing to go into it with our eyes shut. He has noted the increasing reluctance of our people to shoulder European responsibilities, and he is particularly averse to going into an Asiatic adventure which may lead us we know not whither. The problem has been with us for years, long before the outbreak of the war, but whenever it reaches the agenda it is sidetracked and placed in cold storage, where I fear it is likely to remain for a long time, if not forever.

March 9, 1919

While the President was in America and House was taking his place at the meetings of the Supreme Council on March 7, Lloyd George and Clemenceau formally raised the question of the future of Armenia and the disposition of the Rhinelands. House made immediately a report by cable to the President in Washington. He said: "In discussing the dismemberment of the Turkish Empire both George and Clemenceau expressed the wish that we accept mandates for Armenia and for Constantinople."

In his cabled reply, the President instructed House as follows: "I hope you will not even provisionally consent to the separation of the Rhenish Provinces from Germany under any arrangement but will reserve the whole matter until my arrival."

There was not a word about Armenia, which seemed ominous to me. It was clear that House could do nothing until the President returned or until explicit instructions came. It was equally clear, however, that, rightly or wrongly, both the French and the British expect the initiative in the Armenian settlement to be taken by him. Of course, the President went very far in this matter in the Fourteen Points, so far that I do not see how he can draw back, but at the same time it would be manifestly unfair to saddle America with the exclusive responsibility.

March 18, 1919

The President has ordered a report on Armenia—another! And I am it! He asks that Lord Bryce be consulted (that indeed will be easy, as this interesting old Scot practically "parks" in our office). But, says the President, the data which he (His Lordship) submits must be carefully "tested." My main difficulty with His Lordship is to keep him from dragging in Bulgaria—as he admits, the peasant state is a hobby of his—and then of bringing him up to date. He loves to linger on the days when the Mongols lorded it over ancient Armenia and he is fascinated by the problem which he says divides historians. Was Armenia a tributary to Parthia, or merely a client state?

When we get past this we are confronted with the difficulty of describing the geographic situation of Armenia today; and even as it was in the yesterday of the last century is not easy. How can we lay down these metes and bounds which Lord Bryce believes are about to be restored when there are discrepancies of hundreds of thousands of square miles between what might be called the actual frontiers and the traditional boundaries of this ancient people? However, Lord Bryce tells me, and incidentally he tells House, that the President and Lloyd George are in complete agreement that the state they are pledged to re-establish shall, in some way they do not more narrowly describe, extend from the Black Sea to the Mediterranean. How in these circumstances Anatolia is to be "secured and safeguarded" to the Turks, I have no idea and what is more important neither have they.

The Armenians have been "let down" so frequently by the Christian powers that it is amazing to me that they should have any confidence in our promises. Nevertheless they do. The explanation would seem to be found in the words of one ribald observer, "They would rather be crucified than circumcised."

Lord Bryce is strongly in favor of drawing the veil of charity over this story of continued bad faith, but I stand by my guns and insist that an intelligent solution is only possible if we face the facts honestly and squarely. By the treaty of San Stefano [March, 1878], which after their costly campaign the victorious Russians imposed upon the defeated Turks, an end of their long servitude was promised the Armenians. They were assured religious freedom, political autonomy, protection against the murderous Kurds, and all manner of reforms. And this was the only clause of the San Stefano treaty which survived the Congress of Berlin [June-July, 1878] that wiped out practically all the other achievements of the Russian victory and threw the Balkans and the Middle East back into anarchy. It may be recalled, although with blushes, that it was from this Congress that Disraeli returned to London with the announcement, "I have brought you peace with honor." * At any event, he brought Cyprus to the British Empire, doubtless as his brokerage fee.

By 1880 it was apparent that the clause in the treaty that safeguards the Armenians was a dead letter and that the six powers who signed the agreement and had accepted responsibility for its observance should do something; and indeed they did protest to Stamboul, but feebly. The Sublime Porte merely laughed its Jovelike laughter.

"Alexander II, the [Russian] emancipator of his serfs and the liberator of the Balkan peoples, was dead—murdered," explained Bryce. "He seems to have been the only steadfast friend of our unfortunate people. And his successor? He had troubles of his own at home and did nothing about it. Nobody did anything about it. Our job is to find another Alexander II," said Bryce.

"Do you see one on the horizon?"

"We have Lloyd George," and he smiled sadly. "And you have Wilson."

"But now that the war is over and a sort of peace is being arranged, our President is no longer an autocrat. The checks and balances of our system are coming to life again," I commented. "Wilson is no longer omnipotent."

Our memorandum went to the President through House. What became of it? I have no idea.

---

* Neville Chamberlain used these very words on *his* return from Germany. How quickly the facts of history are forgotten, especially when disgraceful.

May 2, 1919

Colonel House told me that the President had decided to send a fact-finding mission to Armenia and he will ask General Pershing to designate a competent officer to head it. He will publish the report and then await popular reaction at home on its findings. Poor Nubar! Poor Aharonian! Unfortunate Armenians! Our promises are out the window, and the reconstituted Armenian state has not a Chinaman's chance.

[In *April, 1920,* the Supreme Council of the Allies, seated still in Paris (the qualifying epithet "War" had been dropped), returned to the charge and formally requested that the United States assume the mandate over Armenia. No attempt was made to describe the geographical limits of what had become a phantom state or the exact whereabouts of these unfortunate people, and Congress took no action in the matter.]

Washington, January, 1922

Thanks to information received from the Honorable Carter Glass, Secretary of the Treasury under the War President, I am able to say that, unlike many who sponsored Armenia at the Peace Conference, Mr. Wilson, at least, stood by his guns. It was our misfortune and not his fault that later these guns did not carry the heavy metal they fired in 1918, when the Fourteen Points promised to a distracted world a new freedom.

An hour or two before leaving for the San Francisco Democratic National Convention (1920) Mr. Glass, who was also mentioned as a candidate for the Democratic nomination, an honor which he sought to avoid, called at the White House to ascertain the President's wishes and hopes as to the party's standard-bearer. Right out of the box the President said: "The nomination of Cox would be a joke."—"To which I fervently assented," comments Glass.

As Glass was leaving, the President said, handing him a slip of paper, "I wish you would get this into the platform." On the train, the senator from Virginia told me, "I read the paper and found it to be a declaration for an Armenian mandate to be assumed by the United States." Written by the President himself on his typewriter and initialed, "W. W.," the suggested plank read:

"We hold it to be the Christian duty and privilege of our Government to assume the responsible guardianship of Armenia, which now needs only the advice and assurance of a powerful friend to establish her complete independence and to give her distracted people the opportunities for peaceful happiness which they have vainly sought for through so many dark years of suffering and hideous distress."

This was hardly a clarion note, but when it came back from the drafting committee, largely through the opposition of Senator Walsh of Montana, it sounded like the squeak of a penny whistle. As placed in the platform, the President's resolution reads:

"We express our deep and earnest sympathy for the unfortunate people of Armenia, and we believe that our Government, consistent with its Constitution and principles, should render every possible and proper aid to them in their efforts to establish and maintain a government of their own."

After a bitter struggle in the committee Glass secured the approval of the Treaty and the Covenant that is written in the party platform; but, as he admits, the opposition to the President's original Armenia policy was overwhelming.

January, 1924

Here is the sequel to this episode which, though tempted, I cannot suppress. General Harbord and his associates made a very intelligent report upon the Armenian problem, but there was no perceptible reaction to it in America or anywhere else. A vague, face-saving clause was inserted in the Versailles Treaty, but it never became operative. It read: "An area to be delimited by the President of the United States is to be given to the Armenians," doubtless for the purpose of "constituting their free State."

The Treaty of Sèvres [1920], with a similar provision, was signed by the then puppet Sultan of the Turks, but Mustapha Kemal rebelled, the Sultan was forced into exile, and the treaty was never ratified. America washed, or tried to wash, her hands of the whole miserable business.

After their crushing defeat by the Turks at Marash early in 1920, the French contented themselves with merely holding on to Syria, which, however, proved to be quite a handful. Kemal, with his reorganized army, was soon in complete control of the situation as a direct result of secret alliances which flowed from the conference which was to put an end to all of them. The Turks attacked the Armenians from the west while the Soviets attacked from the east. Capturing Erivan, the Russians set up a government of Armenian Bolsheviki, and although Lenin had proclaimed the independence of the Armenian lands, Moscow came to terms with the new war lord by ceding to Turkey all the territory that had belonged to her in 1914, plus the district of Kars, which had been annexed by Russia in 1878. The Turks enlarged their frontiers on the east and Lloyd George's and President Wilson's Armenia vanished into thin air.

The Treaty of Lausanne, signed in July, 1923, consecrated the Turkish triumph, and the general cancellation of the peace treaties got under way. Lloyd George called this document "an abject, cowardly, and infamous surrender," and while he himself was not without guilt, the little Welshman was quite right. It may be a redeeming feature of the situation to admit that but few of the Armenians were returned to Turkish slavery. For the most part they had died in battle, or more miserably in concentration camps and in enforced exile. Few indeed survived to realize how mistaken they had been to believe that the civilized world and the churches of Christ would not abandon them to destruction at the hands of their traditional oppressors.

All that remains of the Armenia that the British government promised in 1916 to establish and of which Mr. Wilson dreamed in 1918—the Armenian State extending from Batoum to Baku, from the Black Sea to the Caspian—is a small district around Erivan, and even that today is in the hands of a gang of Armenian Communists subsidized and under the control of Lenin. The high hopes with which the Armenians threw themselves into the war and with which they came to the Conference resulted in disaster, indeed in one of the outstanding failures of the Conference. There are some who take comfort in the thought that another little war was avoided by the complete abandonment of the fragment of the Armenian people who still survived. This is perhaps true, but what a price has been paid! In the future, who will place any reliance on the given word of the civilized nations or in their solemn covenant to save the weak from the criminal aggressor?

* * * *

March—undated, 1919

As a relief to the tragic history of his unfortunate people, Nubar told me last evening a story which ranks with that of Queen Marie Antoinette's necklace and its disappearance, out of which so many mystery yarns have been spun. However, from this incident far-reaching political repercussions are not likely to flow, thanks to the prestige of his powerful father, the great Nubar.

When but a boy, in 1869, the young Nubar participated in all the fêtes with which the Suez Canal was opened and the so-called marriage of the Mediterranean and the Red Sea was celebrated. The announced purpose of the great work was "to spread civilization, expand commerce, and end wars," and consequently all the great ones of the earth were invited to be present. Among those who came in an official capacity were the Earl of Dudley and his wife, whose stately beauty was still remembered when a generation later I lived in London. They came as the favored guests of Khedive Ismail, the great spendthrift and connoisseur of female beauty.

As always when she traveled abroad, Lady Dudley left her famous pearl necklace in the vault of her London bank, only bringing with her reproductions of this and other famous jewels. While away on an excursion to the Fayoum, the necklace disappeared, and before the return of her ladyship the frantic maid called in the police, who immediately ransacked Cairo in search of the precious ornaments and the thief. Also Lady Dudley found awaiting her the secretary of Ismail, who assured her that if not recovered the Khedive would replace the necklace and send it to her with his compliments and his apologies. This placed the Dudleys in a quandary. It was, of course, impossible to admit to Ismail that they had come to his resplendent court and attended a function that would become historic, like the meeting on the Cloth of Gold, with false jewels. No, that could never be. Finally they hit upon a plan. They would on their return to London rediscover the real jewels, advise the Khedive of their find, and beg his pardon for all the trouble that had been caused by the flighty maid, who had failed to bring the necklace to Egypt in the first place.

In the meantime the Khedive, greatly mortified and chagrined at what apparently had happened, sent his secretary to Paris with the commission to duplicate the jewels, whatever the cost.

"Ismail was unfortunate in the choice of his secretary," continued Nubar, "as in many other respects. This fellow was a Turk and not a reliable Armenian or even a Greek as he should have been. This scoundrel came to terms with a famous jeweler who had seen and was perfectly familiar with the Dudley necklace and agreed in a little time to reproduce it for forty thousand pounds. 'Let us say fifty,' whispered the secretary, 'and it is a bargain.'

"While the pearls were being assembled, the secretary got in touch with a Palais Royal merchant, expert in such matters, and had a duplicate made which in due season he sent to the Dudleys in London with the compliments of the Khedive. For some days the Dudleys could neither sleep nor eat. What was to be done? What could they do? In a few days, however, they were delivered from their dilemma. They had the necklace "veted" by their jeweler, who reported that it was a reproduction and not a very good one at that. So Lady Dudley sat down and sent a charming perfumed note to Ismail, assuring him of her eternal gratitude. How magnificently wonderful he had been! There the matter ended as far as she was concerned. The faked necklace had been replaced by a reproduction that was nearly, if not quite, as satisfactory.

"The real necklace, which cost Ismail fifty thousand pounds, was deposited in an Amsterdam bank and the wily secretary returned to Cairo with ten thousand pounds pocket money. Poor Ismail showed him the grateful letter he had received from Lady Dudley and congratulated him upon the skillful way in which he had accomplished his delicate mission. In a few days the secretary pretended to fall ill and had himself ordered to a German spa. But he never went there. Instead he turned up in Amsterdam, reclaimed the necklace, sold some of the pearls, and pocketed the rest."

"And then?" I inquired.

"Then he demonstrated once again that patriotism is the last resort of a scoundrel," said Nubar. "He had heard that some of his cousins, the Turki of Turkestan, had risen against the Russians. He joined them and was killed in the first battle. The jewels, found in his pocket, were turned over to General Skobeleff who commanded the Russians, and he, when he returned to Moscow, gave them to a song bird in one of the cafés who enjoyed his favor."

"And where do you think they are now?"

"I do not know, but I have an idea. Probably the Queen of the

Bolsheviki is wearing them, or, like the thirty pieces of silver which Judas garnered by his treachery, they have just naturally gravitated toward the Soviet treasury."

I should perhaps add that Nubar's opinion of the Lenin crusade is absolutely unprintable.

CHAPTER XIII

Little Denmark Poses a World Problem

December 26, 1918

Pierre Quirielle and several other editors of the *Temps* took me this afternoon to a meeting of the Schleswig Danes in a *salle* of the *Deux Magots* where I found assembled all or nearly all the shepherds of the submerged nationalities. Steed, foreign editor of the London *Times,* was there and was enthusiastically acclaimed when he said that the failure of England in 1864 to prevent the annexation of Schleswig by Germany was directly responsible for the rape of Alsace-Lorraine in 1871. The first Danish speaker asserted that for a time his people had been confident that the great wrong done them by the Prussians would be righted, honorably and without the shedding of blood. "But after Alsace we knew we were in for a long wait, that only a European convulsion would free us."

He was followed by another young Dane who was introduced as the unofficial envoy of the Schleswig-Holsteiners whose name it was not wise to disclose, his family being still in the clutches of the German invaders. "You must not blame us," he protested, "for our neutral attitude during the hostilities. You should recognize how powerless we were, how close to the claws of the German Beast. Our hatred of him goes back to the Middle Ages and beyond. The legend and the prayer that was inscribed in those days on the golden arrow of the Flensborg Cathedral reads 'Lord, protect us from the German Beast who would devour the world.' That prayer was placed there more than three hundred years ago by a patriotic Dane. For long it was unheeded, but now all the world knows that these are true words."

Another member of the committee insisted that language is not a true test of nationality. In his "circle" (neighborhood) he stated many people spoke German as their *umgangssprache*—their everyday speech—who were Danish in blood, in sentiment, and in aspirations. He went on to say: "The children are made to speak German by the carpetbag schoolteachers who are quartered on us, but whenever they can the children twist the words that are put into their mouths. They are commanded to sing

> *Ich bin ein Preuss*
> *Bin froh ein Preuss su Sein.*

But what they really say is

> *Ich bin kein Preuss*
> *Bin froh kein Preuss su Sein.*

He went on to say, "We were promised and indeed for a time received some protection for our language and our schools under Clause 5 of the Treaty of Prague, which Napoleon III insisted upon; but when he fell, and even before, it was ignored and the German wolves, false to their promises, as they always are, sought to devour us."

Several Danes who had been pressed into the German Army now mounted the platform and told how at the earliest opportunity they had passed over to the French, how at first they had been regarded by the Germans with suspicion, which was natural, but how later they had been allowed to fight in the first-line trenches, a dangerous favor which, however, gave them the chance to escape their drillmasters.

The Danish minister to France presided and smiled approval at those who were the most outspoken in their denunciation of the imposed German regime. But for himself he never said a word. So when he called upon me for a few remarks, a message from America, I said I would follow his example—that I too had come to listen, to learn, not to talk.

January 10, 1919

My presence at the Danish meeting has brought me many visitors and I find them without exception charming people. They understand that while the Schleswig problem bulks large with them, it is not a major problem (or at least is not so regarded by many of the delegates); that they must halt at my desk and for the present cannot hope to penetrate into the inner sanctum where the Colonel presides and the major discussions are held. Undoubtedly they have had a hard time during the war years, and they think, doubtless correctly, that their sufferings have been little noted in the outside world. They argue that the Great Powers take a superficial view of their peace and war activities and they insist that they deserve something better than the fame so generally given them as very successful butter and egg merchants. I agree that customers are ungrateful, and they warm up to my memories of the beautiful girls and the handsome dogs I admired in Copenhagen in the tranquil days of long ago.

It was on November 28 that the Danes formally presented themselves and filed a bill of particulars setting forth their grievances and their claims. It is a lengthy document and goes back to the Middle Ages. It is too discursive. I think the Conference will not go back farther than the nineteenth century.

From the very beginning of what is called in all the diplomatic anthologies "the Schleswig-Holstein question," Bismarck appears as the master mind. He knew what he wanted and what he meant to get. He may have expressed an academic interest in the discussion through long decades as to the intricacies of the Augustenburg-Sonderheim-Holstein line and who was and who was not the legitimate Stamm-Herr of the dynasty; one of the pretenders, indeed, he put out of the running with a money payment, a big round sum which must have shocked his colleagues who believed in *"Preussiche Sparsamkeit."* But, it is clear that throughout the discussions and the interminable negotiations he kept his eyes on the ball and in his garrulous old age he set down in his *Reflections* with the frankness which Theodore Roosevelt later emulated ("I took the Isthmus") these words: "From the beginning I kept annexation steadily before my eyes." Indeed, from the very beginning he had his plan for the Kiel Canal and fully appreciated the advantages that would accrue to a war-waging Germany through this unhindered outlet to the Atlantic world and beyond.

Tiring of negotiations which only cloaked his real purpose, Bismarck sent his goose-stepping Prussians over the border and the stout resistance of the Danes was overwhelmed on the bloody field of Duppel in 1864. Austria as the "brilliant second" tagged along, but naturally enough she was overlooked when the booty was distributed. M. Cambon, the French delegate, loses his diplomatic calm as he describes how Napoleon III by his silence gave his consent to this aggression and how Queen Victoria, infatuated with the cousins of her beloved Albert, turned a deaf ear to the suggestions of her wise ministers. "Napoleon at least had an idea," explains Cambon. "He saw that, given the ocean frontage and the naval bases, the brigands might develop into a sea power capable of balancing if not of disputing Britannia's supremacy of the seas. While shortsighted, how right Napoleon was. At Jutland it proved to be a very near thing."

Cambon is more outspoken than any of the other delegates in favor of restoring the stolen territory to the Danes—but he admits he is talking to deaf ears. He holds that the international control of the Kiel Canal is necessary to future peace and tranquillity, of which we are all in such great need. "But do not misunderstand me. I would not 'bilk' the Germans; I would credit the amount they spent in building the canal to our reparation bill. It would prove, I think, the only substantial payment we are at all likely to receive, and that as it were by indirection." More, perhaps, than anyone else Cambon is pessimistic as to the future of reparation payments.

April 26, 1919

While I am frequently told that I exaggerate its importance, that the future of Schleswig and above all the canal is a local problem and one that should be left to the Danes to cope with, I persist in thinking that its future is vital to the peace of Europe and indeed to world security. The Kiel Canal and the surrounding districts that control it should be returned to the Danes from whom the land was stolen in 1866 and their possession of it should be guaranteed by the Powers. Clearly, like Alsace which is to be returned to its rightful sovereignty, the canal and the southern district of Schleswig is a tempting springboard of invasion. It should not be left in the possession of men who are pirates on land as well as on the seas.

But I must admit that many of the Danes here, notably their minister to France, M. Bernhoft, who is their principal delegate, are not ardent supporters of this plan, at least not without certain reservations and conditions. Today the minister called and these are some of the things he said:

"Undoubtedly in 1866 the population of these regions was largely, perhaps overwhelmingly, Danish. Certainly our claim is more fully justified than the claim so often advanced that the population of Alsace in 1871 was exclusively French. The region where the canal was built, and its advanced post and sentinel, the island of Heligoland, had been under our sovereignty (although England seized it a century ago) for many generations, and the people were contented with our rule.

"But we should not lose sight of the actual situation today. Our people have been expelled from the annexed territory in great numbers and others have left of their own accord. As a result, it cannot be denied that the racial complexion of South Schleswig has undergone a radical change in the last sixty years. The prolific Germans have come in in large numbers and the few Danes who remained on their ancestral farms have suffered great hardships. Perhaps another complication of the situation is that many of the inhabitants today who are really Danes, for self-protection pretend to be of German stock; but be this as it may, many, very many Germans are there. We know we cannot assimilate them and most certainly we do not want them within our territory. The Germans outside our frontiers give us trouble enough. We have no desire to come in closer contact. That would be disagreeable for us and undoubtedly most unwelcome to them."

December—undated, 1920

The plebiscites in the disputed districts of Schleswig, which Bismarck promised by the Treaty of Prague as long ago as 1866, were carried out by the victorious Allies in the spring of 1920 after a moratorium of more than fifty years, and apparently with a minimum of rioting and disorder. They were divided into three zones and separate elections were ordered held in each of them. The northern zone voted almost unanimously to return to Denmark, the mother country. The vote in the middle zone revealed a large and very vocal German population in favor of remaining with the Vaterland; in the third zone, which commands the Kiel Canal and the new German naval bases, the recent German colonists or settlers were clearly in an overwhelming majority and so no election was held. The Danes might have claimed both these districts but they let them go, and probably they know what is best—at least for their domestic peace.

When in 1866 this territory was annexed by Berlin in its early predatory mood the inhabitants were Danish, but effective measures were taken to move them out. Many indeed left willingly, but those who clung to their old homes and what they call their "ancestral farms" were soon forced out. Even before the recent "free and fair" elections were held, and most observers agree that they were both, two at least of the Danish delegation told me that they would not be sticklers for their historic rights. The river Eder may have been the racial frontier one hundred years ago but they said, "We face quite a different situation today, and frankly we do not want any districts that reveal a large and vocal minority of Germans. We want none of them within our borders. Our kinsmen who have been submerged by the influx of the prolific invaders may return to their mother country and we will welcome them with open arms. The presence of even a German minority within our borders would mean chronic agitation, later perhaps civil war, and then probably another European conflagration."

Doubtless from the domestic standpoint of the Danes this moderation was wise, but for the future peace of Europe I fear it is disastrous.

December 4, 1943

This tactful behavior, however, did not save the Danes from the midnight aggression which they suffered in the midst of World War II. Once again the Germans showed they had not changed their spots. They were still the wild beasts of the prophecy inscribed on the church tower of Flensborg four hundred years ago. The Kiel Canal and the districts that command it consequently remained in German control. It should of course have been returned to the Danes from whom it was taken by right of conquest as was Alsace from the defeated French. The result of this shortsighted policy is glaringly apparent today. If, as many assumed in 1919, the Danes did not want to take on this responsibility unless a police force under the League of Nations was established, the canal should have been internationalized. I and a few others, notably M. Cambon, the French delegate, at the time were in favor of ousting the Germans from the canal but at the same time of repaying them the construction costs. One of the admirable features of this plan was that it would not have cost the civilized nations a penny nor would it have enriched the robbers by a farthing. It should have been credited, as M. Cambon suggested, to the Germans as a payment on the reparations account, perhaps the only substantial payment they were ever to make.

Another flagrant omission from the Treaty of Versailles was the fact that Heligoland remained in the possession of the Germans. It should be recalled that, as an appeasement gesture in the nineties of the last century, it was ceded to the Berlin government by Lord Salisbury. There was some talk at the time that the Hamburgers wished to make of this mist-ridden island an international bathing beach. It was a graceful gesture, but it failed signally of its purpose. Had His Lordship suffered from an uneasy conscience, the island should have been restored to the Danes from whom it was rudely taken about 1810 when the English admirals were on the prowl for desirable naval bases. Once in their possession, the island, sought as a bathing beach in which all trippers were to disport themselves, was converted by the Germans into a military zone, and in a very short time it became the Gibraltar of the North Sea.

According to the Treaty (1919) these fortifications were condemned and the island demilitarized. But was it? I do not know the answer to this one. The control commissions may have reported what was done, and the Great Powers who were pledged to see that the treaty was carried out may have told their agents not to bother them with their disturbing reports. I do know this was the reception that was given by them to many other reports demonstrating that military and naval clauses in the treaty were honored in the breach but not in observance. But one thing is crystal clear: demilitarized or in the full panoply of its armor, the lonely island jutting out into the North Sea and protecting the entrance to the canal and threatening the insular security of Britain was a great asset to the Germans when once again they went on the rampage. It is a safe harbor for the sinister submarines and the piratical cruisers which, in the early stages of the war, ravaged the seas where once, in war as in peace, civilized practices were observed. When the conference assembles that will terminate this war and prevent the possible outbreak of others in the years to come, it is to be hoped that the canal and the island fortress will be placed in safe hands and not filed away in the dormant files of the United Nations as "unfinished business."

Today I am not alone in thinking that in the face of this and other problems presented at Paris we were infatuated with formulas and disregarded realities. It would have been wiser to have returned the Schleswig districts to their legitimate owners after cleansing them of the alien intruders. This would have entailed some hardship and a few, a very few, decent people would have suffered. But it is a solution, perhaps the only one, to the problem of mixed nationalities who cannot or will not live together as good neighbors. Today it is quite plain that, had this course been pursued, a more stable peace would have resulted than has followed upon the lame plebiscite.

Some thought at the time, and more are convinced now, that plebiscites do not always reveal true conditions and even less that they are an infallible corrective to domestic and international ills. A few days after the orderly proceedings in Schleswig, which I did not witness, I was informed by some observers who were present that the vote was not indicative of the thought and the real wishes of the electorate. Information came to me from sources I regarded as reliable and unprejudiced that many Germans, masquerading as Danes, voted in favor of the return of the districts where they were intruders so that they might escape the heavy taxes which the Weimar government would have to exact to meet the reparation bill and the other imposts which the new people would have to impose if they were to survive. It was also maintained that these Germans masquerading as Danes reserved to themselves the right to show their true colors when the favorable moment struck. No one who is at all conversant with what has happened in the disputed districts since the Prussians marched back in 1941 can deny that these gloomy prophecies were without foundation in fact.

The lesson is that plebiscites are prickly functions and do not always work out as they should. While in 1920 there may have been something "rotten in Denmark," yet even with us, the traditional home of the free and fair election panacea, the results are often disappointing—even at times amazing. The crux of the difficulty seems to be that it is difficult for the voters to concentrate on the main issue and not to be diverted from it by side questions or by personal prejudices. Even with us and with an electorate which we admit is far above the average, here in the land where free and fair elections are sacrosanct, they have been known to result in a fiasco although the expression 'in a national disgrace" would seem more fitting.

Let us look at what happened in our own fair land only a few months later in the same year. Let us recall the words with which, on Jackson Day (January 8, 1920), President Wilson, pointing out the anarchic conditions that prevailed throughout the world, called upon our people through the medium of a solemn referendum to take a stand for righteousness. His trumpet note was: "We must give the next election the form of a great and solemn referendum. A referendum as to the part the United States is to play in completing the settlement of the war and in the prevention in the future of such outrages as Germany attempted to perpetrate."

How little heed was given to this solemn warning—this call to the plain path of duty! By overwhelming majorities the electorate voted for Mr. Harding, not knowing what he had in mind—little caring that, as was obvious, he had nothing in mind. The solemn referendum came to this ridiculous and distinctly discreditable conclusion because, for three years, the voters had been inconvenienced by war conditions—by what in those soft Arcadian days were regarded as hardships—and they turned out in millions to get away from what they had endured, to give the bewildered manikin who preached "a return to normalcy" an overwhelming majority.

Of course the false Danes, the true-blue Germans in Schleswig, were actuated by very different motives. Looking forward to the day when it would be safe for them to show their true colors, they avoided the immediate hardships they saw were awaiting them in the war-torn Reich. When the Prussians came back in 1941 they shouted with joy in many districts. It is true their days of jubilation have been few, but it must be confessed that these clandestine Nazis who masqueraded as true Danes have played a sad role in the army of occupation

CHAPTER XIV

Rhineland Difficulties

December 29, 1918

Yesterday Clemenceau came in for what he called a friendly informal talk. Both he and the Colonel asked me to stay, "to keep us old fellows from straying too far afield" was the way the Tiger put it. He began by explaining the expression of *noble candeur* as applied to the President in his recent speech in the Chamber, to which many ascribe an offensive meaning.

"Nothing was farther from my thoughts than that," explained the Tiger; "I used the words in their English sense. I was applauding his frankness and his loyalty of spirit, but at the same time I wished to utter a word of warning because we are both in a difficult situation and naturally and inevitably we shall view it from different standpoints."

Then turning to House: "Let us survey the scene calmly and deliberately, my dear friend, before the battle begins. America is far away, but we are near to the ravening wolves. America came and saved us, but still you remain far away, and while you were coming think of what we suffered! Our homes and our fields have been ravaged and our mines destroyed. Don't take this as a formal statement, much less a protest. I am simply a tired old man thinking aloud. We are reviving after a world disaster. We in Paris placed our faith in the balance of power and in strong frontiers. Well, as the event has proved, our frontiers were not solid and the political arrangements—well, they were in unbalance. In view of the disaster that followed many today condemn the old system and President

Wilson is their prophet. He and he alone can lead us into the pastures of peace and plenty, we are told. Now I admit I am, even in view of the disaster that has involved us all, still a partisan of the old system, at least until something better is offered and, note this, *has been tested by experience*. I am not an opponent of the proposed League of Nations. Gladly I accept it as a supplementary guarantee, but for today we must have something more practical, something that has been through the furnace of war, even if, as might well be the case, some of the tests have not turned out very successfully."

[I think this is the first indication that Clemenceau had in mind a joint agreement for the defense of the Rhine frontier.]

March 11, 1919

The problem of the Rhine is now the order of the day. Tardieu came in this morning and had a long talk with the Colonel who asked me to be present and, when he left, to draw up a memo of what was said. He admitted that by the Armistice arrangements the Fourteen Points had become binding on France, but he asserted they should be interpreted in the light of what he called "antecedent circumstances." He went into what he called the *historique* of the Rhine problem for the purpose of showing that the present demand for a rearrangement of the frontier had always been a principal war aim of France. He brought with him documents to prove that the question had been taken up with some of the Allies in January, 1917, three months before we entered the war, and that at least with Russia an agreement had been reached. At this time Briand, who was Prime Minister, had instructed the French Ambassador in St. Petersburg to advise the Russian government that in view of the fact that her vital interests were involved France must be allowed a preponderant influence in the adjustment of the Rhine frontier. "In the future," ran this communication, "Germany must not be allowed to touch the Rhine or to secure positions near by which would facilitate future aggression."

Tardieu also revealed a communication which at the same time was sent by his Foreign Office to Ambassador Paul Cambon in London. In it Cambon was instructed to feel out Britain as to the best methods of securing the independence of the Rhine provinces or, in any event, of shielding them from Prussian contact and influence.

However, as the instruction revealed, leeway was granted Cambon as to when and how he should broach the subject. He was not to introduce it if in his judgment it would lead to discord between the principal allies or even to discussion. A few days later the Briand ministry fell and the instruction was not renewed.

But with Russia the negotiations went much farther. M. Doumergue was sent to St. Petersburg with a letter from the President of the Republic to his great and good friend the Tsar in which once again it was affirmed that both Britain and France had agreed to give Constantinople to Russia and also some territory in Thrace that was to be taken away from ungrateful Bulgaria. M. Doumergue brought back from St. Petersburg his *quid pro quo*. The Tsar agreed to support whatever decision France might make as to the future of the Rhine.

"It was not intended to keep these arrangements secret," explained Tardieu. "On the contrary it was planned to publish them *urbe et orbe* at a favorable moment, for instance, when the expected success of the Nivelle offensive was apparent. Indeed a secondary instruction went to Paul Cambon in London advising him that in the opinion of the French government this would be the appropriate moment to inform London of its views, indeed of its decision. But unfortunately Nivelle was not successful and on March 12, 1917, the Tsar was overthrown and all the papers dealing with the matter went into the waiting but certainly not into the "dead" files. So we admit that when Lloyd George came to Paris he was not bound by treaty, open or secret, to any territorial arrangements with France except in regard to Turkey in Asia and also unfortunately on the Adriatic."

Two days later Jules Cambon came in on what the Colonel called a "follow-up" mission. He is an ardent partisan of a division of Germany into what he calls "its component parts." "We must separate the sheep from the goats," he said; "the good Bavarians from the stiff-necked, impossible Prussians. Otherwise there will never be peace on our frontier or for that matter in Europe." His argument is as follows:

"It was the wicked treaty imposed by our conquerors in 1815 that put Prussia on the Rhine. Who can deny that from that sad day to 1870 the inhabitants of these stolen regions have regarded themselves as the unfortunate victims of a detestable diplomatic combination? I hope the right of self-determination will be granted to these people and that in any event the dominance of Prussia will be terminated. Among the Germans, Prussian influence will always be great, perhaps controlling, and this danger must be removed from our frontier as far as possible.

"I cannot see," continued Cambon, "how our plan runs counter to the humanitarian ideals of your great President, and I even think it will find favor in many liberal circles in Germany and perhaps secure the support of some Prussians who must be tired of the recurrent and fruitless wars to which this unsettled frontier condemns them."

The Colonel spends much time reading and pondering over these memoranda. Today he said, "I do not have to tell you that this is 'graveyard stuff.' France won the battle of the Marne and the struggle for Verdun, but now the Battle for the Rhine looms on our dark horizon. How will it end? I confess I do not know."

February 27, 1919

Much to our surprise Clemenceau, unannounced, dropped in on House this morning. He looked rather shaky (he had been shot on the nineteenth) but was in fine spirits. "I have come to pay homage to the American delegation on the birthday of our joint father, the immortal George. Of course I had planned to come on the twenty-second, that is a date I shall never forget, but was prevented by an 'unpleasant incident over which the police had no control.'"

The Tiger was in a rollicking humor and gave amusing accounts of the birthday celebrations in which he had participated during his happy years of exile, as he called them, in New York, in Rochester, and in Stamford. Then he grew serious and the real purpose of his call was revealed.

"My dear House, during many sleepless nights I have cudgeled my brains, what is left of them, for a substitute policy that would be more palatable to Wilson and to you, but I can't find it. There is no other way to secure the security of France than by the annexation of the Rhine lands or the establishment of the Rhenish republic. Wilson told me he could not consider even for a moment direct annexation, so I have come to tell you that after due consideration the French government will insist upon the creation of the Rhenish republic. Those lands furnish easy access to the very heart of France, access that has been availed of so frequently in the past, as the

Prussian invasions of our country during the last hundred years reveal. The keys to France must be in the custody of Frenchmen. I am sorry we cannot accept the American view. We probably would had we enjoyed the same pleasant neighbors as you have during your national existence, but unfortunately we have been up against quite a different breed."

March 28, 1919

The last ten have been crucial days and at times the outlook for the long-sought world settlement has been none too bright. It is most unfortunate that the French and the Italian delegates should be so well informed as to Wilson's increasing difficulties with the Senate and the insistent, indeed the imperative demand that has been served on him in Washington as to the necessity of making a hard and fast reservation in regard to the Monroe Doctrine. At times it has looked as though the Isolationists, far from awaiting the ratification battle at home, have succeeded in choking the Covenant while still in the cradle over here. At the very first meeting of the chief delegates after Wilson's return to Paris (March 14), as is his habit the Tiger placed his cards face up on the table. He told his listeners, who simulated surprise, that unless he secured some hold on the Saar and at least a fairly defensible position on the Rhine he did not think he could present the Treaty for ratification and that if he did he was quite certain that in its present mood the Senate and the Chamber would not ratify it.

The issue was now clearly defined, as Lloyd George and the President were in agreement that they could not accept either the Foch or the Tardieu plan for a solution of these problems. While they differ as to terms, both of these plans aim at a permanent occupation of these frontier districts by Allied forces, a commitment which neither Britain nor America is willing to assume.

It looked as though a stalemate was impending and it must be admitted that it was the resourceful little Welshman who broke it. First he sounded out House with, "I confess I find it natural and even reasonable that France should ask for protective guarantees; in the last fifty years she has been twice invaded by Germany, and it is clear to me why she has been attacked. France is the guardian of democratic civilization on the Continent; she is our bulwark against

Central European autocracy." When this had sunk in, George continued, "Until the League has proved its strength we must stand by France in case of invasion and we must make public announcement of our decision in this regard."

Whatever his real feelings may have been, for some days Clemenceau demurred and talked of counter, more concrete, proposals. Finally, however, he weakened somewhat but insisted upon the temporary occupation of the Rhine bridgeheads by Allied troops, "until the League is seasoned—until it has proved its metal." This is the genesis, in a few words, of the Rhine agreement about which much ink is being spilled and many ponderous tomes are bound to be written.* As none of the parties to it are jubilant, it is probably an excellent settlement. In any event, the deadlock is broken and the other problems will now be taken up. Grudgingly rather than enthusiastically Clemenceau admits that with this guarantee he can steer the Treaty through the chambers, but he asks House, "Can George and Wilson get it through their parliaments?" Clemenceau is well aware how reluctant these bodies are to overseas commitments and responsibilities to be automatically assumed at some future time under circumstances which no one can foresee. House reassures him. He is confident that once the President takes the stump and explains his difficulties and his purpose the American people will stand behind him enthusiastically.

[Under these circumstances, which were clearly beyond his control, the President signed the Rhine agreement. But in view of the hostile reception that the treaty received on its publication in America, he delayed presenting the protocol of the agreement to the Senate. His failure to do so released Britain from its adherence to the agreement, which it only consented to assume in case the resulting responsibility was also shouldered by America. This is the basis of Franklin Bouillon's claim that the ratification of the treaty by the Chamber was secured through misleading and even false representations. To me and to others Clemenceau flatly denied that this was

---

* The basis of the Rhine agreement was: The left bank of the Rhine remained German, was demilitarized "forever," and was to be occupied by Allied troops in three zones for fifteen years, if Germany faithfully carried out all the conditions of the peace. France had allowed the Rhineland to remain under German civil rule on the understanding that England and the United States would sign with her a pact of guarantee, a protocol against German aggression. As the United States refused to ratify it, this guarantee never came into being.

the case. He stated that both before and when signing the protocol, Wilson had told him that the agreement would require the sanction of the Senate; that he hoped to obtain this but could not guarantee it.

In *July, 1920*, in Paris, I discussed the matter with M. Tardieu and he confirmed the information and the impressions I have given above. "Of course the charges of bad faith against Wilson made in some of our papers are absurd and absolutely without foundation, but the unfortunate fact remains that France is left 'holding the bag.' I am not so sure of the good faith of Lloyd George. Why should he have made the assistance of Britain contingent upon the ratification of the pact by Washington? I think that at the time he felt this would be regarded as an entangling alliance by many of your senators, and in consequence be rejected. He saw to it that in this event Britain would be free to act or to stand aside, as she desired. The result is, we think, that the way is left open for future aggressions on the part of Germany. I trust we are mistaken, but we must prepare for such an eventuality, and of course that is a heavy burden on our financial resources and a lamentable conclusion to our war effort. As I recall the circumstances—correct me if I am mistaken—we met in Paris in 1919 to liberate the world from economic burdens as well as from the fear of the Barbarians." Tardieu is distressed and bitterly disappointed at the resulting situation, but he at least does not misrepresent how it came about, as do so many of his countrymen, and some of our own people. "We knew exactly what we were doing," he added. "Clemenceau thought, we all thought, that we should have the Rhineland to safeguard us from invasion. When Britain and America refused this safeguard, we accepted all we could get; that is, the pledge of assistance in case of invasion. We knew that such a pledge required parliamentary sanction in both countries, and while I fear we have been left 'holding the bag,' as you say in America, we were not hoodwinked."]

March 10, 1923

Once again the German propaganda machine is in full operation, and strange as it may seem its bare-faced lies and misrepresentations are carrying conviction in many quarters. The charge of bad faith is hurled at the Powers who signed the Versailles Treaty and, in view of their failure to evacuate the Rhinelands and the other occupied territories, the Germans claim that they are released from the obligations which they entered upon in "good faith." They chose to forget that as plainly stated in the Treaty none of these withdrawals were to be carried out unless the Germans had faithfully complied with all provisions of the Treaty. As a matter of fact, they have not carried out a single one of them or up to the present hour even made an attempt to do so.

[In 1936 Germany marched troops into the demilitarized zone amid feeble but ineffective protests from the League and world public opinion.]

CHAPTER XV

Korea: Once the Land of the Morning Calm

February 5, 1919

All is not quiet along the Seine tonight. Trouble is brewing and it comes from the experts of the Inquiry * who, to the number of two or three score, came over on the *George Washington* with the President determined to put the unruly peoples of Europe, Asia, and Africa in their proper places and make the world safe for democracy. They have served formal complaint to the effect that they are not in the close touch with the President, or with his lieutenant, House, to which they are entitled and the critical world situation demands. Since the day they had the privilege of holding "common council" with the chief of our delegation, our crusading President, on the voyage to France they complain that they have only had one conference with him and that it only lasted five minutes.

This morning, although it was raining cats and dogs, Mrs. House came into the office and said, "I wish you would take my lamb for a walk, under the colonnades of the rue de Rivoli so that he will not get wet to the skin, and tell him one of your stories about life in Korea, which amuse him so much. They must be nice people—at

---

* The Inquiry, organized in 1918 at the suggestion of Colonel House, was composed of men drawn largely from the universities who were informed as to the war aims and the problems that would have to be considered in shaping the peace. Dr. Bowman of Johns Hopkins was the executive officer and Walter Lippmann, the able journalist, acted as secretary. After the Armistice twenty-five members of the organization came to Paris with President Wilson on the *George Washington* and were given varied duties as here described.

least they are not here squabbling and raising 'foreign issues,' which are so perplexing."

This gave me my cue. Mercifully, however, I did not tell Mrs. House that while they had not, as yet, arrived, at least two Korean delegations were on their way to Paris with fully justified complaints against the arrogant Japanese supremacy under which they suffer.

In a few words the Colonel who now came in began to explain the quandary in which the President found himself. "The men of the Inquiry point out that at least once a week Lloyd George convokes the prime ministers from the Dominions, discusses with them the progress of the negotiations, and outlines his plans for the next stage. Why should the President not follow this example with the men of the Inquiry?

"I can only insist," continued the Colonel, "that the over-burdened President would like to do this but has not the time for these meetings in 'common council' of which he speaks so often but so rarely indulges in. But barring these conferences, everything possible has been done for the members of the Inquiry. For the most part they are lodged in the Crillon, they are close at hand for consultation, they have a spacious conference room where they get together to discuss the ever-changing situation, and their reports when they do arrive, not I think as promptly as we could wish, are carefully considered."

Here I thought to rush in with what I hoped would prove a consoling thought. "How natural it is," I argued, "that the men of the Inquiry do not understand what their function is. Like all of us they were totally unprepared for the unexpected war, and now they are taken by surprise, as we all are, by the sudden peace. We are still in the shirt-sleeved stage of our diplomacy. Now in Korea—" Here the Colonel pricked up his ears; "Tell me about that," he said eagerly.

"Well, in Korea," I went on, "while the government has not prospered, it has survived for hundreds of years and its leaders have learned to manage some things better than we do. For instance, in Seoul the high officials just naturally fall into two categories. One is that of the Mandarins-Help-Discuss, the other is that of the Mandarins-Help-Decide. When they are summoned to the palace, in a crown council over which the king presides, the Mandarins-Help-Discuss make the welkin ring with their varied plans and proposals for or against the solution of the pending problem that has been placed before them. In the meantime, the Mandarins-Help-Decide just sit in silence and listen and sweat. It would be a gross breach of etiquette for them to put in a word—even edgeways.

"When their voices have grown husky and their vocal chords are exhausted, the Mandarins-Help-Discuss announce that their last word has been spoken and with great ceremony they withdraw. These lucky fellows now go where their fancies lead them. Some to a monastery to reflect on the possibilities of the future life; others go to some pleasant mountain glade and enjoy a picnic with their lady friends leaving the Mandarins-Help-Decide in the council chamber to face the grim business of decision. If the men of the Inquiry could only be brought to appreciate how fortunate they are in being expected to function simply as Mandarins-Help-Discuss, everybody would be happier and things would move more smoothly. And," I added, "I certainly welcome the advantages of my Mandarin-Help-Discuss position."

The Colonel laughed and evidently told the story to the President for, several evenings later when I was interpreting for him at the Covenant Commission, and was in a decidedly light-hearted mood because M. Bourgeois was down with a cold and could not pontificate, he said, "Mandarin-Help-Discuss! How wise it is for you to appreciate the advantages of your position!"

Unfortunately the yarn got about, and unfortunately not precisely in the form in which I had related it. The men of the Inquiry quite distinctly were not amused, and at times they assumed a somewhat sullen attitude toward those of us members of the Colonel's "family" who inevitably are in closer touch with the kaleidoscopic changes of the day-to-day situation than they are.

Speaking seriously, some of these experts were very competent and their services would have been most valuable if the "rush" and creaking mechanism of the Conference had made it possible to make fuller use of them. But truth compels me to admit that in their number there were misfits as well, and the newspaper correspondents were inclined to poke fun at them, fun which was not always good-natured. One of these mischievous fellows brought out the fact (and fact it was) that while one of the experts had been for six months in the troubled zone, to the elucidation of which he was assigned, these months had been spent in the darkness of a cave where the picture writings of men of an era that even preceded the blossoming of the Cro-Magnon race awaited interpretation. "What enlightening facts as to present-day conditions can you expect from this sojourner in the dark cave?" was the cynical inquiry at one of the Colonel's press conferences. Then, as always, the Colonel loyally supported the Inquirers. "I seem to remember," he countered, "that Diogenes, or some other great researcher, sought and found truth at the bottom of a well. I have no reason to doubt that W. . . met with equal success in the recesses of his cave."

February 16, 1919

"The beautiful, the halcyon days of Aranjuez are over," as the poet sang. A delegate has arrived from what was once known as the Land of the Morning Calm, and so this Naboth's vineyard of the East Asian coast must be classed with the other troubled zones which present so many apparently insoluble problems. In any event it is no longer one of the few sections of the globe to which I can lead my Colonel without the least danger of becoming involved in the labyrinthine discussions of the Conference. The delegate is a Mr. Kim, an authentic Korean if there ever was one. He does not have a topknot or wear a rat-trap hat, but he can quote pages of that wonderful idyl of his native land, the "Perfume of Spring." Indeed, he knows the author of this charming song of youth.

These credentials suffice for me, but as a matter of protocol neither Mr. Kim nor his distressful country have any standing at the Great Assizes, nor will they have a look in at the Conference. The subjugation of his people and the annexation of his land by predatory Japan was formally, indeed it seemed to me at the time cheerfully, recognized by President Theodore Roosevelt and later reaffirmed by President Taft. Indeed, the last-mentioned chief magistrate of the "land of the free and the home of the brave" announced to Washington and to the world that the Tokyo government was in complete control of Korean affairs both in the foreign and the domestic field.

These eminent gentlemen, whose power in the Far East was only exceeded by their ignorance of the situation, "disremembered" a treaty of alliance, defensive and even offensive, which was negotiated with the Seoul government forty-five years ago by one of our roving sailor diplomats. It bound Washington to defend these unfortunate people against all intruders, whatever might be the purpose with which they came. Doubtless this formal instrument was placed in the "dead" files, but even before the encroachments came from benevolent China and later ruthless aggression from predatory Japan, it was regarded by the Koreans (it being among other things the first treaty they had ever negotiated with the Western World) as the charter of their liberties and the bulwark of their independence.

From this instrument, certainly lost sight of in Washington, flowed very distinct personal advantages to a group of Americans with whom I had close contacts during my stay at the Seoul Legation in the fall months of 1895.

It seems to me quite natural, and Mr. Kim assures me such is the case, that the people of Korea should regard the assembly of this Parliament of Man, and the convening of this High Court of world justice, as a heaven-sent opportunity (since Washington had always turned a deaf ear to their pleas) to make known their wrongs to the world and to seek redress. Leaving out of consideration the treaty of reassurance and of benevolent guardianship which our government has long regarded as outmoded—as not even worth denouncing —there is another treaty and other engagements of quite recent date which it should not be so easy to ignore, especially at a gathering where treaty-breakers are to be pilloried and it is hoped punished.

In view of the fact that the war which has cost the world ten million of its best and bravest was fought to maintain the sanctity of treaties and to bring to a strict accounting those who failed to live up to their engagements, yet Japan, the great law- and treaty-breaker in the Far East, sits in the Council of the Great Powers and is not even to be interrogated as to her recent conduct.

Of course Korea is far away and few here know the facts of her situation. Still fewer have any comprehension of them, and yet as a matter of fact it is all very simple. In declaring war on Russia in 1904 Japan proclaimed to the world that she did so to defend and preserve the integrity and the independence of Korea whence came in a large measure her culture, now threatened by the advance of the Russian Colossus to the shores of the Pacific. And after the war she reaffirmed her noble intention. When the treaty of peace was, at the instigation of President Roosevelt, signed and sealed at Portsmouth, one of its redeeming features was that once again Japan agreed to guarantee and to defend the independence of Korea. But see what happened a scant six years later! When the treaty made on American soil with its commitments approved and many think inspired by the American President was thrown into the wastepaper basket by the men of Tokyo, nothing came from Washington, not even a word of remonstrance.

When what they regarded as their opportunity came and the Great Assizes was summoned to meet in Paris, the Koreans bestirred themselves and several delegations at least started for Europe to explain their plight and ask for a fair deal. Of course passports and visas to leave the country were refused by the Japanese overlords, and when mass meetings were held to protest in Seoul and other cities, the unfortunate "agitators" were machine-gunned by the army of occupation to the number of many thousands. It was under these circumstances that the official delegations were prevented from leaving their former kingdom. The result is that the delegation that has arrived, and two others that are on the way, have but very informal accrediting documents and international lawyers are in agreement that they are "stateless men." They, however, represent the two or three million Koreans who have escaped from their oppressed country and found safety and work in China or Eastern Siberia where they cannot be reached by the Japanese police. Mr. Kim represents the refugees in China, while my old friend General Pak, who was my guide and interpreter during my stay in Seoul, represents his countrymen living in Eastern Siberia. Mr. Kim tells me that for lack of funds poor Pak is walking along the rails of the Trans-Siberian and when last heard from was bogged down somewhere near Lake Baikal. Kim, too, is practically without funds, but he faces this unpleasant situation with great dignity.

Later. I have done what I could for Kim. Unfortunately it is very little. It is decided that the Korean case will not even be submitted to our High Court. Despite the fact, the undoubted fact, that the Imperial Japanese minister, General Miura, instigated the murder of the Min Queen (during my sojourn in Korea), and the undeniable fact that his clerks in October, 1895, led the assassins who cut her to pieces, many think that I take a too extreme view of the situation and certainly an impractical one. She was a gallant little woman who would not be bullied or even browbeaten, and so the Japanese murdered her. She may not have been the only "man" in Korea, as many disgusted foreigners at the time asserted, but she was an outstanding one and put to shame the chicken-hearted king, her husband.

Yesterday it was my unpleasant duty to tell Kim, as instructed, that the Korean problem did not come within the purview of the Conference, that its jurisdiction was not world wide as some had believed. My Colonel is sympathetic with my point of view, but he says we must be practical—that if we attempt too much we may fail to accomplish anything. One word of comfort he offered and gave permission to pass on to Kim. If we deal out justice in Europe and punish the criminals here it may prove a leaven of righteousness in other fields. Perhaps later the League will be able to curb Japan when it has less pressing matters nearer at hand to deal with. I hope so, but it was hard to have to tell Kim that there was not even a forlorn hope that he would have his day in court, that Japan, if not a Great Power, is certainly a strong one. He took it very well and seems confident that later, on some not too distant day, the League will at least listen to the grievances of his unfortunate people.

In some respects I fear the New Order is very like the Old. I recall (it is not a comforting memory) what the Russian Ambassador Count Benkersdorff told me of his last talk with that good man and outstanding liberal, Sir Edward Grey, at a critical moment in the affairs of the world at which unfortunately this well-meaning man took the wrong turn. Ignoring the provisions of the Treaty of Berlin, the Austro-Hungarian monarchy formally annexed (1908) the Slav provinces of Bosnia and Herzegovina of which she had accepted the trusteeship twenty-five years before.

"What are we going to do about it?" inquired the Russian Ambassador. Grey hemmed and hawed and then said, "My dear Count, I agree with you wholeheartedly. It is an outrageous breach of faith. But Britain will do nothing about it. Those provinces you have just mentioned are too far away. They do not form a part of our life. Many of our people have never heard of them and few know where they are."

That was quite true, but in those provinces which nobody knew, as a result of thwarted racial aspirations, an explosion occurred, the heir to the treaty-breaking empire was murdered, and a million men of Britain and her dominions died in the terrible war that followed. Korea is far away too, many times farther than was Bosnia, but in it live some twenty million people who are being oppressed and whose enslavement, ten times more severe than anything the South Slavs suffered, may result in another explosion, another World War.

March 15, 1919

Mr. Kim, the unrecognized delegate from Korea, came in today to say good-by. He is naturally very depressed and he has not had even a word from his fellow delegate, and my old friend, General Pak, who apparently is still marooned in the waste places of Siberia.

I did my best to send him off with a word of cheer. While I have the lowest possible opinion of the Yangbans, the official and gentry class of his country, the peasants (and there are nearly twenty million of them) are fine, honest people. They hate the Japanese with what I hold to be a holy hatred, and some day they may strike a blow for liberty and come into their own again. It will not be much, as from what I saw on my last visit, in 1916, the Japanese have stripped the country of everything valuable.

Evidently Kim was comforted by the thought I gave him that unlike our present Peace Conference the field of the League Assembly when it is convened next fall will embrace all the troubled areas of the world. Then the Koreans will have their day in court.

"What a strange world it is," said Kim. "When the Japanese pilgrim, Kobo Daishi, came to us from his volcanic islands hundreds of years ago we gladly opened to him the wisdom of the ages. We taught him the Kingly Way of Life which we had followed for forty centuries. Enlightened he went home and he taught his barbarians how to read and to write. To this day they do him homage at the sanctuary of Koyasan, but it is only lip service. Today these scamps and scalawags, these pirates and landgrabbers, are here and they are accepted as representing a great power while we are excluded from the World Congress. How can anyone in his senses imagine that these swashbucklers will help to make the world safe for democracy?" I did not attempt to answer that one, but I did what I could, perhaps more than the facts of the situation warrant.

"You will have your day in court; the world does not remain static. Do you recall the old Chinese proverb, 'Fullness comes before waning?'"

"I do, I do," he said, "and also that 'waning precedes fullness,'" and with a quick step and an eager eye Mr. Kim went on his way.

CHAPTER XVI

Last of the Genro and the Shantung Unsettlement

March 5, 1919

I strayed from my accustomed beat today and lunched with Baron Makino at the Hotel Bristol where the Japanese delegation, of which he is the leading member (for Prince Saionji never appears), occupies very sumptuous quarters. My excuse for trespassing is that at long last we at the Conference are hearing the East a-calling and also that I came to know the Baron quite intimately when I was secretary at our legation in Tokyo, 1895–1896. Indeed it was Makino who at that time proposed me as an associate member of the American Friendly Society, composed of students who had studied at our colleges and retained kindly memories of our people, despite harassing immigration and school legislation.

In later years Makino became one of the artificers of the Anglo-Japanese Alliance as well as Lord High Treasurer of the Imperial Household. Which reminds me of one of the violent speeches he made at a meeting of the society in which he told a story of "good old Sir Harry Parkes," who in the last century was the idol of the "old China hands" because he preached and practiced the doctrine that the Eastern peoples had no rights that the Westerling was bound to respect.

"A ship arrived at Yokohama," so ran Makino's story, "with cholera on board and our medical men refused practique. But Sir Harry went to the Gaimasho (Foreign Office) breathing fire and

sword, and under threat of war our government yielded; the pas-
sengers landed, also the cholera; as a result one hundred and ninety
thousand Japanese died and the terrible disease ravaged our land for
two years."

Of course I do not know that this crime of Sir "Harry's," beloved
of all the *taipans* of the Treaty ports, can be authenticated, but I do
know that Makino believed it and that it had an unfavorable effect
upon the relations between London and Tokyo for years. I tell the
story to illustrate the truth of the maxim of that wise old diplomat
who said, "Never forget that your enemy of today may be your ally
of tomorrow." And so Makino, with hot passion spent, became an
advocate of the Anglo-Japanese Alliance which in recent years has
so mightily shaped the history of the Far East.

March 16, 1919

The Japanese delegation has suffered in the last week a loss of
prestige which most certainly they do not relish. The Council of
Ten, composed of the ministers for foreign affairs, has been super-
seded in favor of the Council of Four (the "Big Four" for short).
One of the delegates from the Rising Sun Empire sits in with the
Council of Ambassadors and one or the other, generally Makino, sits
in with the other important commissions, but they have no place in
the Big Four. The explanation is that this august body is composed
of chiefs of state or prime ministers, such as Wilson, Clemenceau,
Lloyd George, and Orlando. While it is admitted that both Saionji
and Makino have at various times and indeed repeatedly served as
premiers in Japan, they are not clothed with this authority at present.

House thinks this little and local "exclusion act" most unwise,
based as it is on a mere technicality. The President appreciates the
point and has authorized the Colonel to assure Makino that the work
of the Four will be submitted to him before its final adoption and
that then the Big Four will be expanded into the Big Five. Makino
was greatly pleased by the assurance. Evidently Tokyo had been
harassing him for explanations and for information which from
personal knowledge he was unable to give. He beamed with satisfaction when the Colonel assured him that up to the present the Four
have concentrated on European problems in which they have special
interests, but that the moment the larger world questions are brought
up he will be called in and enjoy equal opportunities and rights. No

one but little Hughes from Australia seeks to hasten the coming of that critical moment. He, however, morning, noon and night bellows at poor Lloyd George that if race equality is recognized in the preamble or any of the articles of the Covenant, he and his people will leave the Conference bag and baggage. Even the President, usually so restrained not to say formal in his language, says Hughes is "a pestiferous varmint"—but still he represents a continent. The President hates to compromise, but as he admitted to House this afternoon: "If we fail to get a perfect peace, of which we could be proud, at least we must not let the world slip back into anarchy."

April 15, 1919

In the early days of the Conference, on one of my walks with Colonel House, I told him that during the years I spent in Tokyo as secretary of our legation I had enjoyed rather close relations with both Count Makino and Prince Saionji.

Colonel House said nothing, but, as is now apparent, stowed this information away in his capacious mental archives to be used later if a favorable occasion should be presented. And the occasion came some weeks later, when the French press raised the question of whether or not Prince Saionji was really in Paris.

The incident did not surprise me as much as it did those less familiar with Far Eastern diplomatic procedure. I was well aware that the Prince had never been at any of the Plenary sessions nor had he put in an appearance at the more intimate meetings of the League of Nations Commission where the solemn Covenant that was to reform a distracted world came under discussion. But these facts did not convince me that the Prince, often spoken of as the last of the Genro, or elder statesmen, was not in Paris. I argued that like all the "boss" men of the East, he preferred to remain "behind the curtain." Wiser than Mr. Wilson, who with his "open covenants openly arrived at" threw himself into the vortex of conflicting world interests, the Prince would remain in seclusion and from this vantage point pull the wires that make the manikins dance.

Spurred on by Colonel House, who thought, as the Shantung and the race-equality problems loomed darkly on the troubled horizon, that the contact might prove useful, I now mentioned to Count Makino my former acquaintance with his "invisible" chief. On the following day, the Count assured me that the Prince retained a pleasant and an even grateful memory of our meeting long ago, and particularly of the often tried and always proved friendship for Japan of my distinguished chief and the United States minister, Edwin Dun. I was further assured that at the first moment he was restored to some measure of health, the Prince would seek an opportunity to renew a friendship which had left with him such happy memories.

Yet days, indeed many days, passed and the desired contact was not established. However, we of the American delegation were not idle and we neglected no opportunity of letting the Japanese know that we were not forgetful of the important contribution their army and navy had made to the common victory. I even slipped to the Colonel the slogan Prince Saionji had pronounced in 1916, and on the following day he passed it on to Makino in his very best dramatic manner.

"If England and France fail to destroy German militarism," said Saionji—and after him my Colonel—"their prestige and power as the leaders of western civilization is at an end."

"And those words," added the Colonel, "are as true today as when they were first spoken. We need you now as we did then, perhaps the need is even greater. The emergency is not passed and we must stand together in making the peace as we did in waging war."

Upon hearing these sentiments Makino's inscrutable face flushed with pleasure and he hastened away, doubtless to report them to his chief, who still remained so steadfastly behind the honorific curtain.

On the following day, Sadao Saburi, the charming secretary of the Japanese delegation, appeared. I felt he had an important communication to make, but at first we talked of this and that. At last the communication came out. The Prince was almost restored to health and he would be delighted to receive me on the following Monday to talk about the old days in Japan and also about the equally interesting present.

An hour before I was to start, under the guidance of Saburi, on my pilgrimage to the shrine of the last of Japan's elder statesmen, the Colonel summoned me to his private study and gave me rather more definite instructions as to what my attitude should be than was his wont.

"Of course," he said, "we want to detach the Prince from the position which Makino, much as I like him in other ways, so stubbornly maintains. If the opportunity presents, we want to start a fire behind Makino and Chinda [ambassador to London, a conference delegate] and smoke them out—of course, in the nicest way possible. But do not mention Shantung or the race-equality matter unless the Prince does.   Deal in generalities—'old days in Japan'—but if he broaches these contentious matters I would suggest that you should be indiscreet enough to say that in the opinion of the President it is wise and indeed indispensable to have the Treaty and the Covenant as concise and as compact as possible—that the spirit that inspires these great documents is more important than the mere number of the articles they contain.   There is a French saying that expresses our thought—"

"*Qui trop embrasse, mal étreint*," I suggested.   "Grasp all, lose all."

"That's it, exactly," said the Colonel.   "We must, of course, settle the great problems in a big way, but the details which take so much time and lead to such passionate discussions we should put aside for a more tranquil moment, and for those who come after.   The passing of time will iron out many a problem that defies the most eloquent appeals today.   I have no doubt that, just as Makino says, Japan will do the honorable thing in regard to Shantung, but I can well under-stand that Japan does not wish it to appear she is doing this under compulsion or even pressure.   And then, race equality: of course, we admit it, indeed, we proclaim it, but there are national traditions, local prejudices, and labor conflicts that unhappily have to be taken into consideration."

At the appointed hour Saburi appeared and escorted me to the *piano nobile* of a very modern and commodious apartment house in the Parc Monceau quarter.   Two Japanese detectives, rough-looking customers they were, rose as we entered the antechamber.   I should say they were heavily armed, though their weapons were not as apparent as they would have been had they been guarding the great man at the gate of his *yashiki* in Akasaka.   Decorously they drew in their breath, Nippon fashion, as they ushered us through a number of empty rooms.   In the last we were detained for a moment, and then a secretary appeared, dressed to the nines, foreign-devil style. He urged us through another door and then closed it behind us.

A subdued, an almost religious light pervaded this room and some seconds elapsed before I caught sight of a tall, slim, and rather ema-ciated figure in Japanese dress advancing with outstretched hands toward me. His coal-black hair had turned snow white and what there was left of it was closely cropped, but his face and forehead were as smooth and unwrinkled as they had been twenty-three years before when he was merely vice-minister in Marquis Ito's cabinet. His countenance was as serene as that of the Great Buddha at Kamakura looking out to sea. And yet, he who greeted me in this friendly way was one of the few men who, uncrippled, had survived the turbulent political battles of the last three decades in Japan.

The Prince began by giving me later news than any I had of my former chief, Edwin Dun. Yes, he was living in Japan, in dignified—and, to him, very welcome—retirement near Oiso. His return to America after twenty-five years of tranquillity in Japan had been a failure. Now he was back in the land he loved so well and where he was beloved. He has a simple country villa, a lotus pond, and a rock garden.

"Of course, the death of his friend, Henry Denison, was a great blow to him," concluded the Prince, "but we do what we can to replace the one who has gone with our friendship. He delights us all with his wisdom and philosophy."

Slyly the Prince made me trot out fragments of my wayfaring Japanese. It was disastrous. I then retaliated and insisted on his English being exercised. It was baffling, and then we had the good sense to place ourselves, unreservedly, in the hands of Saburi, who spoke our language better than any Japanese I ever knew.

"It's a pity," said the Prince, "we make such a mess of our respective languages, for, after all, language is the key to the soul."

He spoke now of Ito, his former political chief and mentor, and I asked him if he recalled a famous lunch given by Mr. Dun at our legation at which all the surviving Genro appeared.

"It was at that feast of reason I had my first personal contact with Ito and Inouye, with Matsukata, and with you."

With a deprecating wave of a small almost transparent hand the Prince said:

"You do me too much honor, classing me with the founders of modern Japan. Even my most indulgent friends speak of me only as half-Genro."

We continued to discuss old days in old Japan, and the princely Buddha became so much like common clay during our gossipy talk that I now ventured an inquiry that had, it is true, political implications.

"I remember the dwarf pine tree from the sacred shrine of Ise in Mr. Mutsu's office at the Gaimasho (foreign office), where we used to discuss foreign affairs and the future of Asia. I would like to know the result of the grafting operations in which he took such a keen interest?"

"They still continue," admitted the Prince, "though Mr. Mutsu has gone. He grafted on the sacred stem shafts and cuttings of pines from Norway and from Scotland, from Russia and from California. As a result of these shocks there were temporary setbacks, but soon the noble Shinto type of pine from Ise prevailed."

Then, thinking, doubtless, that his story was symbolic of unchanging Japan, he added quickly: "But we are getting parliamentary government in Japan now—or almost."

When at last we got away from old days in old Japan, in view of my instructions and other attending circumstances, it was fortunate that Prince Saionji mentioned neither Shantung nor the race-equality clause. He announced that he was in complete agreement with the American point of view on the state of the world as expressed by me. Suddenly, speaking in excellent French, he said we must not let the trees hide the view of the forest, and yet the task of the delegates must not be oversimplified.

"There are vital problems that cannot be ignored," he continued. "One of these problems, and not the least important, is Russia. We should ignore the ephemeral government that today seems to be in control of that great country. That government will disappear I have no doubt, but the expanding genius of the Russian people will remain. To this people we must keep the word, the promise we gave in the stress of war to the Tsar, even though they have disowned him

"To Japan, to all our people, I am not speaking merely for myself, the Conference will have failed of one of its high purposes unless the Russians are placed in control of Constantinople and the Dardanelles. They must have a base there that will give them free access to the warm waters of the Mediterranean. I do not say this merely in recognition of our pledges to the Russian people. I have also in mind the interests of Europe. I am of the opinion that Russia's agricultural produce and her increasing industrial output will revive the devastated economy of Europe as nothing else can, and it is to the advantage of us all to facilitate in all possible ways and by every legitimate means this revival. Please tell Colonel House my thought on this matter. I am sure he will see its importance and I am confident that I can rely on his co-operation.

I did so and I think my report was letter perfect. What the Prince had said filled the Colonel with admiration.

"What a wise old boy he is," was his comment. "Certainly, the outlet on the Mediterranean would keep Russia busy in Europe for decades to come and give Japan for the same period a free hand in Manchuria, in Siberia, and indeed in the whole of Asia. What a boon that would be for Japan—and what disaster for China."

I naturally expressed regret that my interview with Prince Saionji had yielded such a meager harvest, but the Colonel would not agree.

"Not at all, not at all," were the words with which he consoled me. "You have established the fact, beyond the peradventure of a doubt, that the Prince is in Paris, and from 'behind the curtain' is pulling the wires that control the dance of his puppets. To me it seems clear that he and those who think with him are contemplating a general advance on the continent of Asia away from the uneasy islands. And how easy that will be if Russia is engaged elsewhere. No, I think the fair inference from what the Prince said is very important, although not very helpful in easing our present difficulties. Japan is going continental."

[Throughout March the debate between the white and the yellow men continued. Deft penman that he was, the Colonel could not draft a race-equality clause that failed to throw Hughes of Australia into a berserker rage of uncontrolled fury. But when the Monroe Doctrine reservation was inserted in the Covenant at the insistent demand of President Wilson, the Japanese delegation became inactive, and well they might; for now the way was paved for a renewal of the Okuma-Ishii doctrine, and the recognition of their regional ambitions and rights on the east coast of Asia was implicit in the great charter of a new and as we hoped a more peaceful world that was being fashioned.]

April 24, 1919

This afternoon Makino and Chinda appeared by appointment, as solemn a pair of Dromios as I have ever seen. And only a few hours before we had learned that Orlando had run out on the Conference and was speeding to Rome. Makino said he had come in all frank-

ness to announce that Japan would not sign the Treaty unless her informal promise to return Shantung to China, after receiving a pledge
from the Chinese government that Japan would enjoy the same privileges in the returned province as are enjoyed by the other foreign
powers, was accepted as satisfactory by the Conference. Somewhat
sarcastically, Makino said:

"In Tokyo they do not seem to see why we should be the least-
favored nation in our relations with Shantung simply because almost
unaided, with but the nominal support of a British token force, we
rescued the province from the German invaders."

While he retained, as always, his attitude of personal dignity, it is
clear that Makino is "mad" all through. And I am not surprised;
every broken-down newspaperman from the east coast of Asia is here
writing scurrilous articles about the Japanese. Of course I do not believe that Japanese promises are beyond suspicion, yet at the same
time I can see how difficult it is for the Tokyo delegates here to apparently yield to this crusade of vilification. A possible loss of "face"
is involved, and in Asia that bulks large; in fact there is nothing
larger. The Chinese should recover Shantung and I have no doubt
they will, but it would be much easier to persuade the Japanese to
take this proper step if the Chinese press would refrain from its campaign of abuse. Chinda said to me yesterday:

"Does it not seem strange to you that the Japanese forces driving
the Germans out of the holy province of Confucius did not receive
the support of a single Chinaman?"

And I confess it does seem strange, but as I well know the Chinese
are a strange people. You must not measure them with an American
or a European yardstick.

April 25, 1919

Viscount Chinda and Baron Makino came in again today, frock-
coated and very formal. Evidently the activity of the innumerable
pro-Chinese press agents has fully aroused them from the almost Bud-
dhistic calm they had maintained hitherto. Chinda talked with almost incredible rapidity. Makino was impressively silent. Fortunately they left with me a memorandum which explains the purpose
of their visit. It read:

Our duty is to expose the propaganda of the Germans for the purpose of spreading unrest in the Far East and preventing the rapprochement between China and Japan so ardently desired by all the authorities in Tokyo. We denounce these dangerous canards. No Japanese Minister is exerting pressure on China.

And then it reads:

We have no desire to interfere with the Chinese plenipotentiaries. We shall not attempt to prevent China from pursuing an independent course at the Peace Conference. As a matter of fact the Chinese Minister of Foreign Affairs now in Paris (Mr. Liu), when he called on Baron Makino in Tokyo five months ago, promised helpful co-operation in the settlement of Far Eastern affairs and received similar assurances from Baron Makino.*

The only substance to these malicious reports is this. Pending a settlement of the questions between the Government of North China and that of the South, we have decided to make no further advances or loans to either faction. If we did so, clearly it would be regarded as support of one or the other, while of course our wish and our duty is to remain neutral. We await the outcome of the Peace negotiations between the North and the South now in progress. We have not signed a secret treaty with either party or with any of the leaders. On February 2nd there was an exchange of notes; they provide for no cession of territory and there are no secret clauses. We are prepared to return to China the territory of Kiao-chiao, which we took from Germany at considerable expenditure of men and treasure. We are turning it back to China eighty years before the lease the Chinese gave the Germans expires, which we took over from the Germans by right of conquest. In appreciation of this step we ask the Chinese to give us commercial opportunities in Shantung equal but not superior to those which the other foreign powers now enjoy, no more, no less.

Some unofficial Chinese whisper that we propose to occupy Mongolia with the purpose of cutting China off from Europe. All these rumors are base fabrications and are circulated with the purpose of stirring up trouble and strife in the Far East. We shall in the future ignore them because we retain our faith in the integrity of the Chinese people and in the sound judgment of the statesmen assembled here in Paris. Men of this high caliber will not be misled by people who are opposed to a peaceable settlement even when they pretend to have the official support of some faction in China.

It is a thousand pities that Wellington Koo and Alfred Sze are not the leading delegates of China here. They are honorable men and

---

* I fear the unreliable Mr. Liu also received a handsome *cumshaw* for this.

they understand the world situation.   On the other hand, I know Mr. Liu of old and have no confidence in his integrity.   He was in 1900 one of the secretaries of Li Hung Chang in the Peking Boxer negotiations and was known to be open to bribes.   As a result of previous Shantung negotiations, the Japanese have a strong hold on him which, in view of their subordinate positions, Koo and Sze may not be able to break.   To me Liu seems to be as venal as was his remarkable chief, but certainly he is not endowed with the old Viceroy's great ability.

April 28, 1919

The Shantung affair is *res adjudicata,* at least temporarily, like everything else.   The President and Balfour have agreed to accept the personal promise of Makino and Chinda to the effect that Japan will withdraw from the province of Confucius once they are assured that she will not be discriminated against; that her people will retain the same rights and privileges that the Great Powers of the West enjoy—that is, consular jurisdiction under the capitulations, treaty port extraterritoriality, and so on.   My Colonel approves, but most certainly he is not elated over the solution that has been arrived at. The settlement, such as it is, certainly reveals that the system of power politics is not dead but indeed very much alive.

Japan today is a great military power and China, despite her four hundred millions, as a fighting nation for the moment is negligible. Her army has been modernized only superficially and many of her troops are still drilled to fight in the "infuriated tiger formation" that I witnessed from my perch on the wall of the Forbidden City as far back as 1896.   Of course, the argument that has prevailed, although never spoken, is that with Italy withdrawn from the court of the Great Assizes that was to settle all pending questions, with Russia absent and the Central Empires at least temporarily excluded, should the Rising Sun Empire withdraw, our World Congress, or whatever it is, would dwindle to the proportions of a rump parliament.

Baron Makino has given his word of honor that the withdrawal from Shantung will be carried out as soon as it can be done with dignity, and there is no one here whose honor is held in higher esteem than his.   But this is not a personal matter.   It is an international problem of vital and far-reaching importance.   Makino may be disavowed by his Emperor, the son of the Sun Goddess, or he may be thrown out and his commitment disavowed by the Diet. None too cheerfully it has been decided to incur these obvious dangers. At least a majority, if not all, of the delegates are cheered by the thought that for the moment the League has escaped the danger of complete collapse which has been so apparent for the last four weeks.

The Chinese have my sympathy, but how badly they have managed their case! They have spent millions in publicity to prove that the Japanese army is a big bad wolf and a menace to the peace of the world—which everybody knew. Unwisely, too, the Japanese envoys have been vilified in a manner that even I think is unfair and above all clearly a tactical mistake. Certainly the revelations in regard to Japanese behavior in Korea and other submerged countries and the low standard of political morality which prevails in Nippon has not been a surprise to anyone who, like myself, has lived for three years in Japan. Many here think, and I regard them as the more intelligent friends of China, that had not the whole nation been placed in the pillory and covered with abuse, the decent element in Japan, men like Shidihara, would have triumphed and the army of occupation in Shantung would have been withdrawn without too much delay. Now these same people say that the army clique and free-booters assert, "As we are condemned as scalawags and bandits, let us at least hold onto the booty."

The truth as to the wisdom or the "unwisdom" of the decision reached will not be apparent for months, perhaps not even for years. Some console themselves with the thought that the League has survived a critical moment fraught with many dangers. The realization of another one of the President's ideals has eluded him, but the League, while battered, does survive, and the President hopes to fight more successfully another day.

[*1943*. Very slowly and most reluctantly the Japanese did withdraw from Shantung, but only after the Anglo-Japanese Alliance had been abrogated and the Pacific Conference in Washington, 1921, had insisted upon compliance. Today Tojo and his militarists are back in Shantung; they are not there to pay respect to the sage who gave Analects to the children of Han. They are there for the coal and the iron so greatly needed to give life and substance to the East Asian co-prosperity dream.]

May 3, 1919

A Chinese manifesto, in many languages, is being circulated with the connivance and perhaps even with the authorization of Mr. Koo and the delegation. Some of it has gotten into the Paris papers. The anonymous author says that China has been stabbed to the heart in the house of its friends.

"We are surprised, grieved and nonplussed," runs the statement. "After nibbling at the question for weeks, the Big Four turned the matter over to Mr. Balfour, a surprising ineptitude, as he is the sponsor if not the father of the Anglo-Japanese Alliance." It concludes with the statement that Mr. Wilson in consenting to the Shantung settlement has thrown over his own experts who admit that the arrangement, even if it should be merely regarded as a temporary expedient, is most unfair to the Chinese.

May 4, 1919

At his urgent request, I again called on Dr. Morison from Peking who has been advising the Chinese delegation. He is ill with the jaundice and is evidently in a serious condition, but he hopes to leave for England in a few days. He said he did not wish to express his personal opinion, but he thought we ought to know that the members of the Chinese delegation were more furious with Wilson than they were with Balfour, whom they regarded as his cat's-paw. Koo and all of them insist that Wilson said, "You can rely on me."

"We did and now we are betrayed in the house of our only friend." He felt confident the Chinese would not sign and that American interests would greatly suffer as the result of what the Chinese were united in regarding as a base betrayal.

May 5, 1919

Another visit from Williams, who will not be comforted. He is a China expert and an able adviser to the President. To him China is not only important, it is *the* world problem. As a matter of fact, I understand his feelings perfectly. "The Japs have gotten more than they asked for. They should give China, who engineered the deal, the Order of the Kite or some other equally high-flying decoration. That speck of land which they have graciously agreed to give back to China is a dot on the harbor head which they have found of no value and of course give it back, and gladly. Never was a reputation for sweet reasonableness and even generosity achieved at such little cost. But they keep the railroad into the heart of Shantung, not to mention the mines and the other properties which the Germans stole —of course, only temporarily, but that means for the ages. Now the policeman comes along, rebukes the robber, but allows him to keep the stolen property. This railway, with its branches and the tributary lines yet to be built, will give the Japs economic supremacy and political dominance in China right up to the Turkestan frontier."

Williams knows more about China than any man here, but the very fact that he has spent practically his whole life in the Middle Kingdom prevents him, it seems to me, from seeing the world picture. I asked him if he did not think that the fact that at considerable loss in blood and treasure the Japanese had driven the Germans out of Shantung should be taken into consideration and that the Chinese should abandon their silent but very effective boycott of Japanese goods, dating from 1915, in recognition of World War benefits received. He did not think so. He thought even less of my plea that perhaps it would be wise of the Chinese to allow the Japanese the same trading rights in the territory they had at the loss of several thousand dead reconquered, which China had accorded some years before to the Germans in compensation for the murder of two missionaries.

"I am sorry for the poor Japanese peasant, too," insisted Williams. "He is a pawn in the hands of his imperialistic leaders. They are after the conquest of Asia, as a preliminary to world conquest, and their first objective is the coal and iron of Shantung, which they need for their domestic economy as well as for their wider, more far-reaching plans of conquest."

While Williams was still with us word came over the phone from the President's house that as a conciliatory gesture the Tokyo government had agreed to withdraw all troops from Shantung.

"I have no doubt they will do it," said Williams bitterly. "Then they will hire a few starving coolies to throw stones at a passing train or even burn a bridge-and then, of course, the Japanese will be forced to order back their garrisons."

When told that the decision had been practically left in the hands of Balfour, Williams was amazed. "Why, only yesterday, he, Balfour, summoned the Chinese delegates to his hotel and counseled patience on their part, while at the same time he admitted he was disappointed that the settlement had not followed more generous lines. Then he spoke a few 'promising' words which promised absolutely nothing. Of course, China will not give up the province of Confucius without a long struggle. The only thing final about the arrangement is that we Americans have sacrificed the last atom of prestige that we possessed in China."

Later. There is much excitement in Conference circles as the result of the meeting which was called on the evening of April 29 to discuss Chinese affairs. It was held in the famous *salle* in the well-named rue Danton, where so much verbal dynamite is touched off at all seasons of the year. As a matter of fact, the near-riot that developed was not anticipated and probably exceeded in fury the fondest hopes of those who fomented it. In the tranquil days of three weeks ago the meeting was announced under the joint auspices of the Chinese Society for International Peace and the French *Ligue des Droits de l'Homme*. There was reassurance in the announcement that Ferdinand Buisson, a parliamentary dreamer I had often met and greatly liked, was to preside. But when the Shantung negotiations became acute it was thought that the numerous Chinese students in Paris would take control and turn the meeting into an assemblage to denounce the cold-blooded selfishness of Europe and particularly of America in side-stepping all responsibility for the Shantung settlement. And this is exactly what they did.

At the urgent request of Charles R. Crane [the wealthy, devoted champion of democratic China, liberal Russia, and all Slavs everywhere], I accompanied him to the meeting and I went in uniform. It seemed to me that things had reached a sad state when an American officer would think it wise, as he suggested, to go disguised to an assemblage of Chinese. He said that he feared things had come to an ugly pass and he admitted that even he, after all the time and money he had spent in furthering republican institutions and popular education in China, had received in the last few days not a few threatening letters.

Crane talked to the meeting very sensibly for about ten minutes, counseling patience and assuring the students that while the Chinese cause had experienced a setback nothing was permanently lost.

Crane had hoped that his prestige and deserved popularity with the students, so numerous in the audience, whom he had assisted in many ways, would have a calming effect on them, but I am bound to say that this desirable result was not in the least achieved. He was frequently interrupted with insulting remarks, addressed it is true more to our delegation than to the speaker. Then with a sudden idea, which it seemed to me was a most unhappy one, Crane said that he now proposed to yield the tribune to me, whom he described as a man who had lived in China and who, in a certain critical moment during the war with Japan, in his capacity as secretary of the American Legation in Tokyo, and under instructions from the Department of State, had ably protected the lives and the property of many Chinese Nationals who were caught in Japan when the war came. I admitted that this was true, although I protested that the value of my services had been greatly exaggerated by my introducer. In reply to one heckler, while I admitted that I served the American delegation in a subordinate capacity, I denied that I had in any way contributed to the decision that had been reached and that I had no certain knowledge as to its terms. The students and their Chinese friends, male and female, gave me after their first outbreak a respectful hearing, but as I descended from the raised dais the cries that arose from the audience made it quite clear that my appeal for patience and for a continuance of confidence in the Western Powers had failed signally of the hoped-for effect.

Whenever the meeting threatened to get out of hand, and this happened frequently, Louis Laloy, the well-known French publicist, would put in a word of sanity and things would calm down, but only for a moment. Indeed, I must confess that listening to the threats that came from every quarter of the hall against Wilson and his "Japanese friends" I became alarmed for the safety of our President. The young students, boys as well as girls, vied with one another in menacing words and, of course, I could not forget that assassination has become a popular political weapon in the new Chinese era.

After Crane and I withdrew from the platform (where no one sought to detain us) the proceedings were more to the liking of the audience and, I must also confess, more interesting to me. Wang Ching Wei,* a young engineer just back from China, drew a picture, partly in well-chosen English words, of the despair to which the

---

* Later puppet president of China, in the control and pay of the invading Japanese.

people would be reduced when they heard of the Shantung betrayal that I found particularly moving. More violent in language was a charming little lady who was introduced as Mlle. Emilie Tcheng, an art student, who spoke excellent French. She said repeatedly we must change our tactics. "We must stop preaching peace. We must go in for force," and the little coterie of girl students who surrounded her went wild with delight at the new policy she announced. The boy students were a little sulky, for clearly Mlle. Emilie had grabbed most of the spotlight. Then Eugene Cheng, the editor of the Shanghai paper, whom Yuan Shih-kai had threatened to skin alive if he ever laid hands on him, introduced a resolution to be forwarded to the United States Senate denouncing the Big Four, and particularly Wilson. While it was in process of being voted on, unanimously, I believe, I left the hall.

As the meeting broke up after several more fiery speeches from students, which probably it was fortunate we did not understand, the air was one of menace and even of threats to Wilson. Crane, while admitting that their provocation was great, was shocked at the behavior of the men of whom it might be said that many were his protégés and pensioners. He returned with me to the Crillon, and after a talk with the Colonel, and with his approval, I got in touch with Chief Moran of the Federal Secret Service, charged with the protection of the delegation while in Paris, and also with Colonel Starling of the White House police, the President's "shadow." I was glad to learn from them that they were both on their toes and fully alive to the ferment among the Chinese which had so suddenly developed. "We shall do our best," said Starling, "but the President is a hard man to protect. He seems amused when we urge upon him the necessity of precautions here to which he was not accustomed in Washington."

May 9, 1919

Wellington Koo [later Chinese representative on the League of Nations Council and ambassador in Paris and London] came in this morning. Talked for nearly an hour with the Colonel. I was called in to give my testimony as to the meeting. In the end Koo said: "If Peking orders me to sign the treaty, I will sign—otherwise not."

"When the Japanese move out of Shantung bag and baggage, as

they have promised to do, you will be the hero of the hour," said the Colonel encouragingly.

"But I'll be a dead hero," answered Koo. "If I sign the treaty—even under orders from Peking—I shall not have what you in New York call a Chinaman's chance."

I thought this statement quite significant of the situation and passed it on to Moran and Starling of the Secret Service for their information.

"I am too young to die," said Koo as he left us. "I hope they will not make me sign. It would be my death sentence." [And he did not sign.]

CHAPTER XVII

The Conference Runs into Heavy Weather

Note: After my scamper with General Smuts in Southeastern Europe (April 1, to 11), as related in Unfinished Business, *I was back in my interpreter's box for the League of Nations Commission. It may be noted that several entries in my diary bear dates of my absent days. Apparently I drew my information for these from my Colonel's daybook and chronicled these events on the dates when they occurred, even though I was not on the spot at the time.*

April 2, 1919

Some of the newspaper observers, more familiar with political customs at home than with the European scene, are beginning to sniff the air and to whisper that a "deal" is in progress between the mighty men here assembled. They admit it is for the purpose of inaugurating an era of peace and good will between the warring nations, but some say openly that they have gloomy forebodings as to the outcome. They may be right; they look at the situation from the outside and for once that may be the coign of vantage. I shall, however, view the scene as it appears to me from the inside although I do not pretend to know all the moves that are being made on the obscure checkerboard.

It is at least certain that the President returned from America (March 14) with a realistic sense of the obstacles in his path which had been lacking when he left six weeks before. He sees now after his contacts with the opposition in Washington that he is no longer dictator, in a good sense of the word, but that he must plead with his fellow delegates for concessions, even for favors, if the peace ship is not to come to grief on the rocks of a lee shore. He is putting on a brave face to the unwelcome task, but he is no longer absolutely confident of the outcome.

When the President went to America in February with the draft of the Covenant in his dispatch case he thought his troubles were over; that in the future there was to be plain sailing on summer seas. He had persuaded himself that the adverse vote in the November Senate and state elections meant nothing at all.* He placed reliance on the popular support for the great Charter and the adhesion to it of many state governors who apparently supported him in his crusade to bring fair dealing to a distracted world. During his stay of a month at home the President's contacts with senators and congressmen and with those who follow closely the trends of public opinion have opened his eyes to the grim realities. Taft and Root, who at times have given him nonpartisan support, have convinced him that unless he puts over the Monroe Doctrine reservation his whole project of a new world order will collapse. Of course the famous doctrine is not involved in the New World edifice. It is simply a unilateral pronouncement affecting the Americas, but it is developing into a rallying cry for all who oppose Wilson's "idealism," as they call it, and who frankly want to get away from European entanglements and responsibilities. That would of course be splendid—were it possible.

The French and British statesmen are close observers of this change in sentiment, this radical swing of the pendulum, and being human and "patriotic" they will seek to profit by it. They will give Wilson his reservation, they will help him to pacify his opponents, but they will make him pay their price, they will demand their *quid pro quo*. The developing situation has given Lloyd George an opportunity to comment openly and rather boisterously upon what he calls his wisdom in insisting upon what some have termed in contempt his "Khaki election" (see page 255) while the cannon were still smoking from the four-years war. He has said to House several times, "All the world now knows that Britain is behind me. But is America behind Wilson?"

Then both George and Clemenceau admit that they, too, just like

---

* The substantial Republican returns of the November elections lost Wilson the control of the Senate and presented him with a Senate Foreign Relations Committee dominated by his political and personal opponents.

Wilson, are having trouble with parliamentary bodies who will have to be pacified. And there is Italy and Orlando, who concedes that his people are very restive about Fiume. The French Chamber and Senate is overwhelmingly in favor of the creation of a buffer state along the Rhine as a bulwark against future German aggression, or a hard and fast alliance between the Western Allies and America which would give the same security. And then, as always, Poland is a problem and suggested solutions certainly run counter to the Wilsonian principles. Lloyd George makes it quite plain that he wishes to withhold most of Silesia from the Poles. He argues that Silesia, with its ores and its political affiliations, in the control of Warsaw would give France a paramount position on the Continent and that Germany deprived of adequate supplies of coal and iron would no longer continue as Britain's best customer.

In confidential talks with the Colonel, Orlando admits that intrinsically Fiume is not very important, but as a symbol for the flag-wavers like d'Annunzio he asserts it is vital to his continuance in office. "You have Trieste and Venice," says the Colonel, "giving adequate facilities for a world commerce four times as great as Italy has ever enjoyed."

"Quite true," admits Orlando, "but with our World War experiences fresh in our mind we want to, we must, keep the Adriatic as a *mare clausum*, a closed sea, otherwise the superpatriotic orators will declare that our situation is only changed in name but not in fact. To our hurt and embarrassment Yugoslavia will have taken the place of Austria, and everything will be quite as unsatisfactory as before."

House would give France satisfaction on the Rhine, but he opposes the partition of Silesia or even the proposed plebiscite, so dear to Lloyd George for reasons which I have given in detail elsewhere.* He thinks the President should hold out on Fiume or at most accept League of Nation control for a specified period to be followed later on when the situation may have quieted down by a "free and fair" election. But he admits the President will have to yield a point or two or withdraw from the Conference, which would mean a world smash. His choice is this: in the Council of Four he must placate Clemenceau or George, one or the other, otherwise the crusade for peace will end badly.

An amusing story has come from Washington. Cabot Lodge is

* See Chapter VII.

reported to have said, "Wilson's difficulties are wholly imaginary. We can and should shape the Paris picnic according to our wishes as long as we hold on to the lunch basket." That may have been true last fall, but it is not true today. As always, benefits are quickly forgotten and on November 11 last, control of the European situation passed out of the President's hands. Today he realizes it, and some of the most valuable provisions of the Covenant and the Treaty are being jettisoned to save the ship that is making heavy weather.

March—undated, 1919

The Colonel has asked me to "clarify" the situation on the Eastern Front and more particularly in Southeastern Europe, a large order surely. I have sat at the feet of the tacticians and the strategists of the Supreme War Council both in Versailles and on the Place des Invalides, but the result is a crazy quilt. Of one thing only am I convinced, and that is, even these wise men do not know all the answers.

It is quite clear, however, that the French are increasingly nervous over the continued advance of the Bolshevik forces, particularly in South Russia, where from Odessa the French forces were expected to control the advancing flood but did not. A radiogram from the Soviet foreign minister, Tchitcherin, to the Hungarian Bolsheviki has been intercepted and it provokes anxious comment. He claims that the White forces have been held in the North and that in the South the Soviets are victorious and advancing steadily. He concedes, however, that north of Lemberg the Soviet army is menaced by Polish and Lithuanian forces.

Evidently the situation in and around Danzig grows more complicated. To secure the Armistice, vitally necessary at the time to save their shattered armies, the Germans acquiesced in Poland's claim on the port and also conceded to Poland access to the sea by way of the Vistula. Now, according to the French reports, the Germans are seeking to nullify these concessions. They are provoking disorders in Posen and will oppose the landing of General Haller's Polish division should the Entente decide to permit him to land at the Baltic port.

According to French sources, here are some further details of the military crazy quilt. Despite the fact that Poland is an ally of the Entente, Germany is treating her with open hostility, and so the question is today will the Entente be intimidated or will Germany be forced to fulfill the Armistice agreement? Certainly the Supreme War Council does not know all the answers, and while the Big Four examine all these complicated problems they, as far as I can see, make no headway in solving them.

Despite the Armistice, Germany maintains today a large army in and around Mitau in Courland and from this position menaces Esthonia, now in the clutches of the Bolsheviki. Oblivious of the fact that it was Berlin that let loose the Soviet flood in Eastern Europe, the Germans today are doing all they can to convince the harassed populations of the Baltic states that the German army (despite the Armistice, still in being) is the only organized force capable of protecting them from the Red Horde. The French believe, and have much evidence to confirm this belief, that not only did Berlin start the Bolshevik movement by providing it with leaders and with money, but that Berlin directs it today.

To "stop the Horde," to use the expression most often heard here, General Mangin, that famous hard hitter of the 10th Army, is leaving for the East Front in a few hours and other high-ranking officers are going to Poland. The French General Staff insist that Mangin be placed in supreme command of all available forces now in the disputed field so that at last the much-talked-of *cordon sanitaire* may be realized.

I must admit the Colonel was not enthusiastic over my "clarifying" memorandum; but he accepted my final statement that "Eastern Europe is a military crazy quilt—and the Supreme War Council does not know all the answers." Yet, how can they? The information we received from what we must regard as reliable sources is almost always flatly contradictory.

March 24, 1919

Even those of us who are so fortunate as not to be directly involved (we who are only plagued by the repercussions) are well aware that the Armistice commissioners who meet at least once a month at Spa to clarify, implement, renew, and also extend the terms of that document are facing squalls. It is not too much to say that Marshal Foch himself is so disgusted, at least so say his military aides such as Generals Dupont and Mordacq, that he is seriously thinking of dropping the historic instrument into the Seine and beginning all over again. That means, of course, stiffer terms than those laid before the Germans at Compiegne last November.

Mordacq, who is of course closer to Clemenceau than he is to the Generalissimo, says that Foch accepts some measure of responsibility for what he now admits is an almost complete fiasco. He pleads in extenuation, however, that the terms were not what he wanted or what he would have presented had he stood alone, but a compromise document which was the limit of what he could persuade his associates representing the Allied and Associated Powers to agree to. Foch says the delays which they contrive and the back-peddling in which the Germans are so proficient simply mean that they are well aware of the speed with which the English and the American forces are sailing away from France and that they are preparing to reject even anodyne terms which could only be enforced by the war-weary French army. War-weary certainly and even somewhat mutinous many of the French units are growing if we can believe the reports that are coming to us almost every day from the winter cantonments and even from the rest billets in the south of France.

As was to be expected, these long-continued discussions, not to say disputes, resulted in a crisis and it became acute the day before yesterday. Flatly the German commissioners announced that their government would not permit the Polish troops under General Haller to disembark at Danzig on their way to Poland where Paderewski maintains they are greatly needed to establish law and order and to stop the encroachments of the German army, euphemistically called "free corps," now on the rampage in Silesia. And second, they absolutely refuse to permit members of the French military mission in Warsaw to enter, much less inspect, the territory east of the Vistula which they contend is illegally occupied by the Germans. In other words, as Foch advised the Colonel in a snappy memorandum, "The Germans refuse to conform to Article 16 of the Armistice protocol which reads:

"The Allied forces shall have free acess to the territories to be evacuated by the Germans on the Eastern frontier whether through Dantzig or by the Vistula.

"This action means," concludes Foch, "that the Germans now flatly refuse to comply with President Wilson's Thirteenth Point which provides for the creation or rather the restoration of a free and independent Polish state with direct access to the sea—a condition of the Armistice which they so gladly accepted on November eleventh last."

According to French sources the German Commissioners attached to their refusal what is considered here an impertinent inquiry. They are reported to have asked, "Is it true, as generally stated in the Paris press, that the German government will be summoned to sign the Peace Treaty without having been given an opportunity to see, much less to discuss, its terms?"

Foch holds that the inquiry should be ignored. "We are not accountable to the German government for our actions. Granting this request would only lead to interminable discussions," is his comment. House recognizes that the majority of the delegates and the states they represent are unalterably opposed to a face-to-face discussion of the Treaty with the German envoys when they arrive, but he will insist upon giving them ample opportunity to discuss the terms in writing, and he is confident that Clemenceau will comply with his wishes in this matter which he considers so vital. Foch concluded the informal memorandum from which I am quoting with these words: "Whatever decision is arrived at as to these questions, we must prepare for the crisis in our relations which it is now quite evident the Germans are plotting"—in other words the march to Berlin, and it is an open secret that the French divisions that are to participate in it have already been assigned.

Even if the worst comes to the worst and once again the Germans treat a solemn treaty as a mere "scrap of paper," it will be difficult to secure harmonious action from the allied and associated governments. Speaking particularly for the Americans, every one of them from major general to high private wants to go home. Mordacq told the Colonel yesterday that Clemenceau is of the opinion that the Germans are well aware of this *état des âmes* (one of the Tiger's favorite expressions) and that they will exploit it to the limit.

But as a matter of fact the situation is not as simple as this; there are other angles to the problem. None of the Western Powers wish to send troops to the Eastern Front, and without the backing of troops the military commissions which are expected to take charge are powerless; again many of them, most of them in fact, are of the opinion that the German troops which have not been disbanded are the only available bulwark against the encroachments of the Bolsheviki

and would like to send them reinforcements if it could be done without loss of "face."

So, though regrettable, it is natural that the Germans, far from
growing more amenable, are getting more cocky with the passing of
every hour. With their excellent sources of information they probably know that many of the control officers have reported that if the
Germans carry out the disarmament to which they are pledged nothing but an Allied army could prevent the Moscow people from overrunning Poland and parts of Rumania, certainly Bessarabia. Indeed
it was only yesterday that the propaganda bureau of Trotsky announced that a reunion of all the Soviets will take place in Warsaw in
April and that the revolutionary movement in Bessarabia and Wal-
lachia is spreading rapidly. Paderewski is constantly sending the
Colonel frantic appeals. He insists that only the arrival of men and
of ample munitions can save the situation. He reports that the Bolshe
are drawing nearer to the Dniester every day and that the more
radical wing of the Ukrainians is getting out of hand in Eastern
Galicia.

It is certainly a pretty kettle of fish, and Foch admits that even if
they are enforced, and he claims that many of them are completely
ignored, the articles of the Armistice protocol are not strong enough
or elastic enough to control the situation. Even before the President
left for America (February), Foch in a rather indirect manner suggested that something would have to be done: For instance, that a
rather broad interpretation should be placed upon some of the Armistice provisions.

But Wilson, as was to be expected from a man of his integrity, absolutely declined to accept the suggestion or even to consider it should
it be formally advanced. His answer was, "If the arrangements
which we made are faulty, well, that is our lookout. I certainly will
not agree to slip in provisions at this late day, however helpful they
might prove. If it is a bad bargain, we must stand by it." Mordacq's
comment—whether it is personal or inspired by Clemenceau we do
not know—is, "If we cannot hold the Germans to the terms of the
Armistice, what is the use of continuing to discuss the terms of the
definite treaty, which cannot but prove even more unacceptable to
the same unreliable gang?" The answer to this is not broadcast but
whispered under one's breath, that "there is a no more reliable gang
within sight."

April—undated—probably 22, 1919

A busy week, but as far as I can see nothing, or next to nothing, has been accomplished. In the matter of prestige, and nothing can be more important, I fear the Supreme Council has lost out. Germany refused to let Haller and the new Polish army disembark in Danzig and the Council did not insist—although it blustered and said it would. It ordered the Poles and the Ukrainians to stop their destructive and most uncivilized warfare, and yet it goes on tragically. It is now apparent that Smuts went to Budapest to urge upon Bela Kun the advisability of withdrawing from the shrine of good St. Stephen, offering to ease him out in a comfortable and orderly manner; indeed he was invited to come to the Conference, but the little "piker" refused to budge and the Rumanians are pushing ahead and apparently are giving the Hungarian *putsztas* a taste of fire and sword with which they have had no experience since the days of the Turkish Horde. And the Russian Kolchak? Well, he has acknowledged with thanks the rifles and the many supplies he has received from the Allies, but as yet no official answer is forthcoming to the eight questions concerning his future policy which the Supreme Council submitted to him. Little wonder then that many here are saying, paraphrasing the *mot* of the Prince de Ligne in Vienna, 1815, "the Conference talks but accomplishes nothing." At least we do not dance.

And I am afraid those men who the sailors call my "wild tribes" are not making any particular headway. The Greeks of the Euxine Pontus have been in several times and have talked again in a fascinating way of the glories of those ancient Greek cities of Trebizond, of Samsoun, and of Tripoli (in Syria). They want an Asiatic republic of Black Sea Greeks attached to the Athens government by some loose form of dominion status, but even Venizelos, venturesome as he is where Thrace and the Smyrna vilayets are concerned, shrinks from this responsibility.

The Albanians saw the President on the seventeenth; at least Essad Pasha did, and his hopes are high although he admits that the President was noncommittal. Essad insists on complete independence and claims the support of all the Albanians in the United States. Unfortunately the Albanians at home are far from unanimous. A very stately gentleman named Turkhan Pasha has arrived and he brings a petition which indicates that his people want Italian protection but nevertheless are violently opposed to an Italian protectorate!

In one direction, at least, the atmosphere has been cleared by a forthright statement from Clemenceau of what I fear is an ugly fact. Always constituting himself the champion of the lesser states, who he thinks are not getting their rights, M. Hymans of Belgium drew from the Tiger the remark, "After all, the rights of the Great Powers have to be considered. Indeed, we who put twelve million men in the field are the arbiters of the world, and no one more than M. Hymans should gratefully acknowledge our power and responsibility."

*   *   *   *

March—undated, 1919

Yesterday House told me that he now realized that the only possible peace would not be the ideal settlement he had hoped for.

"One of our handicaps is that, at least in the eyes of Europe, the President has been in a measure discredited by the result of the November election. The American Congress is now in the hands of those who do not view the situation eye to eye with the President; and worse, much worse, the Foreign Relations Committee of the Senate is, to say the least, unfriendly to the Wilson policies. Between November the tenth and twelfth (1918, the Armistice intervening) we lost the ball. By some it is argued that we should have bound our allies by more definite terms than we did before victory was achieved; but what a poor crusade that would have been if we had shown the same want of confidence in the word of our allies as we did in the promises of our enemy. And after all, they did accept the Fourteen Points. As a result of our discussions, which reveal a distinct want of unanimity, the enemies of the President are greatly encouraged and the violent attacks upon him at home are having an unfortunate effect in Europe. Naturally it is being said, 'Wilson cannot even carry his own people with him; he is no longer omnipotent—even in America.' "

March 11, 1919

Lloyd George came in and had a long talk with the Colonel. The purpose of his coming was to say that he was willing to state that in case of another invasion of France by Germany Britain would come to her aid. "But," he added, "I want to say definitely and finally that we are not willing to maintain an army for an indefinite period on the Rhine."

"In that position we are in complete agreement," said House.

Then George began on another task.

"House, if you will allow me, I want to speak to you on a personal matter."

"Go ahead," said the Colonel.

"I have been lambasted by Northcliffe and his henchmen for having held what they call a 'Khaki election' and so securing a parliamentary endorsement in the hour of victory when the people could not deny anything to the government that had weathered the storm. They even say, these people who were not so very helpful in winning the war, that by this 'trick' I secured a new lease of power that in calmer moments the people would have denied me. This was not my purpose, and I want to tell you what my thought really was. I think it will merit your approval.

"I knew—how could I help knowing?—that I had the people of England and indeed of the Empire with me in support of my war policy one hundred per cent. But after November 11, the course to be pursued was not so clear. New problems were presented, and the main one was how to win the peace. I went to the people, told them what I had in mind frankly and openly, and they endorsed my policy. Northcliffe says I am a political trickster, but what would he and those who take orders from him have said if I had not gone to the polls and consulted the people? I think I did right and that I am much stronger now with my renewed mandate from the people than is Wilson with his Congress arrayed against him. Clemenceau also is stronger because he has secured several votes of confidence in the Chamber, and today only Wilson is threatened and is in danger. For this I am profoundly sorry. We in England do not wish to see him weakened; we need him almost as much as we did last spring when we were fighting with our backs to the wall and the outlook was none too encouraging."

"The effect of the November election is greatly exaggerated and partly, at least, misunderstood over here," protested House. "By and large, our people support the Wilson policy; there were in the election local issues and tactical mistakes which lend themselves to the misunderstanding of the result so prevalent in France and in England too. There should, of course, have been no partisan appeal in the President's election manifest. However, the people are with him, and when the time for decision comes Congress will be with him too."

House had made a brave showing, but after Lloyd George left he was not so cheerful:

"There is much in what George says," he admitted ruefully. "The hot fit is over and the President is not as strong as he was. We should have secured a preliminary peace within three weeks of his arrival in Paris. It should not have taken us much longer to have laid down the public law of the new era we hope to enter upon. Now we must do what we can, and I am confident we shall succeed. Every day of delay and hesitation is against us. But while regretting these delays and hesitations, I see and frankly admit that there were difficulties and obstacles to quick action. Ours was not an easy task. Perhaps the greatest was the question, 'Would the Republican Weimar government survive, and would it be able to suppress the Spartacist revolt in Germany?' Undoubtedly these people were in close touch with Moscow and were receiving substantial support in money and munitions from them, and as late as January their movement seemed formidable. More than once Clemenceau said to me, 'It is wise to wait and watch and see. What possible use would it be to make peace or any other arrangements with governments such as those of Ebert's and Lenin's, which may not survive; let us make haste slowly.' "

March 21, 1919

Several days ago the President's indignation at the way in which many of the senators are hampering his activities, the strong impression which he brought back with him from Washington, blazed out. To Lansing [secretary of state] he said (March 17), "I must free myself from the servitude which many of the senators seek to impose upon me, and for this reason I have decided to accept the time-saving expedient, which hitherto I have rejected, of a preliminary treaty."

Lansing admitted that he was disturbed and shocked at the proposal. "While I must make a careful study of it, my first impression is that a preliminary treaty, even though provisional in character and merely to serve as a stopgap until the general treaty is signed, would have to be submitted to the Senate. So, while time might be gained here by this expedient, it would be lost in Washington where we would have to face two battles in the Senate instead of one. However, it is a matter that requires the most careful consideration and I advise submitting it to our legal advisers."

The report of Miller and Scott * then consulted was in the hands of the President in a very few hours. They agreed that the plan was unconstitutional. They held that "the status of war cannot be changed into the status of peace so far as the United States is concerned, except by a treaty consented to by the Senate." They fortified their opinion by citing a number of precedents drawn from our diplomatic history.

The President accepted this opinion in silence and immediately abandoned his plan. Later he is reported to have commented, "Lawyers! They can tell you a dozen ways how a thing cannot be done but not a single one how it can be done." House says there is not a word of truth in this gossip which he says is simply embroidered on the President's well-known dislike of the legal profession. I trust that the news of what the President had in mind will not reach Washington, where of course it would be regarded as another, if futile, attempt to kick over the senatorial traces.

April 12, 1919

In view of certain unpleasant incidents, it is now advisable to turn back the clock, or rather the calendar, to a period some months ago. On December 9, as requested, House radioed the President, then at sea, the tentative programme of his reception, for he was due to arrive at Brest three days later. Among the proposed arrangements was this: "The French and Belgian governments are most insistent that you should make a tour of the devastated regions, and accordingly the French government is making arrangements for you to take a trip through Northern France and Belgium which, beginning December 26, will occupy three days."

The President vetoed this arrangement. Instead, while awaiting the opening of the Conference, he visited the courts of St. James and the Quirinal and received the thanks of the monarchs and the peoples who had by American intervention been saved from destruction. When these courtesy calls had been paid, House was strongly in favor of the postponed visit to the devastated regions and the battlefields without delay, and Clemenceau offered to act as the President's cicerone.

---

* Hunter Miller and James Brown Scott of the legal staff.

To this the President made no reply or simply begged the question. When ripples of dissatisfaction became noticeable in the French press, about January 5 (the President was even reproached by some of the papers for what one of them termed his "Olympian indifference to suffering"), House took up the project again and urged the President to give it his attention. By this time the President was irritated and it was clear that some of the criticism of his inaction had seeped through the almost sound-proof walls of the Paris White House. "House," he said, "I have come to Europe to do what I can to repair the damage resulting from this savage war. But looking at the ruins and examining the scars will not be helpful in the work of restoration which awaits us, and I am confident that such a tour would not be conducive to the frame of mind we must all pray for if the peace negotiations are to succeed. I should think the French people would know that nothing could make me despise the Germans more than I do now."

When it became apparent that the President was not going to make the excursion, or had at least postponed it to some quite distant day, the French press, provincial as well as Parisian, became indignant and this indignation was expressed in unrestrained language. There are some who maintain that the resulting campaign of—well it approached vilification—was inspired by the French government, but I do not think so. For once, in my judgment, the newspapers were a true mirror of French public opinion. Many of them printed with approval the demands of the *Depeche* of Toulouse, a most influential paper, which said and repeated almost daily, "Wilson must emerge from his study. He must see with his own eyes what we have suffered. *Enfin* he must get in touch with the realities of war." The President realized at last that he had been unwise and in early spring paid the skimpy visit which would have sufficed in December. While of course other grievances have been added to the score, and for these the President was not solely responsible, I am confident that the delay in making the pilgrimage to the martyred cities and the devastated provinces started the outburst of ill-feeling with which he has to contend now.

[*September, 1919.* In my judgment, in his attitude and in his handling of this matter the President made three mistakes and these three were all that it was in his power to make. First, he should have made the excursion when invited and when the French people expected him to make it. And when criticized for the omission and the criticism was couched in outspoken and indeed in most unseemly terms, he should not have yielded to it and paid the visit. Third, when he did yield and made the excursion he should not have allowed it to degenerate into a perfunctory and a most ungracious affair.]

March 30, 1919

I was told by House to take an early opportunity of calling to Clemenceau's attention the undoubted fact that the changed attitude of the people of Paris toward Wilson and the more or less unfriendly attitude of the French press was again having an unfortunate, indeed a deplorable, effect in the United States. I had this opportunity today and availed myself of it and fortunately I found the Tiger in a mellow mood.

"I agree with House; public opinion in France is not reasonable, but how natural this is in view of the fact that Wilson is opposing the minimum of our demands," he said. "But these outbreaks while not unnatural are above all, as I see it, unwise. Tell House that I understand the situation and that I shall take care of it. I shall get Martet to assemble those blatant editors in my office and I shall give them a talking to that they will heed and long remember! However disappointed they may be by more recent developments, the French people should not forget that in all human probability without the assistance of America and Britain France would no longer exist. What wouldn't the Germans have done to us had they won? I shudder to think of it. True, I would have fought them to the last gasp with my back to the Pyrenees, but tell House I'm obliged for his timely reminder. In spite of present disappointments, I shall see to it that our people and our press shall demonstrate that they have not forgotten the wartime assistance which we received and thanks to which we are still an independent nation."

Within three days the intervention of the Tiger bore fruit, laudatory articles appeared in many of the papers, and as of yore crowds gathered about the President's house and cheered his goings and his comings.

I hope this incident is closed and that the French press will show some degree of respect for the President to whom they owe so much, but I doubt it. It is, however, only fair to say that the French are not the only people who are prone to forget benefits received. There are many such assembled here. In conversation and even in fairly serious London papers there have appeared criticisms of the make-shift merchant ships which at our expense and to save Britain from starvation we built in improvised shipyards.

April 4, 1919

The attacks on the President, and what is more important the mis-representation of the peace policies which he pursues, have broken out again with vitriolic force in both the provincial and the metro-politan newspapers. There was, it is true, an outbreak of this nature toward the end of January but, with the consent of the President, House put an end to it by announcing in one of his newspaper con-ferences that as apparently his views were not understood, Mr. Wil-son was thinking of making a full statement of his hopes and his fears in a Plenary session of the Conference to which the world press would be admitted. As this was the very last thing that the French govern-ment wished to have happen, the brakes were put on and the anti-Wil-son philippics vanished from the front pages. Today, however, as it is known that the President does not view the situation on the Rhine in the same light as does Clemenceau and that he is most reluctant to sanction the three five-year periods of occupation by the Allied ar-mies which Foch insists on, columns of billingsgate are filling the papers once again.

Today we placed the collection of these diatribes which Frazier and I had culled before the Colonel. He was more angry than I have ever seen him and having arranged a call on Clemenceau by telephone he went to see him at the War Ministry. He was back an hour later and evidently greatly pleased with the result of his talk. "I told the Tiger that as far as they aimed at the President or myself these attacks left us both indifferent, but as the United States was also misrepresented and her motives aspersed this press campaign was damaging the good relations between our respective countries and that was serious—something I was sure he could not countenance. The Tiger agreed with me and called in General Mordacq and his young secretary, Jean Martet. In my presence he told them that the relations between America and France were excellent, indeed they were the hope of saving the world from anarchy. 'You must call up every paper and press agency in Paris and inform them that these attacks must cease.'"

Then the Tiger and the Colonel talked about more agreeable matters for ten minutes or so and as he left the Ministry we heard the uproar from the telephone booths. "Figaro *alloo! Alloo!* Matin alloo!"

April 5, 1919

The effect of the Colonel's visit has been magical. Every paper in Paris, at least all that have come to our notice, print eulogies of the President this morning and of House, "that loyal friend of France." What a press it is! With the Colonel's permission I am destroying the file of recent press attacks, but as I do so I come across the record of the almost delirious praise with which his arrival on these shores but a few short weeks ago was hailed. Excerpts from two of these I place in my diary. I begin with that of Henri Lavedan of the French Academy in *L'Illustration.* It reads:

We have seen him; we have admired him; our descendants in their turn will wonder at it all, and the work of President Wilson will remain one of the legends of history. President Wilson will appear in the poetry of the coming ages, like unto that Dante whom he resembles in profile. Future generations will see him guiding through the dangers of the infernal world that white-robed Beatrice whom we call Peace. . . . It was for peace and justice that he went to war. This man of law, this jurist of Sinai, this Solomon of Right and Duty, has never failed to subordinate his conduct, and that of the States of which he was the absolute representative, to the dominant sentiment of Justice. He was possessed by it as by a good demon. Nothing was to be desired, nothing was to be done— but Justice. . . .

The time will come when we shall see statues of him in those United States of Europe whose union he strengthened in the teeth of the perils and necessities of war. And these statues, whether they be in France, Italy or England will not show him in military habit or booted and spurred like Washington and Lafayette but will present him as a student, a humanitarian. . . .

But before he is made memorable in bronze and marble, let us salute in our hearts, in the temple of our gratitude, the image of this forever memorable man. Honor to President Wilson, High Priest of the Ideal, Leaguer of the Nations, Benefactor of Humanity, Shepherd of Victory and Legislator of Peace.

And now for a few of the trumpet notes that came from Romain Rolland.

You alone Mr. President are endowed with an universal moral authority. All have confidence in you. Respond to the appeal of these pathetic hopes! Take these outstretched hands, help them to clasp each other. Help these groping peoples to find their way, to establish the new Charter of enfranchisement and of union whose principles they are all passionately if confusedly seeking.

Descendant of Washington, of Abraham Lincoln! take in hand the cause, not of a party, of a people, but of all! Summon to the Congress of Humanity the representatives of the peoples! Preside over it with all the authority which your lofty moral conscience and the powerful future of immense America assures to you! Speak! speak to all! The world thirsts for a voice which shall leap over the frontiers of nations and of classes. Be the arbiter of the free peoples! And may the future greet you by the name of Reconciler!

April 3, 1919

I wish it were as easy to refute all the attacks upon the President's leadership as it is the one that is most often advanced here today. We are told that he threw a monkey wrench into the machinery of the Conference by taking no notice of the French programme that was submitted to him in Washington last November by Ambassador Jusserand. While this paper was merely informal and suggestive, I could understand that the French might have been miffed by the way it was ignored; but as a matter of fact the French never mentioned it, and it is the English, and particularly the Balliol boys, who maintain that at this moment the President "torpedoed the Peace Ship."

And the Germans, how they hate Wilson! I wonder if they will ever know what the Vaterland would have looked like but for this man whom they denounce today as a "sanctimonious traitor." It would have been unrecognizable.

April—undated, 1919

Our closet philosopher who dreamed a beautiful dream and became President is now at grips with stern realities. They listened to him while the world floundered in the welter of war and the New Jerusalem he pictured as our goal seemed most inviting, but today with the danger passed, or so at least many think, the old selfish desires reassert themselves and apparently with redoubled force.

Further, many are convinced that they understand the international situation and the needs of their people better, much better, than the amateur from across the seas.

While others are not far behind, the Italians with their *sacro egoismo* are the worst sinners against the New Course; they are not the only ones, but clearly they are the most shameless. They crawl before the President for another loan "to set the world going again" and yet are ever busy to torpedo his plan to make the world a decent place for civilized folk to live in. They are hysterical in their demand for Fiume, although the only promise it gives them is the certainty of war with the Yugoslavs, sooner or later.

The President had a long and anxious talk with the Colonel today. He looks wretched. The illness which laid him low for days after his return from America was evidently more serious than Grayson will admit. To me he looks like a man due for a complete breakdown unless he is relieved of his burden of responsibility. No one dares to tell him this, least of all Grayson whose role with so many presidents has been to tell them only what they wanted to hear.

March 24, 1919

The change for the worse in the President's physical condition since his return from America is increasingly noticeable and is being generally remarked upon. The tic on his left cheek that is so disfiguring and to me so alarming has become almost chronic. Evidently the President is in a highly nervous condition and the confidence that animated him as he left for Washington is gone. He has been to see House twice since his return, and the subject of these conferences is how best to introduce the Monroe Doctrine reservation, demanded by the Senate, into what had been hopefully regarded as a closed covenant, signed and sealed. This sop to the Senate is a delicate matter because it will again open the floodgates of discussion. Not that any of the powers with the exception of Great Britain care in the least about the Doctrine; for over here, as at home, there are millions who have not the remotest idea what it means or can be fashioned to mean when the occasion arises.

But undeniably the insertion of the Monroe Doctrine reservation will open up another period of "trading" and all the uncertainty that goes with it. Even Lord Robert Cecil, who has been an indispensable supporter of the President in all the League of Nations fights, has been instructed by Lloyd George to once again, as during the Armistice proceedings, bring about a naval "understanding" with America. The Admiralty wants some assurance that the Washington plan to outbuild the British will not be enacted into law or if it is that the plan will not be carried out. House and Cecil are closeted daily, but even the almost invariably cheerful Colonel admits that the problem is a difficult one. How in the world can he go bail for what the Congress may decide to do under circumstances which as yet have not developed?

The physical change in the President is emphasized by a certain peevishness of manner. One of the first things he said to House on his return was, "*Your* dinner to the Senate Foreign Relations Committee was not a success." The Colonel might have countered with the view held by so many observers in Washington that the dinner might have been more successful had not the President's manner been so glacial and "superior." At least one senator has written that they were treated by the President as though they were being reproved for neglect of their lessons by a very frigid teacher in a Sunday School class. But this would not have been in the House manner, so he simply said, "Yes it is very disappointing—but in the long run the people will see that the charge that you hold yourself aloof from your constitutional advisers is without foundation. You offered the opportunity of a conference to the people who hold, as they have the right to hold, very different views from yours. You gave them an opportunity to question you and they declined to avail themselves of it. It might have been more successful. I had hoped it would be, but this point you scored: Back from the firing line, you placed at their disposal all the information you had. It was to be had for the asking, but apparently they did not want it."

House is evidently distressed by the bitter attitude of the President and his unfriendly remarks as to the motives of the hostile senators; but, if possible, he is more distressed by the President's physical and mental condition. Unfortunately others, many others, have noticed the change.

Yesterday General Mordacq, chef of Clemenceau's *cabinet*, came in with Tardieu, and after speaking to the Colonel about routine matters Mordacq said, "M. Clemenceau is very greatly perturbed at the President's condition. He is evidently overworked and has the greatest difficulty in keeping his mind on the subject under discussion. Often even early in the morning he seems quite *vidé*, and then nothing is done. Clemenceau thinks that the President in addition to his tremendously exacting official tasks is spending too much time in social matters which are also exacting. Knowing your close personal relations, M. Clemenceau thought you might suggest to the President that he cut out his jaunts with Mrs. Wilson and the social activities which take up so much of his time and evidently so much of his strength—at least until the more pressing questions have been adjusted."

The Colonel replied that perhaps he could intervene in this matter but that most certainly he would not. Tardieu listened with an approving air to the General's words but said nothing. On the following day, however, he said to House: "It is of course a most delicate and difficult matter, but what we fear is that the President is near a physical breakdown and of course that would be a catastrophe for us all."

April 16, 1919

Some of the President's "liberal minded" admirers (last year in Washington by many they were denounced as parlor Bolsheviks) are today, I find, criticizing him severely. They assert that he has entirely abandoned his policy of "open covenants, openly arrived at" which endeared him to them and that now in consultation with the three war lords of Britain and France and Italy he is, in "Star-Chamber" proceedings, reshaping the world and that the hundreds of millions of people who are involved are not having "a look in" much less a say about it.

The evidence they advance is based on the undoubted fact that the famous Council of Ten, composed of the foreign ministers of the Allied and Associated Powers, which filled the scene in January, has to all intents and purposes been dissolved. Yet in reality it has not been dissolved; from time to time a contentious bone is thrown to its members. But the great and vital problems are reserved for the Big Four. The President is made responsible for this change in course or method, and there is some truth in the charge. On several occasions he became very angry because of the leaks that emerged from the Council of Ten, which some of the correspondents insisted on calling the "cave of the winds." It was soon apparent that ten foreign ministers, each with an axe to grind, accompanied by at least two secretaries and an unlimited number of "experts," could not be expected to maintain strict secrecy.

As a matter of fact, the original resounding slogan which traveled around the world was greatly misunderstood. The President had never proposed that publicity should be given to the proceedings of the Conference until decisions had been arrived at. While not an able negotiator like House, and averse to caucus proceedings which House favors and enjoys, the President probably knew how unpalatable it would be to a minister of foreign affairs to have it heralded at home and abroad that he had failed to put over a point of view which was dear to his government and which he had been instructed to insist upon. One might imagine that such knowledge was rudimentary, but the history of the Ten demonstrates that it is a lesson which many of its members found difficult to digest. As House knew, "face saving" was only possible in secret sessions. All the delegates have to recede at times from their original stand and accept compromises (and this will also be the fate of the President of the United States who, since November 11, is no longer the undisputed lord of the world).

"The result of our labors we shall trumpet to the world," says House, "but the details of how they are arrived at should be, and must be, veiled out of consideration for those who have failed to secure all that they wanted. In my political experience I have found it difficult to persuade a statesman to accept defeat while the light of publicity beats upon his fevered brow, but privately, most of them are quite reasonable."

To meet this situation the Big Four was invented. Here the danger of leaks is greatly reduced but there is another danger. Practically no record is kept of the discussions; the four great personages are likely to recall only what they wish to remember, and when it comes to registering the decisions arrived at, disputes may arise. As a matter of fact this very thing has happened, and House fears that in escaping the frying pan the negotiators may have fallen into the fire. However, only one thing is certain, a world settlement cannot be arrived at in a few hours or overnight. It is going to take time and most certainly it will not please everybody. The birth pangs will prove painful and the ordeal will leave scars.

* * * *

Undeniably for some days the ship of international state has been wallowing in the doldrums. "All our quartermasters are whistling for a sail-filling wind," confessed the Colonel today, "but unfortunately they each want it to come from a different direction." The press, national and international, is in an angry mood, and while the Conference is really doing nothing the charge is heard in many quarters that with Star-Chamber procedure the Big Four or the Big Three are plotting atrocious things. Agreement there is on one point in the newspapers, and that is to the effect that the slogan of only a few short weeks ago, "Open covenants openly arrived at," has been thrown overboard.

This is far from being the truth, but perhaps it is not more disastrous than a frank confession of the truth would be, for the fact is that the unhappy pilots who were expected to steer the craft bearing the comity of nations into a restful haven after the storms and turmoil of war are at their wits' end and at the ragged end of their patience too. Although the reefs ahead, and indeed on every quarter, are plainly visible, most of the delegates are wrangling over selfish interests, and all thought of the common good would seem to have fled.

But the charge of undue secrecy is absurd. Here in Paris are entrenched some thirty or forty discordant peace delegations (and as many more who have not been invited to participate), and each and every one of the recognized delegations has been given its day in court and some of them have had at least a week. The spokesmen of these delegations before they appear before the perplexed Peace Tribunal issue copious communiqués to the press setting forth their desiderata, the maximum that they hope for, and at times the minimum that they will accept. And after the hearings are over the impressions received, which they are to carry home, are also given the widest publicity. It is true that much of this is not printed in the popular political press because apparently it is all so complicated and because there is so little interest in the details. London, Paris, Rome, and Washington are indeed united in a desire for peace, but alas, each wants, as is said so often and with truth, a peace *à son guise*.

Le Temps and several of the other more serious papers here try to be helpful but they are not overly successful. Each afternoon *Le Temps* runs three or four columns under the invariable rubric, "*La Organisation de la Paix.*" Even a hasty glance at the Conference table reveals the fact that the doves of peace that assembled here in January are fast developing into veritable fighting cocks, and most of them sport on all occasions their steel spurs. For every difficulty that is ironed out a score of complications resulting from a clash of what are held to be vital interests puts in appearance.

The Colonel is not dismayed. "Full speed ahead" is still his cheerful slogan, but he is well aware that little progress is being made. In the sessions of the Great Four discussions are increasingly violent and there have been several "squarings off" which with lesser men would be regarded as altercations. The truth is everyone would like to go home and President Wilson is not the only one who has threatened to do so with his request to be informed when the *George Washington* could reach Brest. Yes, the weary statesmen would like to go home, but they cannot bring themselves to confess failure or to admit that all the high hopes with which they came together have gone a-glimmering. That must not be, and the Colonel is determined that all present must make fast their moorings to the Covenant and trust that those who come after will be able to clean up the mess. "Even reduced to bare poles," he argues, "the Covenant will give the world a chance to reflect before plunging into the abyss of war again."

April 14, 1919

There came a telephone call this morning from Charles Seignobos, the historian and eminent professor at the Sorbonne. He said he wanted to see me, and breaking several less important engagements I had him in my office within the hour. Probably I had expected to revel in the optimism as to the outcome of the Conference which he displayed, as my diary proves, only two weeks ago. If I did, I counted without the recent depressing developments. Like Professor Denis he is a champion of the little peoples, the submerged nationalities as we call them here. But today he did not go into that. Their situation he summed up with the words: "They have been brushed off. They are being ignored by the Great Men. They are entirely ignored or relegated to committees which have little knowledge of and no authority to solve their problems."

He listened patiently when I agreed with him, at least in part. Then I said, "The President has had to throw overboard some of his plans and panaceas. He is concentrating on saving the League and the Covenant from enemies open and concealed. If he fails, the little fish in the stormy seas will indeed be out of luck."

CHAPTER XVIII

Wind-Up in Paris and a Two-Way Mission to Washington

May 7, 1919

The ceremony this afternoon in the Trianon Palace Hotel in Versailles when the peace terms were handed over to the Germans was most certainly not a pleasant spectacle. Indeed it has proved almost as unpleasant for the victors as it must have been for the vanquished. The Tiger stood on his feet and was formal and dignified as he handed over the historic document, but unfortunately the attitude of the German plenipotentiary was contemptuous and the long rambling discourse which he read was in the worst possible taste. He remained seated throughout the ceremony and no explanation was offered for what many considered a gross discourtesy.

The general verdict seems to be that in the peace campaign the Germans have suffered another "defeat at the Marne." As he listened intently to the diatribe of hate that issued from the trembling lips of the speaker the President's face was a study. For the first time since he came to France it betrayed passion and at the end he is reported to have said, "Now I'm ready to admit that I hate the Germans." "Beasts they were and beasts they are," was Balfour's comment. "How in the world can we contrive to live in the same world with them?"

House was greatly distressed and as is his habit tried to take a kindly view of the incident. "The man must be mad or ill or drunk. But what a calamity, whatever the explanation may be. He has played into the hands of those who would wipe the German people off the face of the earth and made the task of those of us who seek to establish an understanding that might lead to friendship simply impossible."

I lean to the opinion that Brockdorff-Rantzau, German minister to Denmark throughout the war, was both ill and drunk. For weeks we have heard of the enormous quantities of cognac he consumes daily and but a glance at his deadly white face, his sunken chest, his hollow shoulders reveals what must have been his physical condition for a long time past. Cambon thinks that personal pique had something to do with the sorry exhibition. "He hoped to play the role of Talleyrand at the Vienna Congress and instead he was placed behind a stockade. How wise that precaution was he probably does not appreciate. When you recall the atrocities the Horde committed on French and Belgian soil it is almost a miracle that our Sûreté were able to protect this representative of frightfulness from what I can only admit would have been just retribution."

The Colonel asked me to drive back with him from Versailles. "Our work is over," he said, "although some details may have to be adjusted. Some of our demands are harsh, but if we remember what took place in Belgium, in northern France, and elsewhere they are only what was to be expected. I shall try to 'iron things out' [his favorite expression], but of course we shall not make a complete job of it until the League gets down to work under more favorable conditions.

"What I am now hearing from Washington is, I must admit, disquieting. What we have accomplished here is, I fear, not well understood there. I see some defects, too, and I am aware that in some respects we have not lived up to our ideals, but we have been dealing with men and not with angels. As the treaty carries with it the machinery for its correction, before it is ratified and before the Covenant is generally recognized as the hope of our civilization, I think it unwise to point out and dwell upon the defects and the shortcomings of our work, although I am aware at least of some of them. I had thought of going home myself, but the President told me yesterday that I must remain until the treaty is signed and that then he wanted me to go to London as his representative on the Mandate Commission: 'I shall want you to curb the land-grabbers who will gather there,' the President said.

"I want you to be with me," added House, "and in the meantime in a few days I shall ask you to go to Washington, secure your discharge from the army, and above all keep your ears and your eyes open. When I reach London I shall cable you to join me, and I hope you will."

I told the Colonel I would be glad to fall in with his plans. I had been separated from my family for more than a year and, as the war was over, I had hoped and indeed expected that normal conditions would be resumed. Mrs. Bonsal had not been allowed to come to Paris, the rule excluding the wives of those in the armed forces having been rigidly enforced. The Colonel said he was very grateful that I was willing to absent myself from the crowning day of our work, which would be when the Germans signed the treaty in Versailles. I told him to dismiss any thought of this from his mind; that I personally would prefer to be in Washington on the great day.

That evening I had a séance of an hour with the Colonel in which he emphasized the favorable aspects of the negotiations, which he wished me to impress upon senators and others. He read me excerpts from letters recently received from Philips of the State Department and from Tumulty in the White House; both were evidently depressed at the outlook for ratification and said so quite frankly. He told me to make what preparations were necessary and that in a few days he would ask Chaumont for my travel orders. I was delighted and walked on air for several days and then, as so often the case before, there ensued a period of uncertainty and delay.

May 16, 1919

In the bag which the courier from Washington brought this morning there was more bad news, and for a time the Colonel was depressed over the political situation at home. But soon he was arguing stoutly, "Everything will come out all right once the 'Governor' returns and gets in touch with the people. How the days have slid by! How long he has been away!" At last it is plain the Colonel is growing anxious over the bitter battle for the ratification of the treaty in the Senate, even now under way, although as yet the exact terms of the great document have not been settled upon here.

This seemed an opportune moment to broach my personal problem that had hung fire for ten days, so I said, "When do I shove off?"

"Let's take a walk," answered the Colonel, and soon we were strolling in the gardens of the Tuileries as so often before when decisions had to be reached. After a few moments of silence the Colonel began:

"When, as we returned from Versailles on May 7, I asked if you were willing to go to Washington, I thought, indeed we all thought, the Treaty would be signed in two weeks at the latest, and so if you went you would not be missing the great scene in the Hall of Mirrors. But there have been delays and, as you know, the fault is not entirely with the Germans. Some weeks may elapse before the final text of the new world charter upon which I think the fate of civilization depends is settled.

"I wrote Frank Cobb about it and he too wants you to look over the situation in the Senate, which he thinks needs watching, but I must tell you that he also cabled it would not be fair if you, whom he calls the veteran 'events man,' were to miss the historic moment at Versailles—one which you have earned the right to witness and to chronicle. And Frank is right on both counts. They need light in Washington, particularly under the Capitol dome, and you could bring it. On the other hand, the sacrifice I would be asking of you is too great."

I helped the Colonel all I could. "On the great day," I argued, "I would only be an idle spectator, one among hundreds. I have seen all the great actors at close quarters when they were not on dress parade. The pageantry will not escape the camera and what they may have to say will be carried to the ends of the earth. But at home in Washington, as a Mandarin-Help-Discuss, I might be useful."

The Colonel seemed to waver, so I advanced with what I hoped would be a winning argument. "Of course it will be a great spectacle, but frankly on that glorious day I would rather, much rather, be at home with those from whom I have been separated for so many months of these war-racked years. I would prefer to share the rejoicings of the home folks than to see the illuminations and the fountains playing in the town of the French kings."

I then told him some of the personal and very cogent reasons why I wished to return home, reasons which hitherto I had not mentioned from fear of in some slight measure inconveniencing him. But now that the text of the Treaty was in the main established, I would like, indeed I was most anxious, to get out of harness—and here was presented the opportunity.

Colonel House then went on: "As you know, every mail brings me letters from Washington and even more of them from politically pivotal states as to what the outlook will be when the Treaty reaches the Senate. They are interesting, far from reassuring, and so contradictory. So my thought is (if I let you go) that while in Washington getting out of the army, which I understand requires at least two to three weeks, you would have an excellent opportunity to inform yourself as to the real situation there and to spread light as to the many difficulties we have had to contend with here. You have many contacts and I shall be able to suggest others—men who will play their part in the ratification struggle, and certainly nothing could be more helpful to the President and to me than to have the situation both here and there clarified. As you know, the President in several respects has revised the Covenant to conform to the wishes of some of the hesitating senators, but as you also know at least two of their suggestions he has not thought it advisable to comply with. What the feeling is in the Senate and what the score is likely to be when the senators come to vote on the question of ratification is most important. Indeed I think it is the most important question in the world today. I hope you will be able to shed light on it—if I finally decide to let you go."

Seeing that my fate still hung in the balance, knowing my Colonel's weak side, I now shot my bolt. "I am raring to go," I insisted. "I do not care to see the Hall of Mirrors in gala dress. I want to witness the miracle of spring in northern Westchester to which I have been so long a homesick stranger. I want to feast my eyes on the white oaks, to hear the spring floods from the Stony Hills rushing through our gorge, to breathe in the perfume of the balsam pines. . . ."

I had indeed grown lyrical, and that my Colonel could never resist. He put his arm affectionately upon my shoulder and said, "I think you ought to be there when the Great Captains capitulate, but I shall never forget your willingness to miss it and go to Washington." [And he never did.]

May 17, 1919

This afternoon the President came in and paid the Colonel a long visit. Then the Signal Corps men who are tinkering with his private telephone to the Paris White House came in also, and so the great men adjourned to my room. Soon it was quite apparent to me that they were engaged in drawing up a confidential memorandum, what the Colonel called "graveyard stuff," and so, not wishing to eavesdrop, I withdrew.

When the President had left I returned to my desk and the Colonel expressed regret I had not stayed with them. "We have been drawing up a memo," he said, "which is to be transmitted to leading men at home who are in need of light. It is right up your alley. It contains many talking points that would be helpful to you in the contacts I hope you will make while in Washington. If what came in the bag this morning is based on fact and not on fanciful fears, friends and foes alike are in great need of information, in need of what the President calls 're-education.'"

For an hour or two we sat over the memo and I took many notes, stressing certain phrases which the Colonel regarded as bugle calls. About half of them, particularly those dealing with the treatment of the suppliants at the Conference, I reproduce here.

Emphasize [wrote the President] that this treaty, is not intended merely to end this war. It is intended to prevent all wars. It is unique because it seeks the redemption of the weak nations and not the aggrandizement of the strong. For the first time in history the rights of those who cannot enforce them, who cannot stand alone, are safeguarded. We are fighting for the oppressed nationalities who submerged or standing alone could never have secured their freedom.

Poland alone could never have won her independence. Unaided Bohemia could not have thrown off the yoke of the Austro-Hungarian overlords. The Slavic peoples of the Balkan Peninsula were often crushed when, standing alone, they asserted their nationality and demanded freedom. The little nations were always suppressed by the old alliances and by those who battened on the balance-of-power principle.

We say now that all these people have the right to live their own lives under governments which they themselves choose to set up. That is the American principle. I was glad to fight for it and I believe the American people will back us up. There is a disturbing element, I admit; some among the so recently "redeemed" say they want and indeed must have certain positions strong from a military point of view, but I claim, indeed I insist, that when we have established the League of Nations they will not need those key military positions. If it fails, I admit the military view will prevail—also that there will be no peace.

I maintain we are not merely punishing Germany for her hideous crimes and for the great wrongs she has committed. We are seeking to rectify the age-old wrongs that characterize the history of Europe. There are some I frankly admit that we cannot take up, some which most certainly ought to be righted. We cannot take them up for the moment because we can only deal with the countries which were engulfed in this war. But the turn of those people will come—and soon. At them the Covenant is aimed. It is their plank of salvation.

The feature of our achievement most worthy of praise is the fact that this is the first treaty *not* made by the Great Powers exclusively in their own favor. I claim that we have secured world-wide endorsement of the fundamental American principle: that nobody has the right to impose sovereignty upon anybody else; that every people must be its own master. We are giving this boon of free choice to people unfortunately placed who unaided could not have won it. And the Covenant is the bulwark as well as the sword and buckler of this achievement.

It is true that, while amazing, ours is not a complete victory. Many delegations wanted to be heard by the Peace Conference and many, very many of them, had very real grievances to present, grievances which should be carefully weighed and promptly redressed. But unfortunately in some instances we had to point out that these matters did not come within the present area of settlement, and so, with our hands fully occupied by the immediate tasks, we had with regret and real sorrow to turn away from problems which should be discussed and must be settled in the way in which world opinion has definitely decided to act.

All these matters are taken care of, or will be shortly I trust, by Article XI of the Covenant, which is my favorite article because it is full of promise and gathers up all the loose ends. This article says that any and every question that affects the peace of the world is everybody's business and that it is the friendly right of any nation to bring before the League any problem that is likely to disturb the peace of the world or the good understanding between the nations upon which future peace depends. We proclaim and we shall maintain this position: that every nation has the right to present any of these problems to the League whether, and please mark this, whether the problem concerns the nation that rings the alarm bell or whether it is merely a matter of general concern.

What a change that is! Here it seems to me indeed a miracle has been wrought. Recall for a sad moment what has been hitherto the state of international law. Under it no nation has enjoyed the right to call to the attention of the civilized world any problem that did not directly affect its own national interest. If it did it would be told, and how often that has happened, to mind its own business. Today the prospect is very different. Under our Covenant there is not an oppressed people in the world that is not assured a hearing before our court and all must know what that will mean if the cause presented is just.

By now all must appreciate what obstacles, what cunning pitfalls to the goal of peace, the secret treaties presented and are still presenting. Now it is agreed that there shall be no more of them. Here indeed our victory is complete.

Regretfully I admit there are some shortsighted and I think weakhearted people who say, "It is not our business to take care of the weak nations." No, but it is our urgent business to prevent war, and if we do not take care of the weak nations there will be wars—world wars. Ours is not a combination for war as some misled or ill-informed people assert. Ours is a combine of nations for arbitration and for open discussion, and war only follows if the piratical nations persist in their aggression. And weigh carefully how powerful are the weapons of peace that our agreements place in the hands of those who follow the path of righteousness. We boycott the would-be aggressors. Their commerce is interrupted; they cannot communicate with the world. They are shut in; they are ostracized and entrance to their territory is forbidden. Until they repent and see the error of their ways they are cast out of the comity of civilized nations. With these powerful weapons in our hands I do not think it will be necessary to go to the battlefield. No, this is not a war document. Our Covenant will secure peace in the only way it can be secured.

I must admit the President looked wretched and evidently he is very tired, but there is still plenty of fight in him. It is a thousand pities he was not given an opportunity to recuperate from that strange illness that overtook him early in April. My chief told him that I was leaving for Washington in a few hours with the purpose of getting out of the army, and then as the Colonel put it to "spread enlightenment." The President thought both were excellent ideas but offered a word of caution. "Tell him," said the President, "that no more changes in the Treaty will be considered. Here I am. Here I have dug in."

I thought the President, basing my opinion upon what I heard and upon the memorandum which the Colonel later showed me, defended his work intelligently and sympathetically, and I find myself believing that once he gets home, mounts the rostrum in Congress, and resumes contact with the people, he will dispel the many doubts and fears and the honest misgivings which were voiced in the bagful of letters which came to House from Washington yesterday. The President has the gift of carrying conviction.

[The memorandum from which these notes were taken was never used as a whole nor was it, so far as I know, ever published. In *July, 1920*, Colonel House told me that the President had used it as the source book for his brilliant speeches during his tour across the country in *September, 1919*, which ended so disastrously for the President, for the people of the United States, and for all peace-loving nations.]

When later I went in to say good-by I found my Colonel in the *salle* where the new world charter had with so much difficulty been drafted. All that was water over the mill, and now he was as busy as a bee with other matters. Two young naval officers were displaying bunting and bringing together red stripes and blue bars out of which, following the Colonel's suggestions, the standard which is soon to fly over the new world where peace and plenty should reign was being fashioned. He asked my opinion as to one of the combinations of colors to which he was favorably inclined, but I stalled. "It's like a woman's bonnet," I stuttered, "it all depends upon the features beneath it."

"True, true," commented my Chief, "but the new world we are inaugurating must have a braw brave flag."

Then he led me into his study. "You are off on a two-way mission of the utmost importance. You are to take information to where it is needed and in a few weeks I hope you will join me in London with good news, which is also greatly needed. There we shall work out the mandates that have been decreed by the Conference in rather general terms. We shall select the trustees and the guardians for those unfortunate and long-submerged peoples who as yet cannot be expected to stand alone. It will not be easy to put the decrees of the Council of the Great Powers into practical shape. We shall have to be realistic, perhaps we shall have to be 'tough.' We are, as I have said so often before, not dealing with angels but with men who have survived four years of barbarous warfare and have not come through it unscathed. Tell them in Washington we must do our part. We cannot, even if we would, crawl back into our shell. We must keep the flag that gives promise of peace flying, flying high! Else, as you know from your contacts here better than most, what will happen."

This new mission was very welcome to me. And I was glad it had been finally decided upon. It fell in with my deep-felt wishes. As a bearer of important dispatches and armed with what were, to say the least, unusual credentials which promised quick transit through the port of embarkation, I reached Brest within forty-eight hours.

But one last scene in Paris as I drove to the station filled me with regret. My cab was held up by a dashing troop of cuirassiers, with flowing horse-hair plumes, who were escorting to the Peace Table the belated delegation from Abyssinia, or rather from Ethiopia, as the land of Prester John and the Lion of Judah is generally called here. The delegates were all tall, magnificent-looking men, dark of skin but with Aryan features and robed in long white gowns.

These latter-day suppliants have come as Homer describes in his great songbook from "the most distant land of the Ethiopians." They are or rather were then, as the Greek bard sings, "the remotest of mankind." But how changed is our world! The once-secluded Ethiopians are right in the midst of things today. How our so-called civilized world has grown in space and how it has dwindled in transit time!

This was the thirty-eighth delegation that had come to the Great Assizes asking for peace and suing for justice. I would have liked to help them as I am confident they had very substantial grievances against their encroaching neighbors. I took what comfort there was in the thought that had I stayed on I would have proved in all probability as little helpful to them as I have been to my other friends. I could only hope that "clear-eyed Athene" would have pity and guide them with her wisdom. They will certainly need it.

New York, May 30, 1919

Within an hour after reaching the old Breton port, where only a few months before we had arrived with such high hopes, it was brought home to me that we had not made the world safe for democracy, at least not in Brest. The stevedores' strike had developed into a long succession of riots. Apparently the police were either unreliable or inefficient and marine soldiers had been brought in from the French fleet to restore law and order. Occasionally the rip-rap of musketry fire reverberated through the damp and foggy streets. I was told the strikers had hoisted the red flag and were singing the Internationale hymn. However, I neither saw the red flag nor heard the revolutionary hymn. Our town major and the transport officer were greatly depressed. The town major mumbled something about the war having been won by Moscow and called my attention to the instruction to all Americans. We are to keep off the streets as much as possible.

All units and organizations as they arrived were being marched out along the narrow duckboards to the dreary cantonment in the suburbs, always enveloped in wet mist and surrounded by a sea of mud. In view of the exceptional orders that I brought with me (in military language they announce that the first transport sailing would have to carry me or else—), I was permitted to billet myself in a dark room not far from the dock from where I could keep an eye on all shipping. With the credentials which I carried for the nonce I was an important person and, knowing how transitory was my importance, I determined to avail myself of it to the fullest extent for the few fleeting moments that it lasted.

However, I agreed that I would not wander around the streets after curfew. Many men and at least two officers had been slugged and robbed for this indiscretion. But in the afternoon, with my teeth chattering (in May!) and the water dripping from the walls of my room, in desperation I sallied forth. The desultory firing continued and the streets were quite deserted. When it began to rain, and this time it was real rain, I took refuge in an estaminet. In front it displayed the cabalistic lettering Y.M.C.A. (to which it had no right). With this reassurance I entered. At least this place was not out of bounds.

Inside there were two doughboys; one was tossing down drinks of a mysterious character. He was a North Carolinian and he announced to all who would listen that he lived on the Tar River in God's country. With each drink he became more melancholy. Suddenly he said, "Colonel, we hev made a big, a mighty big mistake.

They sandbagged my buddy last night and took all his dough. We have saved the hides of a lot of anarchists and what are we getting out of it? We are getting sandbagged and short-changed."

The other soldier when he opened his mouth revealed a glittering array of gold fillings and the fact that he came from the deep, the far deeper South. "Mebbe, mebbe" he said. I said nothing.

That night I boarded the *Imperator*. A great gaudy ship that had been the German *Vaterland* I believe and had been interned in Hoboken when war was declared. On board when everyone, even the thousands of soldiers down below near the double bottoms, were preparing to enjoy such comforts as were available, a rumor, a rather alarming rumor, spread and it turned out to be true. The engines of the *Imperator* were of a new and complicated character and our machinists had been forced to admit they did not understand them and could not make them work. Twenty-five interned German engine-room men had been brought on board from the fleet at Scapa Flow and—of course they would sink the ship when we put to sea.

"I have thought of that," said our naval commander, "and I have placed guards by the life boats and the rafts. I have told the Germans if anything happens they would go down with the ship—admittance to the life boats would be *strengst verboten.* So I do not think we have anything to fear from sabotage."

Ten days later we crawled into New York harbor and once again saluted Liberty, firmer than ever on her tall pedestal. The experimental engines of the *Imperator* were not a success; it was clear they would not revolutionize marine techniques. Even the Germans from Scapa Flow (before the scuttling of the fleet) did not understand them. The Kiel technicians admitted sadly, "They looked 'wunful' in the shop and they worked 'buful' in the Basin," but out on the stormy Atlantic *"nicht so gut."*

Perhaps in this there is a lesson to all of us who took part in drawing up the Treaty in more or less serene surroundings. I wonder what will happen when it gets out into the stormy seas that lie ahead.

(Subsequent entries in the Diary, describing things heard and seen in Washington and London, in Paris and Berlin, appear in *Unfinished Business,* Doubleday, Doran and Company, Inc., 1944.)

Appendix

POINTS, PRINCIPLES, PARTICULARS, AND ENDS

I give here in full the Points, the Principles, the Particulars, and the Ends with which President Wilson proclaimed his crusade and which most naturally loomed large on the horizon of the Oppressed Nationalities, who, coming to Paris in great numbers, hailed our President as their Messiah.

THE POINTS

V. A free, open, and absolutely impartial adjustment of all colonial claims, the interests of the populations being equally considered with the equitable claims of the governments.

IX. Readjustment of Italy's frontiers along clearly recognizable lines of nationality.

XI. Restoration of the Balkan States and international guarantees of their independence and integrity.

XIII. Polish independence on a racial basis, with access to the sea and international guarantees.

THE PRINCIPLES

II. No more bartering of peoples and provinces as mere chattels and pawns in a game.

III, IV. Every territorial settlement to be made in the interests of the populations concerned and (4) utmost satisfaction to all well-defined national aspirations.

THE PARTICULARS

I. Impartial justice to all without discrimination.

III. No leagues or alliances within the general and common family of the League.

THE ENDS

I.   The destruction of any arbitrary power anywhere . . . that can disturb the peace of the world.

II.   Settlement of every question on the basis of a free acceptance by the peoples immediately concerned.

IV.   The establishment of an organization of peace to check every invasion of rights.

1946

More often than the Fourteen Points and the supplementary injunctions, it seemed to me that the words which Wilson spoke to the Council of Worker and Soldier Delegates when they took control in Russia in 1917 were hailed by the suitors and suppliants who crowded the reception rooms of our Delegation as their compass and guiding star of hope.   To these new men the President had cabled while Russia was in the birth pangs of a new national life:

"The day has come to conquer or submit.   If the forces of autocracy can divide us, we shall be overcome.   If we stand together, victory is certain and also the liberties which only victory can secure. . . .   We are fighting for no selfish object but for the liberation of peoples everywhere from the aggression of autocratic forces."

We did not stand together, and after much misery and travail the terrible battle with all its hideous losses had to be fought over again.

APPENDIX B

PRINCIPAL DELEGATES TO THE PEACE CONFERENCE

THE UNITED STATES OF AMERICA

The Honourable Woodrow Wilson, President of the United States.
The Honourable Robert Lansing, Secretary of State.
The Honourable Edward M. House.
The Honourable Henry White, formerly Ambassador Extraordinary and Plenipotentiary of the United States at Rome and Paris.
General Tasker H. Bliss, Military Representative of the United States on the Supreme War Council.

THE UNITED KINGDOM OF GREAT BRITAIN

The Right Honourable David Lloyd George, M.P., First Lord of the Treasury and Prime Minister.

The Right Honourable Andrew Bonar Law, Lord Privy Seal.

The Right Honourable Viscount Milner, G.C.B., G.C.M.G., Secretary of State for the Colonies.

The Right Honourable Arthur James Balfour, O.M., M.P., Secretary of State for Foreign Affairs.

The Right Honourable George Nicoll Barnes, M.P., Minister without Portfolio.

THE COMMONWEALTH OF AUSTRALIA

The Right Honourable William Morris Hughes, Attorney General and Prime Minister.

THE UNION OF SOUTH AFRICA

General the Right Honourable Louis Botha, Minister of Native Affairs and Prime Minister.

Lt. General the Right Honourable Jan Christiaan Smuts, K.C., Minister of Defence.

THE FRENCH REPUBLIC

Mr. Georges Clemenceau, President of the Council, Minister of War.

Mr. Stephen Pichon, Minister for Foreign Affairs.

Mr. André Tardieu, Commissionary General for Franco-American Military Affairs.

Mr. Jules Cambon, Ambassador of France.

Mr. Raymond Poincaré, President of France.

THE KINGDOM OF ITALY

Prime Minister V. Orlando.

Baron S. Sonnino, Deputy.

THE EMPIRE OF JAPAN

Marquis Saionji, formerly President of the Council of Ministers.

Baron Makino, formerly Minister for Foreign Affairs, Member of the Diplomatic Council.

Viscount Chinda, Ambassador Extraordinary and Plenipotentiary of H.M. the Emperor of Japan at London.

Mr. K. Matsui, Ambassador Extraordinary and Plenipotentiary of H.M., the Emperor of Japan, at Paris.

THE KINGDOM OF BELGIUM

Mr. Paul Hymans, Minister for Foreign Affairs, Minister of State.

THE KINGDOM OF THE HELLENES

Mr. Eleutherios K. Venizelos, President of the Council of Ministers.
Mr. Nicholas Politis, Minister for Foreign Affairs.

THE POLISH REPUBLIC

Mr. Ignace J. Paderewski, President of the Council of Ministers, Minister for Foreign Affairs.
Mr. Roman Dmowski, President of the Polish National Committee.

THE KINGDOM OF RUMANIA

Mr. Ion I. C. Bratianu, President of the Council of Ministers, Minister for Foreign Affairs.

THE KINGDOM OF THE SERBS, THE CROATS, THE SLOVENES

Mr. Nicholas P. Pasitch, formerly President of the Council of Ministers.
Mr. Milenko Vesnitch, Envoy Extraordinary and Minister Plenipotentiary of H.M. the King of the Serbs, Croats, and Slovenes at Paris.

THE REPUBLIC OF CZECHOSLOVAKIA

Mr. Eduard Beneš, Minister for Foreign Affairs.

(This is not a complete list of all delegations or all delegates, but of those featured in this book. A glossary of other outstanding personalities in these pages follows.)

Glossary of Names

ABDUL HAMID II. The "Red Sultan" and the last to reign in Turkey. He was deposed by the revolutionary movement that started in Macedonia.

ASEFF. The mysterious figure who during the Russian Revolution sold his services both to the government and to the revolutionists, and who in the end cheated both the gallows and the assassin by dying in his bed.

BELL, GERTRUDE. The charming Englishwoman who had lived long in the Middle East; called the Arabs "my people," and was regarded by them as their "mother."

BLISS, GENERAL TASKER H. Served as the American delegate to the Supreme War Council before the Armistice and later as the Army representative on our Peace Conference Delegation.

BOUILLON, FRANKLIN. An important member of the French Chamber; an opponent of Clemenceau. He was the first to announce that the American Senate would never ratify the Peace Treaty.

BOYD, COLONEL, U. S. ARMY. The able military secretary of General Pershing. His early death was a great loss to the Army.

BROCKDORFF-RANTZAU, COUNT. Scion of an old Holstein family; a votary of power politics. He was the unfortunate choice of the Weimar government as German representative at the Conference.

COBB, FRANK. The able editor of the New York *World;* a valued adviser of the President and Colonel House during the war and at the Conference.

CRANE, CHARLES R. The Chicago merchant who became a liberal supporter of all Democratic movements whether in Europe, Asia, or Africa.

DAVIS, NORMAN. One of the economic advisers of the American Delegation. Later Assistant Secretary of State and Chairman of the American Red Cross.

EDWARDS, MAJOR GENERAL CLARENCE. He commanded the 26th or "Yankee" Division, which was the first of the National Guard divisions to reach the front.

HLINKA, FATHER. A leading Slovak priest. He was an ardent fighter against Austrian domination and later the leader of the movement to separate his people from the Czechs.

HORODYSKI, PAN. A charming Pole who acted as liaison officer with the Peace Conference when Paderewski was absent.

IONESCU, TAKE. Leading liberal statesman of Rumania; a staunch supporter of the Western Powers throughout the war.

ISWOLSKY, M. Entrusted with many diplomatic missions under Tsar Nicholas; Ambassador to France; twice Foreign Minister.

KERENSKY, A. Succeeded the Provisional government of Prince Lvoff and was in turn overthrown by Lenin and the Soviets.

KOO, WELLINGTON. The youngest and the most talented member of the Chinese Delegation. President Wilson said he spoke English in the way Macaulay wrote it.

LAWRENCE, T. E. The young archaeologist who developed great talent for desert warfare. With Emir Faisal he led the great ride of the Arabs from Mecca to Damascus.

LVOFF, PRINCE. A member of one of the feudal families but a convinced democrat. He headed the short-lived Provisional government after the deposition of the Tsar.

MASARYK, THOMAS G. Leader and inspirer of the Czech Liberation movement and the first President of the Republic, an ardent admirer of President Wilson.

MIRKO, PRINCE OF MONTENEGRO. Second son of King Nicholas. His role in Vienna, where he was caught at the outbreak of war while attending his ailing wife, is still a matter of dispute among the Serb factions.

NUBAR PASHA. The son of the great Nubar who played such an important rôle in Egyptian history; an eloquent exponent of the Armenian cause. At the Conference he represented the Armenian communities of Egypt.

PILSUDSKI, GENERAL JÓZEF. Polish soldier who first joined the armies of the Central Empires and later fought with the Western Powers. He was an opponent of Paderewski and for years was dictator of Poland and an enemy of its democratic regeneration.

PLEHVE, WENZEL VON. Minister of the Interior and head of the repressive government in Russia under Tsar Nicholas. His assassination was carried out by Boris Savinkov.

SAVINKOV, BORIS. An active participant in all the revolutionary movements in Russia, before and after the fall of the Tsar. He became Minister of War under Kerensky. His hatred of Stalin, who engineered the "ouster," warped his judgment of that great revolutionist.

SEIGNOBOS, CHARLES. Learned historian and professor at the Sorbonne, Paris.

STEFANIK, GENERAL. The outstanding Slovak soldier. For a time he commanded the Czechoslovak forces in Siberia. The manner in which he met his death after the Armistice is an apple of discord among the West Slavs to this day, unfortunately.

SYDORENKO, M. Chairman of the principal Armenian committee; eloquent advocate of the Armenian claims; unfortunately, but little heeded.

SYKES, SIR MARK. British traveler and authority on the Middle East. His sudden death during the Conference delayed the solution of the problem to which he had devoted his life.

Index